Quarto.com

© 2025 Quarto Publishing Group USA Inc.
Text © 2025 Mike Hembree

First Published in 2025 by Motorbooks, an imprint of The Quarto Group, 100 Cummings Center, Suite 265-D, Beverly, MA 01915, USA.
T (978) 282-9590 F (978) 283-2742

All rights reserved. No part of this book may be reproduced in any form without written permission of the copyright owners. All images in this book have been reproduced with the knowledge and prior consent of the artists concerned, and no responsibility is accepted by producer, publisher, or printer for any infringement of copyright or otherwise, arising from the contents of this publication. Every effort has been made to ensure that credits accurately comply with information supplied. We apologize for any inaccuracies that may have occurred and will resolve inaccurate or missing information in a subsequent reprinting of the book.

Motorbooks titles are also available at discount for retail, wholesale, promotional, and bulk purchase. For details, contact the Special Sales Manager by email at specialsales@quarto.com or by mail at The Quarto Group, Attn: Special Sales Manager, 100 Cummings Center, Suite 265-D, Beverly, MA 01915, USA.

29 28 27 26 25   1 2 3 4 5

ISBN: 978-0-7603-9317-8

Digital edition published in 2025
eISBN: 978-0-7603-9318-5

Library of Congress Cataloging-in-Publication Data
Names: Hembree, Michael, 1951- author.
Title: Petty vs. Pearson : the rivalry that shaped NASCAR / Mike Hembree.
Description: Beverly, MA : Motorbooks, 2025. | Includes bibliographical references and index. | Summary: "In Petty vs. Pearson, veteran motorsport journalist Mike Hembree examines how the co-dominance of drivers Richard Petty and David Pearson helped propel NASCAR from regional curiosity to national phenomenon"-- Provided by publisher.
Identifiers: LCCN 2024046585 | ISBN 9780760393178 (print) | ISBN 9780760393185 (ebook)
Subjects: LCSH: Stock car drivers--United States--Biography. | Petty, Richard, 1937- | Pearson, David, 1934-2018. | Stock car racing--United States--History. | NASCAR (Association)--History.
Classification: LCC GV1029.9.S74 H434 2025 | DDC 796.72092/273--dc23/eng/20241106
LC record available at https://lccn.loc.gov/2024046585

Cover design and layout: Justin Page
Cover image: Smyle Media
Endpaper image: Dick Conway

Printed in China

For the grandest of grandchildren—
Maggie, Gus, Hope, and Harper Lee

WHAT COULD BE MORE BEAUTIFUL THAN PETTY AND PEARSON, RUNNING FLAT-OUT, DIXIE-STYLE, BELLY-TO-THE-GROUND, CHASING A HURRYING SUNDOWN?

Atlanta Journal sportswriter Bill Robinson, November 1967

CONTENTS

FOREWORD: TWO OF THE BEST, BY TERRY LABONTE | 8
PREFACE: THE RIVALRY THAT FUELED THE SPORT | 10

Chapter 1
PETTY TO PETTY | 22

Chapter 2
MILL HILL KID | 30

Chapter 3
BRIDGE TO THE FUTURE | 40

Chapter 4
NORTH TO CANADA | 46

Chapter 5
DAYTONA DEBUT | 50

Chapter 6
VICTORIES AND VIOLENCE | 60

Chapter 7
CHAMPIONS AT WORK | 70

Chapter 8
IT'S VERY GOOD TO BE THE KING | 86

Chapter 9
FUN WITH FORDS | 96

Chapter 10
MEETING WALLS | 110

Chapter 11
SMOKIN' | 122

Chapter 12
DUEL AT DAYTONA, PART 1 | 140

Chapter 13
DUEL AT DAYTONA, PART 2 | 150

Chapter 14
TRIUMPHS AND TROUBLES | 164

Chapter 15
FINAL FLAGS | 184

Chapter 16
LAST LAPS, LEGACIES, AND THE HALL OF FAME | 204

Epilogue
THE DEBATE | 222

SOURCES | 234
ACKNOWLEDGMENTS | 236
INDEX | 238

FOREWORD By Terry Labonte

Two of the Best

In early 1968, my parents bought a brand-new Ford Torino and the salesman gave me a poster of David Pearson's Holman-Moody Ford. I hung it on the wall in my bedroom, and my interest in NASCAR began.

Back then, some NASCAR races were televised via closed circuit in movie theaters. The 1968 Daytona 500 was to be shown live at a theater in Corpus Christi, and I talked my dad into taking me. It was the very first NASCAR race I ever watched. The thing that always stood out to me about that race was Richard Petty's roof coming loose on the windshield and the King climbing out of the car during a pitstop and working on it himself. Sitting there watching the race in that movie theater, I thought that was the coolest thing I'd ever seen in my life. It was something an eleven-year-old kid could only dream about.

Somehow, ten years later, I ran my very first NASCAR Cup Series race in Darlington, South Carolina. David Pearson won the pole, Richard Petty finished third, and I finished fourth.

I admired all the drivers I raced against, but David Pearson and Richard Petty always stood out. When I started racing in NASCAR, David was on a limited schedule driving for the Wood Brothers. He might not have been at as many races, but when he did show up, you knew he was there. He was always competitive and someone we all had to try to beat. Early in my career, I would try to follow David in that No. 21 car, but I couldn't keep up with him. He was one of the smoothest drivers I'd ever seen.

Not only was David one of the best drivers I ever competed against, but he was also one of the coolest guys I'd ever been around. We had an opportunity to race in the 24 Hours of Daytona together in the early 1980s. David and I were riding to the racetrack, and I had the schedule and realized we had missed practice the night before. We had gone to dinner and missed it. David, just as cool as you could imagine, said, "Oh, don't worry about it. I doubt that thing [car] makes it to dark anyway." And you know what? He was right. The engine failed when David was behind the wheel, just before dark. I knew, in that moment, this guy knew what he was talking about.

Back in the early days, at the short tracks, when they opened the gates to fans, there would be a big crowd of people on pit road. When I first saw that, I wondered what was going on. Turns out it was Richard Petty sitting there signing his autograph until the last person got one. Not just that one race, but he did that every race. That says a lot about the type of person Richard Petty was and is.

In 1996, I was able to tie (and later break) Richard's record for most consecutive starts in the Cup Series. I remember thinking to myself, this might be the only record of Richard Petty's anybody could tie. Several years later, in 2008, I filled in for Kyle Petty driving the Petty Enterprises No. 45 for six races. It was so cool driving a special car for a special team. And it was cool listening to Richard tell stories about the early days in racing. You could mention a race and he knew every detail of it, which was amazing to me. I was just proud to be mentioned in the same article as Richard Petty, much less drive for him. The guy won seven championships and 200 races and made thousands and thousands of fans happy with his autograph and picture. He really is the King.

David and Richard were two of the best drivers our sport has ever seen. It is amazing that they finished first and second sixty-three times in their careers. Just imagine how different the records might look if one of them hadn't raced. I can't think of any two people that did more for our sport than David Pearson and Richard Petty.

> *Texas native Terry Labonte, a member of the NASCAR Hall of Fame, won the Cup Series championship in 1984 and 1996. He raced in NASCAR's top series from 1978 to 2014, winning twenty-two times. He was named one of NASCAR's fifty greatest drivers and later one of the sport's seventy-five greatest drivers.*

PREFACE

The Rivalry That Fueled the Sport

A couple of hours before they would race again on a NASCAR track, Richard Petty and David Pearson sat side-by-side in the prerace drivers meeting. Before the meeting opened, Petty leaned toward Pearson's right ear and said, "You ain't worth crap."

A week later, Pearson caught Petty off guard, walked by him, and said the same thing, "You ain't worth crap."

It was a running joke, a shared laugh between two of the greatest drivers in motorsports history. Rivals. Both were worth millions; their talents clear in ways even beyond the dollar figures and statistics. Petty would total 200 NASCAR Cup victories; Pearson would win 105. Between them, they recorded ten Cup championships.

Across the years, they had the sport's biggest rivalry, battling for stock car racing's high ground hundreds of times. They crossed swords at numerous crossroads as NASCAR grew and prospered, and they finished their decorated careers heavy with honors and glory.

Long-time NASCAR official Mike Helton witnessed the Petty-Pearson rivalry as a fan, years before he started working in the sport. "Richard and Petty Enterprises needed someone," Helton said. "If they beat everybody hands-down, then his success was not as valuable as it was when he had to fight to win races. David Pearson and the Wood Brothers was the group that made that happen, and NASCAR was the beneficiary. I think it (their rivalry) is the standard, which makes it the most dominant. When you start talking about rivalries, that's where you start. For NASCAR, the rivalry that fuels our sport today is David and Richard."

Perhaps surprisingly, the fact that they so often raced each other (and, on so many last laps, no one else) for wins didn't put Pearson and Petty at war. Their rivalry was not colored by hate or animosity; their fierce battles—even the toughest ones—did not lead to fists in faces. Their engines were the loudest thing about them.

Their relationship was mostly friendly, leading to the kinds of practical jokes and humor that made the rough and risky sport of auto racing a bit lighter. Prior to a 1966 race at Bowman Gray Stadium in Winston-Salem, North Carolina, Petty strolled over to Pearson's No. 6 Dodge, handed Pearson, who was already buckled into the car ready to race, a 25-pound (11-kg) piece of lead and said, "Hey, do something with this." Lighter cars run faster, of course.

No other driver pairing over NASCAR's first seventy-five years sizzled like Petty-Pearson (or, in the minds of Pearson fans, Pearson-Petty). In the 1960s and 1970s, if a disagreement among fans in the grandstands turned into an exchange of fists, chances are one wore a Petty T-shirt and the other a Pearson cap. And alcohol might have been involved. It was like Yankees–Red Sox with pistons.

Of course, other driver rivalries colored NASCAR's history as challengers appeared alongside Petty and Pearson on racing's high road. Dale Earnhardt would emerge from a North Carolina mill hill to rattle the sport. Darrell Waltrip would charge in to become a rival of Earnhardt and Cale Yarborough, a fierce South Carolinian who knew no fear. Waltrip and Yarborough traded fender paint and insults, Yarborough eventually labeling Waltrip with the interesting nickname "Jaws" because of Waltrip's penchant for aggressively sharing his opinions. Bobby Allison would fight both Petty and Waltrip for first place—and would fight Yarborough (literally) on Daytona's infield grass. Petty and Allison raced their way through some classic short-track disagreements in the late 1960s and early 1970s, showcasing some intense racing and wrecking that ended in a truce because both sides considered it too dangerous—and too expensive. Jeff Gordon, Jimmie Johnson, Tony Stewart, and other greats would join the fray at the top.

The Petty-Pearson rivalry reached deeper than any other. They created one-on-one drama on track in NASCAR's growing years, and on many Sundays, a few Saturday nights, and some other weekday events, they were one-two approaching the final miles. A victory over the other was especially treasured.

"One time at Talladega," remembered long-time Petty crew chief Dale Inman, "we had the first pit and Pearson and the Wood Brothers pit was close. When Richard and David went by on the last lap, we couldn't see who won from where we were, but Maurice [Richard's brother and engine builder] said over the radio, 'We finally beat them sons of bitches.'"

It was that kind of rivalry. Wins were always welcome but wins over Pearson or Petty were special for the people involved on either side.

In the beginning, though, long before they would become racing superstars, there was the reaper shed and the cotton mill. They produced Richard Petty and David Pearson. The reaper shed provided a foundation and the cotton mill a place from which to escape. Farm and factory—the central units of the Carolina Piedmont landscape present during the mid-twentieth century.

Lee Petty, Richard's father, farmed the family's land in central North Carolina, near Randleman. His neighbors did the same. Tilling the earth was as much about feeding the family as it was about trying to make an extra buck. Thus, the reaper shed, a tiny enclosure barely big enough to shelter farm equipment, came into effect.

Along the way, Petty and his brother, Julian, picked up the racing game, and Lee, who was smarter than the average guy riding a tractor, figured out there was money to be made in this new thing. The reaper shed, topped by a tin roof, soon became a rudimentary race shop. "There was a tractor in there," Richard Petty said. "We just pulled it out and put a race car in." Farming became secondary. Adjacent to the reaper shed was a bloody board the family used for butchering hogs. The need for it soon disappeared.

Lee's sons, Richard and Maurice, also chose fast cars over slow tractors. After Lee made his choice, there was little debate for them. They grew up consumed by the sport, knowing and living little else; they, too, would be racers. By 1955, both were working long hours in the Petty shop.

A three-hour drive southwest in Spartanburg, South Carolina, teenage David Pearson was on a path like other youngsters his age in the area. He quit school and went to work in the Whitney cotton mill near Spartanburg, following his father. Pearson wanted money faster than a high school education might provide, but he quickly decided that long shifts in the heat and noise of mid-century textile work were dreadful and would not do.

As a kid, Pearson had walked to a nearby dirt track—at the Piedmont Interstate Fairgrounds in Spartanburg—to watch stock car races. Heroes of the day like Cotton Owens, another Spartanburg resident, raced on the dirt of the old horse-racing track, and Pearson was enthralled. Later, he determined this was something he could do. Other people did it. Why couldn't he? After his cotton mill experience, this determination became less of a dream and more of a goal.

For those reasons (and others) and over a series of years, the greatest rivalry in NASCAR developed. Petty vs. Pearson. The King vs. the Silver Fox. No. 43 vs. No. 21. Petty blue vs. Purolator red and white. Fire vs. fire.

Beginning in the 1960s and lasting into the 1980s, their bristling competition, playing out on short backwoods bullrings and giant modern superspeedways, produced lightning and thunder of the highest order and race finishes that still spark debate. As they battled, the universal eye of television began taking notice.

They were giants.

Petty was NASCAR's rookie of the year in 1959, and Pearson won the same title in 1960. Those back-to-back honors started a road map to the future. They were off to the races.

From Columbia, South Carolina, in 1963 to Charlotte, North Carolina, in 1977, Petty and Pearson finished one-two in sixty-three NASCAR Cup races. Pearson won thirty-three of those and Petty won thirty—numbers that Pearson's disciples will point out early and loudly in conversations about the drivers' relative abilities. Petty fans will counter that he won more races overall and in the 551 Cup Series races in which they both were entered, Petty finished higher in 290 to Pearson's 261.

On February 15, 1976, at Daytona International Speedway, the Petty-Pearson rivalry reached a dramatic summit. They were nose-to-tail entering the final lap of the Daytona 500, with no other challengers in sight. Pearson, calm and assured despite 498 miles (801 kms) of hard racing, led in his red-and-white No. 21 Mercury, all his thoughts concentrated on keeping Petty behind him. Petty, who had studied the ins and outs of Pearson's car over the final miles, waited for the moment.

It was the last minute of a long afternoon. With thousands standing and leaning toward the best view in the long frontstretch grandstands, Petty pulled alongside Pearson in the fourth turn and their cars met, sending both into the outside wall. Petty's car came to a stop and stalled. Pearson kept his engine running by depressing the clutch, chugged across the finish line at about 30 miles per hour (48 kms per hour), and won the race. Across the grandstands, in the crowded infield, and in living rooms around America, the amazement level spiked. Pearson had won in ridiculous fashion, a finish so zany a scriptwriter would have been too embarrassed to submit it.

The earth shook that day in Daytona Beach.

Pearson and Petty were in the right time and place to have a big, two-pronged impact on the sport. NASCAR showed exponential growth in the 1960s, pushed along by Petty and Pearson, who would combine to win half of the sport's championships in the decade (Petty in 1964 and 1967, Pearson in 1966, 1968, and 1969). They were key players as stock car racing spread beyond its Southeastern base and steadily edged into the television world. Their rivalry was juiced in the 1970s as major corporate sponsors lifted the sport to new heights and spread money across the table (and, occasionally, under it).

The Pearson-Petty dynamic fit perfectly into the automobile manufacturers' struggle for dominance in stock car racing, particularly in the 1950s and 1960s when the concept of "Win on Sunday, sell on Monday" was a slogan of sorts in the car industry. Ford, Chrysler, and General Motors spent millions in pursuit of success in the NASCAR playground, and Detroit designers and engineers produced passenger cars in part with racing in mind. Car builders bought newspaper and magazine ads boasting of wins on the NASCAR circuit. Sports followers outside the auto racing world sometimes found it bizarre that fans might enjoy rooting for a specific brand of automobile on equal terms with lining up behind individual drivers. This concept is not nearly as important in twenty-first-century racing, but in NASCAR's growing years, it was a vital part of the sport.

Much of the Ford vs. Chevy vs. Plymouth phenomenon came from the post–World War II years when many Americans were upwardly mobile and had the ability to buy cars. At drive-in restaurants and in high school parking lots, boys boasted of the power of their Fords. Someone in a Chevrolet took up the challenge, and on some back road they tore off into the night, side by side in a dangerous drag race for neighborhood honors—or maybe five bucks and a hug from the prom queen. This competition naturally carried over into stock car racing, as Ford owners pulled for Blue Oval racers and Chrysler owners lined up behind Plymouth and Dodge drivers. With Pearson driving Ford products in the late 1960s and 1970s and Petty driving Chrysler-built machines, the two became the faces of the fight. Petty discovered how rabid devotees of the cars could be in late 1968 when he announced that he would be leaving Chrysler to drive Fords in 1969. Petty Enterprises was flooded with letters of protest, many addressed simply to "Richard Petty, Randleman, N.C." A sample from a fan in Clifton, Virginia: "I am extremely disappointed that you switched to Ford. As a Petty/Plymouth fan for many years, I plan to stick with Plymouth and forget the name Petty. Richard Petty is the Benedict Arnold of stock car racing. How could you do this??"

The Petty-Pearson saga produced some amazing finishes and some tense moments (two in particular), but they remained friends throughout their competitive years—and beyond. They were like Magic Johnson and Larry Bird, Arnold Palmer and Jack Nicklaus, or Tom Brady and Peyton Manning.

Despite their similarities—both were Carolina country boys whose racing styles showcased consistency and grit above flat-out speed and aggression, Petty and Pearson were very different people. And they drove through their racing years with different approaches and in varying circumstances. Petty drove virtually his entire career for the Petty family team; Pearson jumped from team to team, enjoying success at most stops. Petty was the outgoing superstar, an Everyman for the times; Pearson drove fast but didn't connect as easily with fans and media.

Raised in a racing family, Petty learned the sport's ins and outs at an early age and worked at building a popular image, even in his fledgling years. He began signing autographs almost as soon as he began turning fast laps and as he began winning races and drawing fan attention, he spent hours after races chatting with those who had bought tickets to see him run. In 1974, an open house at the Petty team shop in the North Carolina countryside attracted 35,000 people. Three years later, Petty's fan club had about 15,000 paying members, including chapters in Germany, England, and South Africa.

"Richard would always go the extra mile like that with the fans," Pearson said. "He smiled for pictures and signed autographs and was in the middle of everything. I didn't like doing that. I used to hide to keep from talking to people, and I'm sure that hurt me in the long run. I just didn't feel comfortable doing it. To start with, I was a little bashful and was afraid I'd say the wrong thing. A little old mill hill boy goes to the race and all those news people come scattering around you—you don't know what to say or do."

Pearson was introduced to racing as a fan—and a nonpaying one at that. As a kid, he climbed trees to see over the fence at the Spartanburg track, and any other interests he might have had disappeared in the noise and calamity of those dirt-track days. Bashful and shy in public, in part because of his decision to drop out of school, he raced a different road than that paved by Petty. Pearson's exploits and successes attracted followers, but, as he admitted years later, his general reluctance to engage with fans and media hurt his career. He wasn't unfriendly, but he didn't seek the bright lights. While Petty zoomed into superstardom and spread his name across the sports world and beyond, Pearson succeeded in relative isolation, his star shining in a smaller universe.

"David came from a mill town and had little education, and I think because of that it kept him from opening up," Petty said. "He was very open to people who knew him, but he wasn't open to strangers. I think sometimes he felt uncomfortable in a crowd. I never paid it any attention, but I grew up in a different environment. I grew up in the sport and around the people. He didn't. He had to work into it."

Kyle Petty, Richard's son, said Pearson once told him that he regretted not following Richard's lead with fans. "He told me, 'If I had to do it over again, I'd be like your dad,'" Kyle said. "'I'd sit there and sign autographs. I'd cater to the fans. I would change that.' David just didn't have that personality. He's the guy who sat at the back of the room."

Kyle might have added that Pearson was also the guy who raced from the back of the room to the front of the field.

When the engines were cranked, Pearson and Petty played with fire on equal terms, and their fenders reached for the same spaces across more than two decades of racing. They raced each other for the win on a regular basis, but they didn't engage in a feud. They weren't into fisticuffs or butt-whippin'. What they had was a face-to-face, bumper-to-bumper confrontation that was ongoing year after year—the very definition of a rivalry.

"I always enjoyed running with Richard," Pearson said. "He knew what he was going to do all the time. I mean, he wasn't radical. He wouldn't go in a corner real deep one time and the next time back off way early or something like that. He did the same thing every time. That's the reason I enjoyed running with him, I guess. If you beat him, you knew you beat a good one."

Petty often described Pearson as the best in the business. "I agree with Richard," Pearson would reply.

THEY WEREN'T INTO FISTICUFFS OR BUTT-WHIPPIN'. WHAT THEY HAD WAS A FACE-TO-FACE, BUMPER-TO-BUMPER CONFRONTATION THAT WAS ONGOING YEAR AFTER YEAR.

Simply because the Cup schedule is so much shorter than in Petty's heyday, it is extremely unlikely anyone else will reach his 200 wins. He raced full-time virtually his entire career; Pearson was mainly a part-timer, interested mostly in big-money races after several years of running the full schedule. Thus, Petty started twice as many races as Pearson (1,184 to 574), giving him many more opportunities to stack victories. Pearson's winning percentage (18.3) topped Petty's (17.0). Petty won seven championships to Pearson's three, but Pearson ran lengthy schedules in only four seasons.

Both men had extended runs of greatness and moments of brilliance. In 1967, Petty won twenty-seven races, including ten in a row. In 1973, Pearson raced eighteen times, winning eleven and dominating the series' superspeedways. There were seasons in which each seemed unbeatable.

Pearson, said his former crew chief Leonard Wood, "could sense what was going to happen and be ready for it. A lot of drivers drive no further than the end of the hood and don't see the danger ahead of them. He could figure out a lap ahead where drivers were going to be and what kind of trouble they were about to get in."

Pearson also had remarkably good vision. He said he could glance across Daytona International Speedway's massive infield while he was on the frontstretch and pick out which cars were on the backstretch. It gave him advance notice of what to expect on the road ahead, he said.

Pearson's celebrated strategy of holding his cards close to the vest until near the end of races often succeeded. As sneaky as a night predator, he typically used the first three-quarters of a race to settle somewhere in the top twenty, feeling out the strength of other drivers in different parts of the track. When it was time to challenge for the win, he pushed toward the front. He proved repeatedly that the race is not always to the swift.

When challenged, however, Pearson could rise to the occasion at virtually any point in a 500-mile (805-km) chase. At a race at Talladega Superspeedway during Pearson's golden years, a track sponsor offered a huge fishing boat to the driver who led the fiftieth lap. Pearson's party, including his cousin, Danny Pearson, passed the boat on their way into the garage area before the race. "David looked at the boat as we walked by and said, 'I'm going to win that boat for Glen [Wood, the team owner],'" Danny Pearson said. "On lap forty-eight, he was about twelfth. On lap forty-nine, he was fifth. On lap fifty, he was a good way out in front."

Bobby Allison, a brash newcomer who became a threat to the supremacy of Petty and Pearson, watched Pearson's method of operation with interest. "The rest of us, we couldn't stand to be back there in fifth or tenth when we knew the car could be leading," Allison said. "David could. He had taken care of his car and protected his tires, and so his car was really way better to go those final laps than the rest of our cars were."

Petty also evaluated Pearson's style. "He was one of the most relaxed drivers ever," he said. "He just went out and did his thing. He didn't drive on adrenalin. Bobby [Allison] and Cale [Yarborough] did, but that was their personalities. Pearson was relaxed. He had confidence that he could do whatever he needed to do. He didn't have to strain to drive. Day in and day out, on all different tracks and different kinds of circumstances, he probably had more natural talent than anybody. He made everything look easy."

Dale Inman said Petty "respected Pearson and Pearson's driving more than anybody out there."

In his NASCAR Hall of Fame press conference in 2011, Pearson said he had fun racing Petty. "I knew what he was going to do every lap," he said. "Of course, he did me. Don't ask me who, but there are some of them out there that you didn't know what they were going to do the next lap. You can't really race somebody that way, or at least you don't feel safe racing with them that way. Like Richard, I knew exactly where he was going to back off every lap. That way, you could figure out where and when you could pass him, if you could. One of you was going to be better than another through a certain corner. Whatever corner it was that you were the best in, that's where you got to pass."

Petty was more of a frontrunner than Pearson, but he was also a calculating driver. Almost every time he drove onto the track during his peak years, he had one of the best cars in the field—sometimes one so well prepared that the rest of the starters had little chance. Petty worked that advantage to the limit, the best evidence of that being his 200 victories and consistent presence in the top ten.

Other drivers occasionally outsmarted Pearson and Petty, but such circumstances were as rare as snow in Florida.

When Darrell Waltrip showed up in the early 1970s to challenge the stock car racing establishment (which certainly included Petty and Pearson), he looked on with a bit of envy.

"They were pretty equal," Waltrip said. "I watched them race each other a lot. I was still struggling trying to figure out what I wanted to do and how I was going to do it. I would ask David questions. He would tell me the truth. I'd ask somebody else, and they'd tell you a damn lie. Maybe he told me the truth because he knew I couldn't beat him. He knew I was going to get into trouble and he tried to keep me from it. Richard and I were never friends. I felt like he felt like he was privileged, that he had certain advantages that other people didn't have. I don't think Pearson bought into that too much. I don't think he really cared."

Petty and Pearson remained friends throughout and following their careers. "They always had respect for each other," NASCAR's Mike Helton said. "You knew they appreciated each other. They were going to race each other hard, but they had a mutual respect that bonded them and kept it from being uncomfortable."

Larry Pearson, David's oldest son, said his father's relationship with Petty became more important after the 1977 death of driver Bobby Isaac, Pearson's best friend in the sport. "When Bobby died, he became close with Richard," Larry told *The Scene Vault* NASCAR podcast. "They were not brothers, but they acted like it. They were really friendly and close. And they never raced each other dirty. You have to earn respect. Daddy knew if he was going to win, he had to beat Richard."

Many years after their racing ended, Pearson called Petty "one of the closest friends I have. We wouldn't fuss. We have beat and banged a lot, but we never did spin each other out for meanness to win the race. We would nudge them or move them over, you know. You can move a guy over without spinning him out, and we would do that. Get him sideways a bit and go on, but wrecking him for meanness or spinning him all the way out or something like that, no, we didn't do that."

So often, as sundown beckoned and the laps wound down, it was Petty-Pearson gliding toward the finish. Together.

"They ran first and second sixty-three times," Kyle Petty said. "Show me those numbers with anybody against Dale Earnhardt, anybody against Jeff Gordon. Nobody went after it like those guys. When they both showed up, chances are that it would wind up between them. It's funny to me today when two drivers will get in an altercation and you pick up Monday's paper and it's a rivalry. You don't make a rivalry in one race. A rivalry is twenty years."

In addition to being rivals, Petty and Pearson were teammates—sort of. In a 1964 race on the Watkins Glen International racetrack in New York, Pearson was forced to the pits when a crash near him sent debris into his windshield, propelling splinters of shattered glass into his right eye. Petty, who had fallen out of the race early with a blown engine, jumped in Pearson's car. The No. 6 Cotton Owens Dodge finished sixth.

"THEY RAN FIRST AND SECOND SIXTY-THREE TIMES. SHOW ME THOSE NUMBERS WITH ANYBODY AGAINST DALE EARNHARDT, ANYBODY AGAINST JEFF GORDON. NOBODY WENT AFTER IT LIKE THOSE GUYS."

Five years later, in the Volunteer 500 at the Bristol Motor Speedway (formerly the Bristol International Speedway from 1961–1978 and then the Bristol International Raceway from 1978–1996) in Tennessee, Pearson scored the win with relief-driving assistance from Petty. The race, the first since the half-mile (0.8-km) track was banked steeply in the turns, was held on a 104-degree (40°C) afternoon. (It was the same day, incidentally, that American astronauts Neil Armstrong and Buzz Aldrin became the first humans to land on the moon.) Pearson, wrestling with the flu, turned his Holman-Moody Ford over to Petty (also a Ford driver that year) after leading laps 183–344. Pearson's car won by three laps.

"Today, if you're driving a Chevrolet you can't get in a Ford," Petty said. "Back then you would get in two or three different cars. It didn't make any difference. You were trying to help out your competitors, trying to get the best out of the car."

It was another day in which Petty and Pearson were successful—this time, oddly enough, in the same car.

Eleven-year-old Richard Petty stood and watched with a certain amount of awe—and a certain amount of dust in his eyes—as Oldsmobiles, Fords, Buicks, and Hudsons whirled around Charlotte Speedway.

June 19, 1949. Looking at that time and place from the perspective of a lens far in the future, it was a day of insanity. On a nondescript three-quarter-mile (1.2-km) dirt track pockmarked by holes and ruts, Bill France Sr. had corralled a ragtag collection of drivers, all of whom knew the dangers they were about to address and none of whom much cared. More remarkably, some of them had brought (or borrowed) new cars fresh from the post–World War II factories in Detroit to race in wild abandon for most of a thoroughly unpredictable afternoon.

It was a circus of uncertainty, a carnival of highwire thrills, and a junkyard in motion.

It was the very real beginning of the vision France, a sometimes racer and a sometimes race promoter, had formed years earlier. If people enjoyed watching daring men and the occasional woman race on dirt bullrings in old jalopies rebuilt from dying or dead street cars, wouldn't they rush to see those same drivers compete in new sedans? Wouldn't that be an irresistible show?

The answer, on this day, clearly was yes—a loud yes. Thousands of spectators saying yes with their dollars. The crowd estimate ranged from 13,000 to 22,500. Traffic moving in and around the track property the morning of the race was crazily snarled.

"There were fans here at 6 a.m. that day," said David Allison, standing on the track property many years later. His father, Carl, operated the track, which was located near the Charlotte Municipal Airport (now the Charlotte Douglas International Airport). (The much larger Charlotte Motor Speedway, located on the other side of the city, would open in 1960). "They came from everywhere. Cars were parked as far as 4 miles [6 km] away. We had people climbing trees to see. Daddy would crank up a chainsaw and go over there. He wouldn't actually cut the trees down, but they would come out of them anyway."

Joining Lee Petty, Richard's father, in the field were future racing stars Curtis Turner, Buck Baker, Herb Thomas, Red Byron, and Tim Flock, among others.

But wait . . . was it smart to take practically new passenger vehicles and subject them to this sort of punishment, perhaps never to be able to use them to ferry the wife and kids to church again? It was one thing to bang around a grungy dirt track in an old jalopy that had been modified into a semblance of a race car; it was another to drop a sleek new Lincoln coupe with shiny black fenders sparkling in the sun and its very presence shouting "Money!" into a hellish terrain better suited for military maneuvers.

Still, there they were. Dozens of new or nearly new representatives of Detroit factory labor whipping around the track at astonishing speeds and sending clouds of dust in all directions. There was no escaping the grit and grime—or the adventure. Even though the day brought the heat of mid-June, there was a certain chill to it.

For young Richard Petty, there was no need to run, no idea of plugging his ears with his fingers, and no thought of escape. This was a little bit of heaven. He watched as his father, who had picked up the racing bug on trips with his brother Julian to watch dirt-track events near Greensboro, North Carolina, charged through the turns and down the short straightaways. Lee ran wide open and fearless and with little concern for the plight of the hulking Buick Roadmaster that carried him through the fog of competition. Lee had little concern for the car in large part because it wasn't his. Like several other drivers on that next-to-last day of spring outside Charlotte, North Carolina, he had borrowed the car with the hope—but not the promise—of returning it fully intact.

"We got in the Buick in Greensboro and drove it to Charlotte," Richard Petty said. "Daddy pulled it up to a Texaco station and put it up on the rack and changed the oil and greased it up, checked the air in the tires and took the muffler off. We drove the rest of the way to the track."

Lee Petty was one of thirty-three adventurers wheeling around Charlotte Motor Speedway in what was the first race of Bill France's newest idea—a thing he called the Strictly Stock Series. There had been automobile races across much of the United States in the years before World War II, but France's audacious plan to put new cars in competition was a bold departure from the norm. Heavily advertised around the region, the race was a financial success even before the first engine fired to life.

There *were* issues, however.

The dust was so bad even early in the race that drivers counted poles or posts along the track to know when to whip the steering wheel because they sometimes couldn't see to the next turn. This was standard operating procedure at some tracks.

"It was so dusty that when you went by the grandstand and went all the way around that track, when you came back you'd run through the dust you had stirred up the lap before," said Tim Flock, who would become a star on NASCAR short tracks. "We took masking tape, probably a hundred rolls, and taped the bumpers and all the chrome all across the front of the cars to keep the rocks from really beating it up, but when the race was over with, that front end was beat up.

"When they dropped them flags back then, it was dog eat dog. We weren't worried about no points. We were worried about making enough money to take home to feed the kids."

It was a wild day for the Petty family. The panhard bar broke on the Buick, and Lee crashed and rolled the car several times halfway through the race but finished seventeenth. The accident happened quickly, and Petty's body bounced around inside the car as the Buick slammed into the dirt surface. He needed a few stitches to close a head wound. Lee and his two sons, Richard and Maurice, surveyed the damage. "We tore that car up so bad," Maurice remembered, "that they couldn't get it on a wrecker. They had to put it on a dump truck."

Through the haze of that calamitous race day, Richard Petty could see his future. It smelled of engine exhaust, tire rubber, and Carolina red clay, and it was good. Petty had no idea at that moment how good it would come to be.

Lee Petty had driven a delivery truck and worked as a salesman for a biscuit company. The work was boring and the money wasn't good. Racing held promise, he figured. He rolled the numbers around in his head and decided, at thirty-five years old, to change course. He could raise a family doing this. Racing cars was about bread and trophies, but mostly the bread.

Lee jumped onto the NASCAR train and rolled on. At Daytona Beach, Florida, in the 1950s, drivers with fast cars and grand ambitions gathered to test themselves against others of the same persuasion. After running wild on the hard-packed beach sand in February 1954,

Petty came home to Level Cross, North Carolina, with what NASCAR called an Official Certificate of Speed, verifying that Petty had reached 123.41 miles per hour (198.61 km per hour) in what NASCAR described as the "measured mile" along the beachfront. The certificate was signed by Bill France Sr.

Lee had joined NASCAR five years earlier, two days before the Strictly Stock Series debuted at Charlotte. His membership number was 0-53. By handing over his $10 and joining, as outlined by his membership card, he agreed "to do everything in his power to further the sport of stock car racing." Benefits included a NASCAR decal for his car, a membership pin, and regularly distributed bulletins.

Kyle Petty, who also would race for the family team, described Lee's decision to trust the Pettys' future to racing: "[Lee] saw racing as a way to earn a buck—a better way to make money and put food on the table for his young family. Nothing more, nothing less. That's what racing was all about for him. You can drive past all the farms around where they lived in Level Cross, and those are fifth- and sixth-generation farmers. That's their life. Racing is where my grandfather went. So, Richard Petty grew up in it. It's his life. And it's just like being a farmer. You have good years and bad years. Sometimes it rains. Sometimes it doesn't."

It would rain for the Pettys. It would pour.

From Lee Petty's moment of decision into the first decades of the 2000s, racing was largely one thing for the Pettys—business.

"It worked for the family, and it's still working," Richard Petty said in a 2022 interview. "When Daddy made that decision in 1949, we're still living off that—the whole Petty crowd and thousands of people who worked with us or for us. There's no telling how many people were influenced by that decision."

"My grandfather came through the Depression and knew what it was like to have nothing," Kyle Petty said. "The family lived in a construction trailer. They were dead dirt poor. Then they found out you can race and win 150 bucks. My God, you can feed the family for a month with that. It became all about putting food on the table."

After the Charlotte race, Lee bought a 1949 Plymouth coupe—it was relatively light and relatively inexpensive, about $1,000—with the idea of going big-time racing. He bought a set of tires for $19 at

Montgomery Ward, a major retailer of the day. The tires typically would last for several races. Purpose-built racing tires were still somewhere in the future.

Lee quickly became a regular as NASCAR rolled through its first Strictly Stock season. He scored his first victory in the seventh race of the eight-race 1949 season, finishing five laps in front of the field in a 200-lap event at Heidelberg Raceway, a half-mile (0.8-km) dirt track near Pittsburgh, Pennsylvania, on October 2. Leading all but four laps, Petty won $1,500. This was big money to take home to North Carolina.

Petty won at least one race every year through the 1950s and earned series championships in 1954, 1958, and 1959 as he established himself as one of the fledgling sport's first reliable stars. "Lee was as tough as anybody I ran against," said Buck Baker, who had more than a few postrace "discussions" with the Petty patriarch. In those early days, the infield fights sometimes lasted almost as long as the races.

Richard and Maurice had childhoods similar to those of other boys in their farming community in central North Carolina. Richard remembers attending the local Methodist church and playing kick the can with other kids in the yard after services. Richard, Maurice, and their cousin Dale Inman raced wagons and bicycles in the woods near the Petty home. The Petty family didn't have a television during the kids' younger years, and there were no luxuries.

"We lived on a dirt road, and there was no electricity, no running water, no indoor plumbing," Richard remembered. "But we didn't think we were poor. It was the same as the neighbors. If you wanted water, you went out to the well and got it. If you wanted to take a bath, you heated the water and put it in the tub. We did have a radio. After supper, we'd turn the radio on for an hour or so and listen to *The Green Hornet* or *The Lone Ranger*. That was a big thrill."

There were difficult days along the way. The Petty home burned to the ground in 1943 when Richard was in second grade. His father got a construction trailer and turned it into a makeshift home.

"It was all about survival," Richard said. "Back during the war, you couldn't get building materials. The only way Daddy was able to get stuff was through the black market. That house was built under the table. He had a guy down the street build it."

Richard played basketball, baseball, and football at Randleman High School and even found time to be in the marching band. He was good at stick-and-ball sports, but it was very clear very early that his future rested in his father's tire tracks. His first experiences behind the wheel came in 1954 as he put a Chrysler through its paces on the back roads of Randolph County—this before he had a driver's license. He also remembers steering the family's 1938 Ford in a farm field at age five. By fourteen, he was working on engines in the Petty shop. Early on, he had designs on becoming a racing mechanic, but those ideas soon faded and he announced to his father his desire to drive race cars. Okay, Lee said. The qualifier was that Richard had to wait until his twenty-first birthday.

It was like waiting for Christmas.

Richard made his NASCAR debut July 12, 1958, in a Convertible Division race at Columbia Speedway, a half-mile (0.8-km) dirt track in central South Carolina. The track was a favorite haunt in the 1950s for drivers who one day would dominate NASCAR superspeedways, and it was a logical place for Lee Petty to choose for his son's baptism of fire. After Richard turned twenty-one, Lee pointed to a tired Oldsmobile in a shop corner and told him to get it ready to race.

Lee Petty was a cantankerous sort. He gave his sons advice (more often commands), but he wasn't a touchy-feely father. He was old-school before anybody knew the term. I made it on my own, he figured, so can the boys.

"I don't know that I ever heard my dad say, 'I love you,'" Richard said. "I don't ever remember him putting his arm around me or hugging me or any of that stuff. I can remember as a little kid that he played ball and stuff with us or wrestled around on the floor with us. But once we got into the growing-up part of the deal, it was 'Work on this car' or 'Go mow the yard' or 'Move that car' or 'Change the oil in it.' It became more of a business deal than a father-son relationship.

"It was good for me. That's the reality of life. I was able to grow up real quick in the real world, not in the family world—even though we were family, and it was a close family as far as the business part. As far as hanging out together, we didn't do that. But that was society at that time. It was tough for everybody.

"My parents grew up in the Depression, so every penny that came in, they made it count. What we had was the necessities. We didn't have any extra, but our neighbors didn't have it, either."

The Pettys often compared their situation with the farmers who were their neighbors. As soon as farm children were old enough to work in the fields, many were given chores. The Petty kids did theirs in the shop.

Having gotten the okay from Lee, Richard, Dale Inman, and crew member Red Myler hauled the Oldsmobile convertible south out of Level Cross. They arrived at the track on the outskirts of South Carolina's capital city later than they anticipated, giving Richard time for only a few practice laps. Lee and Maurice Petty were not there for the big moment because they had traveled to Asheville, North Carolina, where Lee was running a Cup Series race.

"I looked forward to seeing if I could do this," Richard said. "Me and Dale had worked on cars our whole lives. We put a bunch of wedge in the car and ran sideways when I had to. There wasn't a lot of setup. It was about going out and running around the racetrack and learning how to do it. It wasn't about racing anybody because I didn't know how to. I got lucky and didn't run into anybody."

That Saturday marked the first time Richard had driven a race car on a track. He qualified a respectable thirteenth. Then, to his surprise, he finished the 200-lap race.

Petty, driving car No. 42, finished sixth, five laps behind winner Bob Welborn.

"I wasn't nervous," Petty told reporters after the race. "But I was a little scared. I think I should have done a lot better."

Bob Talbert covered the race for the Columbia newspaper, *The State*. "Lee Petty's little boy made his debut with the flourish of a veteran," Talbert wrote. "On the eve of his maiden voyage, he was joking with other drivers, a typical Petty trait. He didn't appear to be nervous or excited. It was as if he was taking a Sunday afternoon spin in the family car."

It was a small start to something that would become very big.

Soon—in fact, very soon—the big time would call. Rivalries awaited— one in particular.

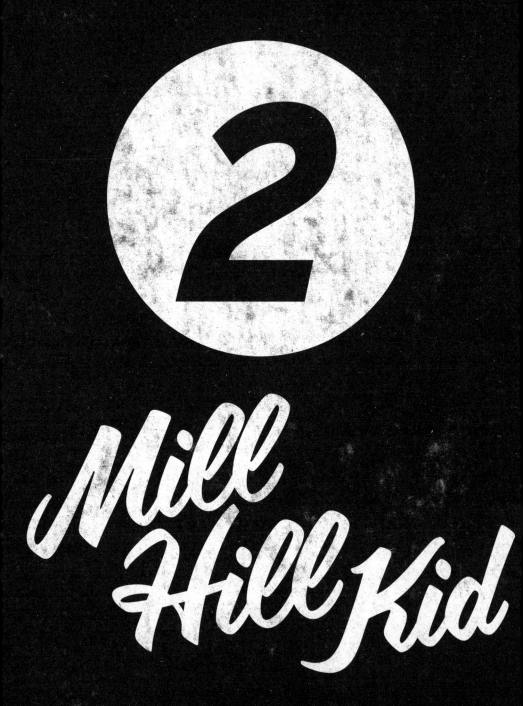

Many of stock car racing's oldest tracks were connected to city or county fairgrounds. Racing—first with horses and later with automobiles—was a part of the package when locals visited the fair to ride the carousel, grab some cotton candy, and admire the nephew's prize heifer in the livestock barn.

Such was the case at the Piedmont Interstate Fairgrounds in Spartanburg, South Carolina. The annual fair typically is held in October, and people from Spartanburg and neighboring counties in South and North Carolina (thus "Interstate") have made it a part of their autumn celebrations for decades. For many years, auto racing on the dirt track adjacent to the fairgrounds was a popular, almost mandatory, part of fair week. Fairgoers remember riding the Ferris wheel and being able to see the race cars rolling around the track when the wheel reached its peak. The track gained noteworthy status in 1953, when the almost-new NASCAR Cup Series (then Grand National) came to town. The Spartanburg track was a mainstay of the series until 1966, and it became a favorite of many drivers. There was a devoted fan base, and drivers of that era remember spectators passing a hat through the crowd to collect money for drivers whose cars left the track damaged.

This was the landscape that attracted David Pearson to auto racing. A Spartanburg native, he climbed trees outside the fence as a kid to watch drivers stir up dirt on the old track. To a kid from a mill hill village, it was fascinating stuff.

Spartanburg businessman Joe Littlejohn knew that lure well. Littlejohn was one of eight children of cotton mill and farming parents in Spartanburg. In 1938, he was operating a barbecue restaurant and tavern in town. A lover of fast automobiles, Littlejohn and several of his friends became interested in the racing that was occurring on the hard-packed sand of Daytona Beach, Florida, and they drove a couple of cars south to try out this new thing. The idea didn't make any sense, but that didn't matter.

Soon, Littlejohn was running blistering speeds along the Daytona sand. There was a mix of thrill and danger to it all, just the recipe for young men looking to live on the edge. Littlejohn became friends with Bill France Sr., who had taken over promotion of the beach racing. Nine years later, Littlejohn was one of three dozen men France invited to a series of meetings that resulted in the formation of NASCAR and a bold new horizon for stock car racing.

After driving in the Daytona races and experiencing the excitement building around them, Littlejohn saw an opportunity. He was convinced that automobile racing would sell in Spartanburg. He approached the Spartanburg city council about revamping the fairgrounds harness-racing track for automobile racing. The city fathers were astonished.

"They said, 'What in the world do you want to do—kill everybody in Spartanburg?'" Littlejohn remembered in an interview many years later. "I said, 'No, I'm not planning on hurting anybody.' They finally agreed to let me use it."

PEARSON NEVER FULLY ACCEPTED THE FACT THAT HE WAS A NATIONAL SPORTS CELEBRITY, A HERO TO HUNDREDS OF THOUSANDS OF RACE FANS.

Admission for the first race Littlejohn promoted at the track, held November 11, 1939, was seventy-five cents.

Littlejohn continued to schedule races at the fairgrounds, and the noise and excitement attached to such unpredictable events eventually drew a young David Pearson to the track—or, more precisely, to trees surrounding the track, where he had free viewing. "I thought that was the greatest sight in the world," Pearson said. Years later, he would kid Littlejohn, his mentor, that he never paid a penny to watch Littlejohn's races. But clearly many other folks did.

Pearson grew up as the son of textile-mill workers in a modest home near Spartanburg. He was one of six children of Eura and Lennie Pearson. Three died in infancy. David, born December 22, 1934, would become one of the most famous athletes to call Spartanburg home and a racer of international renown. Eventually, visitors rolling into town from Interstate 85 would travel along David Pearson Boulevard, which runs past his childhood home. Accepting that honor, Pearson said the road would have no speed limit.

Many years after his 1989 retirement, David Pearson sifted through the mail at a small desk near his kitchen. It was a typical Tuesday batch. Long after his racing days, Pearson still got autograph requests almost daily. Some arrived addressed simply to "David Pearson, Race Car Driver, Spartanburg, S.C." Post office workers knew.

"They keep coming," Pearson said, shaking his head. "It never fails to amaze me."

That was David Pearson. He never fully accepted the fact that he was a national sports celebrity, a hero to hundreds of thousands of race fans, and one of the greatest athletes ever produced by the state of South Carolina. Because of Pearson's racing exploits across the country and at the highest levels of auto racing, the name of his town—Spartanburg—appeared in newspaper accounts in every state and beyond. The town, once a railroad hub (thus its nickname, Hub City), was put on the map by Pearson, some said.

To his friends, his family, and himself, he was just David. There was no veneer, no artifice. That he could do one thing better than virtually anybody else who had ever tried it was kind of matter-of-fact. Racing and winning were just the things he did. He expected to win every time he flipped the switch to crank a race car engine. "He never left the house thinking he wasn't going to win," said Ricky Pearson, one of his three sons.

He did win—105 times at the NASCAR Cup Series level and many more times in other sorts of race cars across the spectrum of motorsports. It's likely that he could have succeeded at the top level of any sort of racing he chose. Fortunately for NASCAR, and unfortunately for those who would compete against him, his path led to stock car racing.

Pearson's career could have been as a linthead, the derogatory term some used to identify cotton-mill workers in the mid-twentieth century. He quit school to follow his father into a job at the textile mill in Whitney, near Spartanburg. This was not unusual in the Carolina Piedmont in the 1950s as older teenagers—many hoping to buy their first car—saw factory work as a quick way to earn money. The textile industry provided employment for thousands across the Carolinas and Georgia in those years. Like many others, Pearson's ancestors had moved from the Appalachian Mountains early in the century, leaving behind the uncertainties of hardscrabble farm life on rocky mountain landscapes to work in the often-punishing noise and grime of the textile mills. The work was hard and often dangerous, but the pay was steady and the textile companies usually provided cheap rental housing for employees. The Pearsons moved to Whitney from North Carolina in part because David's father had been recruited for a spot in the workforce. The elder Pearson was an outstanding baseball pitcher, and baseball was a big thing in the textile world. Mill officials often hired workers based on their on-field talents. Having a winning baseball team often was high on mill owners' priority lists.

David Pearson's job, known then as "taking off cloth," involved handling big swaths of cloth, hour after hour, day after day, on the 3 to 11 p.m. "second shift." The rolls weighed about 600 pounds (272 kg). The job gave him a window view of his buddies hanging out at the nearby service station, and that, more than anything, made his textile career a very short one. When he looked back on those days, he said he couldn't stand to watch his friends having fun while he toiled away. It was only a matter of weeks before Pearson closed the mill's doors behind him forever.

In the weeks that followed, Pearson picked up odd jobs, working in his brother Bill's automobile body shop, pumping gas at a service station, roofing houses, and briefly driving a garbage truck. Foremost on his mind, though, were cars—and the faster the better. Pearson bought an old, used-up Ford for $40, and he and some friends worked on the car, beating out the fenders and trying to turn it into a race car. They drove it around the neighborhood, often detouring onto ballfields or other wide-open properties to see how fast it might go, kicking up dirt in the process. Pearson was the only one in the group who wanted to drive the car. He had the wild gene.

Word of Pearson's interest in racing spread to Bill Tomlin, who lived in nearby Woodruff, South Carolina, and was a regular at area dirt tracks. One day in September 1953, Tomlin hauled his race car to Pearson's house, stopped out front, and asked Pearson if he'd like to drive his car. Pearson, then eighteen years old, needed about one second to say yes. He wanted the fun and he needed whatever trickle of dollars might appear from the adventure. He had responsibilities as a husband, having married Helen Ray of Gaffney, South Carolina, in February 1952, when he was seventeen. She and Pearson had met at a drive-in restaurant on the east side of Spartanburg.

Pearson raced for the first time at Confederate Motor Speedway, a dusty dirt track in Woodruff. Details of that landmark event have been lost to history, but Pearson later said he finished second in a heat race and second in the feature.

"I remember one thing about it," Pearson told writer Jim Hunter. "It was fun. There weren't any guardrails and the track was a quarter-mile [0.4-km] dirt. The only reason you put rollbars in your car was because everybody else had them."

Pearson won $5.22. "I thought I was the luckiest person in the world," he said.

It was a very slow start, but he was on his way to being very fast and earning much bigger numbers.

"I liked racing on dirt," Pearson said in an interview in 1991. "There's a lot of skill to driving on dirt. I think that's the best way to learn. You just touch a guy enough to break him loose a little to get by him. You don't have to knock him out like a lot of people do. You can do the same thing on asphalt and make it look so easy like you didn't mean to do it. Some people can do that, and nobody ever knows the difference except the two drivers. They know.

"At the [Spartanburg] fairgrounds, you could actually sling it sideways and throw mud up in the stands, just messing around in practice. It looks good, and it's a good show, just going through the corners sideways like that."

Helen Pearson remembered watching her husband and a friend, Gerald Pruitt, transform junkyard cars into race cars. "He sat up half the night, sometimes all night, working," she said. "I was pregnant with our first son [Larry] at the time. I would sit out in the garage behind his father's house and keep the coal heater going while he worked on the car."

In the early years of his driving career, Pearson jumped at the chance to race cars owned by others, in large part because he didn't have the money to build a competitive car of his own. One of those owners was Harley Hill, a Spartanburg-area racer who often stopped to fuel his race car at the Spartanburg service station where Pearson worked. Hill's son, Mike, who many years later would become a winning NASCAR crew chief, remembers riding to those races as a kid.

"Daddy would pull his old '40 Ford into the station there on Asheville Highway in Spartanburg, and David would pump the gas," Mike Hill said. "I was just a little kid. I would hear David hollering to Daddy, 'You need to let me drive this car.' Then he would reach inside the car and tickle me."

Pearson's pleadings worked. In the summer of 1958, the Hill family traveled to Myrtle Beach, South Carolina, for their annual summer vacation, and Harley Hill left the race car with Pearson, telling him to run a few races while they were gone.

"The whole time we were at the beach Daddy was dragging me up and down the highway looking for a newspaper to see if we could find the results from some of those little tracks," Mike Hill said. "We never did, but when we got home we found out David had won every race he ran. He gave Daddy envelopes with money he had won. Daddy put those envelopes in a drawer at home, and I would go in there and look at the money sometimes. I remember thinking, 'That's a lot of money.' I'm sure he split it with Daddy."

Hill grew up near the Pearson family and graduated from high school with Larry, Pearson's oldest son. At Spartanburg High School, Hill remembers being assigned to write a biographical paper about a famous person. Paul Riddle, the student sitting behind him, chose legendary drummer Buddy Rich for his paper. Riddle would go on to play drums for the Marshall Tucker Band, a Spartanburg-based rock and country music group that reached international stardom.

Hill wrote about David Pearson.

"I was over at their house all the time as a kid," Hill said. "Helen fed me pimento cheese sandwiches. There was no better person than Helen. I'd go over to their house all the time and just stare at all David's trophies. That's one of the things that got me into racing."

While Pearson was spinning in the dirt at local short tracks, he had one ear on the racing at Darlington, only a few hours but a world away in the lower part of South Carolina. In those years, he could only dream of what it might be like to race on a huge asphalt track.

"I guess the first time I heard about it, it was just listening to the races, you know, on the radio," Pearson said. "And I'd be out under a shade tree or something, working on an old car and hear them talking about running Darlington . . . the doors and the stripe rubbing the guardrail to get around it, running about 130 mile-an-hour [209 km per hour] or something like that, and I'd say, 'Boy, them boys is crazy doing something like that,' you know, rubbing a wall running that fast."

How aggressive was Pearson in the early years?

Very, according to Willis Smith, who was wrecked by Pearson, an encounter that led to a lifelong friendship.

WHILE PEARSON WAS SPINNING IN THE DIRT AT LOCAL SHORT TRACKS, HE HAD ONE EAR ON THE RACING AT DARLINGTON, ONLY A FEW HOURS BUT A WORLD AWAY.

"It was in 1957 at Golden Strip Speedway in Fountain Inn [upstate South Carolina]," Smith said. "I was picking up some rides here and there at tracks around, and Pearson was there in his No. 16. The first heat race probably had about twenty cars, and we drew for starting positions. I drew the pole. It was fifteen laps, and Pearson was in the race. My car wasn't that great, but we took off and I led the first eleven laps. I should have never looked in the mirror, but I did, and David and 'Ozark Ike' Williams were right behind me, running side by side. They were good, and I was surprised it took them that long to get through the field. I'm thinking that I'll get out of their way and finish third and get into the feature, and I'll be happy. I pulled down, and Pearson never backed off. He ran slap into the back of my car. I flipped six times, end over end, tore it up big time."

Smith and Pearson had a "discussion" after the race, Smith said. "After I told him that he wrecked me, with his sense of humor he said I was in his way," he said.

Smith wasn't hurt, but the crash was unsettling, particularly for his wife, Virginia. "She was at the track and was pregnant with our daughter," Smith said. "We had heard the old tale that if a woman got scared suddenly when she was pregnant that she could 'mark' the child in some bad way. When I wrecked, people said Virginia grabbed her face. That worried me bad, about what was my child going to look like. Of course, she turned out beautiful."

Smith had begun running South Carolina dirt tracks in the mid-1950s a few months after a stint in the Army. Pearson already had a reputation in the area. "People would tell me how good he was," Smith said.

Pearson was a few years away from edging into primetime. On dirt tracks scattered across the Carolinas, his star was rising. He picked up a nickname: Little David the Giant Killer.

Brothers Tom and Pete Blackwell, who operated Greenville-Pickens Speedway, a track between Greenville and Easley, South Carolina, which became one of NASCAR's premier half-miles (0.8 km), heard reports of Pearson's successes elsewhere and invited him to race there. He was an immediate star, winning the track's featured Late Model championship in 1959 and putting an even stronger foundation under his reputation as a short-track wizard.

"I never will forget," Pearson said. "Every time you win, they [NASCAR] sent you a little checkered flag decal. That was the year I'd won so many races I had them all around the hood and up over the top. It'd just tickle me to death to get one of them little ol' checkered flag stickers."

It was about more than tiny stickers, of course. Once he started logging wins regularly, Pearson figured he was making about $150 a week driving race cars. That was good income, he said, unless he wrecked a car and had to invest more in new parts.

Next came the call from Columbia Speedway in central South Carolina, where Ralph Earnhardt (Dale's father) and Bobby Isaac were kingpins. "They were winning most of the races, and up in here [Greenville-Pickens] I was winning most of them, so they got me to come to Columbia to outrun Earnhardt. So, I went down and I won the race," Pearson said. Paul "Little Bud" Moore, who ran against Pearson in Columbia, said Pearson's cars were some of the most solidly prepared in the race fields.

As word spread about Pearson's skills, car builder and driver Banjo Matthews convinced Pearson to race in Asheville, North Carolina, a big switch for the young driver because the track there had an asphalt surface. "I said, 'Banjo, I've never run on asphalt before in my life,'" Pearson said. "I won the race. I went back the next week. I said, 'I can do this again!'" Didn't work so well. He demolished his car.

It was all a big learning curve—those hard runs into the first turn after the green flag—for David Pearson, but he was an excellent student on the short tracks of the day.

Bigger things—bigger tracks, bigger money, and bigger competition—were ahead.

Jack Smith, one of stock car racing's pioneer drivers, started running fast cars on short tracks in 1949, NASCAR's first Cup season, and saw the dramatic changes in the sport over the next half-century. A Cup race winner twenty-one times, Smith raced against all the sport's early stars and became one himself as the NASCAR traveling circus bounced from one backwater dirt track to another.

In 2001, not long before his death and almost forty years after his retirement, Smith offered some perspective on what racing had been and what it had become. He definitely was a proponent of the "old days were better" point of view, a perspective that permeates the ranks of the 1950s- and 1960s-era drivers.

"There's very few of the drivers today who would have been successful back in the old days," Smith said. "They don't know how tough it was to get out of a car and blood be running out of your hands. You didn't want to do it, but if you wanted to make a living you had to keep going. I don't think they could sleep in a car all night at some track and then race it and then tow that car from Charleston, South Carolina, to Jacksonville, Florida, to Savannah, Georgia, to Martinsville, Virginia, and run at all those places. I don't think there are many of them who love it enough to stay with it."

Those times were hard. The men had to be harder. Buck Clardy, another 1950s-era racer, said the action often continued well past the checkered flag. "You kind of made up the rules as you went back then," he said. "I've seen twenty-six drivers fighting in the infield at Greenwood [South Carolina], and twenty-four of them didn't know what they were fighting for."

They rolled on despite the obstacles, even when money was an issue. "You'd take the house payment money and go buy tires for the race car and hoped you made enough money in the race to get the house money back," Clardy said.

Buck Baker remembered racing on the old Charlotte Fairgrounds track while dealing with a steering issue. "I had a steering wheel to break on me, and I drove with a pair of Vise-Grips the rest of the race," he said. "I had them in the car, and I clamped down and turned with the grips. Didn't go as fast as normal but finished the race. I thought it was dangerous, but I didn't pay much attention to it. It was just the idea of finishing or outrunning somebody."

Racing was a dark art of sorts.

Lee Petty traveled those same roads and raced through many of the same tough circumstances. In 1958, racing for the national championship, he faced a dilemma near the middle of the season, a challenge that would be considered ridiculous in the modern NASCAR world.

The schedule for what would later become the Cup Series was oppressively long that year—fifty-one races scattered across the country. Petty needed as many starts as possible to gather as many points as possible. One of the men racing him at the top of the standings was Jack Smith, who, as he mentioned, was known to race until his hands bled. In that world, there was no retreat, no surrender.

NASCAR's wacky approach to scheduling made Petty's task difficult. The series would race May 30, a Friday, on the one-mile (1.6-km) oval at Trenton, New Jersey. Only two days later, a 190-lap race was scheduled on the road course at Riverside International Raceway in California. Petty, in first place in the series point standings, intended to race in both events. Participation in every race was not required to qualify for the seasonal championship, but missing a race entered by his closest competitors could cost Petty in the search for a title to pair with the one he won in 1954.

Setting the stage for Petty to race in both events required a family effort. While Lee traveled to Trenton, his sons Richard and Maurice were assigned to drive a second Petty race car from the team shop in Level Cross, North Carolina, across the country to Riverside. After competing at Trenton, Lee would fly cross-country to race the car at Riverside.

The plan took a slight turn when Richard hurt a shoulder "goofing around in the front yard," said Dale Inman, at twenty-one years old already one of the team's major players. So, Inman and Maurice Petty drew the assignment of delivering the second No. 42 car to California. They didn't tow the race car—they drove it.

To say the least, it was quite a trip.

"So Maurice and I lit out for California somewhere in the middle of that week," Inman remembered. "We put the toolboxes and wheels and jackstands and a spare gear or two and luggage in the car with us. Filled the trunk up with stuff and headed out. We took a mattress so one of us could sleep while the other drove. The car had two headlights and one rear light. No turn signal. No brake lights. No windshield wipers. We got stopped by police seven times, but mostly the officers just wanted to know what was going on, so we didn't get any tickets. We were rolling along at about 120 miles per hour [193 km per hour] through the desert and lost a right rear hub coming into Willcox, Arizona. We jacked it up, put another tire on and limped into Willcox. We slept in the car that night and then drove on."

Lee Petty finished third at Trenton, flew to the West Coast, and finished fourth in the car that was waiting for him at Riverside. He drove fifty of the fifty-one races that season, winning seven times and earning his second national championship.

After the Riverside race, Maurice Petty and Inman made the return trip to North Carolina in the No. 42 car. This time, it had *42* on the sides, leftover numbers from the race—one car, one driver, two delivery boys, one fourth-place finish, and a trip almost from sea to shining sea.

The day after arriving home, they went back to work in the Petty shop, a long adventure behind them. It was not a big deal, they said later, just part of keeping a winning team on top during those seasons.

In the early years of the second generation of the racing Pettys, Maurice, who was almost two years younger than Richard, also got his chances behind the wheel. He drove in twenty-six Cup races between 1960 and 1964, scoring no wins but seven top fives. He was twenty-second in his final start, April 12, 1964, at the Occoneechee Speedway in Hillsborough, North Carolina, a race ironically won by David Pearson. Richard Petty finished twelfth. On August 3, 1960, there was a Petty extravaganza. At Dixie Motor Speedway in Birmingham, Alabama, Richard finished second, Lee third, and Maurice eighth. It was the only time the three Pettys raced together.

"Maurice wasn't bad," Inman said. "I remember him running at Hillsborough [a fast 0.9-mile (1.5-km) dirt track]. They had watered the groove pretty good before the race. They threw the green flag and had a big wreck before they got to Turn 1. They stopped the race to clean up. Richard and Maurice got through. When they came around, I went over to Richard's car and he said, 'I'm OK, go and check on Maurice.' Maurice said, 'I can't see.' I cleaned the inside of the windshield and the outside, and it didn't help. We finally figured out there was mud and dirt all over the inside of his glasses.

"He finally quit driving. He had turned over one time at Columbia. He never was that gung-ho about it. He was content looking out for Richard and building engines."

Stock car racing was undergoing a revolution of sorts as the 1950s ended. The massive Daytona International Speedway would open to acclaim—and to a Lee Petty victory—in February 1959, and other big tracks soon would follow. NASCAR was outgrowing its childhood and new stars were needed to succeed the sport's pioneers, men like Lee Petty, Herb Thomas, Tim Flock, and Buck Baker.

One of them would be Richard Petty, who, as the 1958 season began, was eagerly awaiting his first shot at NASCAR's top series. Following not far behind would be David Pearson, who was still banging around the Carolina dirt tracks, racing at higher levels not yet a target. "Pearson, when he came on, he came on pretty quick," Dale Inman said. "I was well acquainted with him early on."

On November 30, 1959, Richard Petty, then twenty-two and newly married to Lynda Gayle Owens, completed an information form for the NASCAR News Bureau, which was building files on drivers as part of its public relations efforts. Petty listed his height at 6-2, his weight at 190, his hair and eyes as brown. His hobby, other than racing? "Handwriting." Had he had any accidents? "Several."

Petty's penmanship on the NASCAR form was immaculate, in stark contrast to most of the other drivers who scribbled their responses. He used the flowing, florid writing style he had learned in a class at business school. He was practicing the art of signing his name with a flourish, a kind of gift he would give everyone who approached him for an autograph for the next six decades. And counting.

Earlier in 1959, on July 18, Petty had scored his first race win. The landmark victory occurred in NASCAR's Convertible Division, a largely experimental series that lasted from 1956 to 1959, at Columbia Speedway in South Carolina. Petty had made his driving debut at the same track in a convertible race on July 12, 1958.

Records show Petty winning the Columbia race in July 1959 over veteran drivers Jack Smith and Glen Wood. The top three finishers were the only drivers on the lead lap at the finish of the 200-lap chase.

Over the course of the next few years, Petty would become exactly what NASCAR needed as it grew from its dirt roots to bigger tracks and broader acceptance. He became a personality, in many ways a bigger-than-life figure. Although Lee Petty was a great manager and an accomplished driver, it was his son who would become the torchbearer during the sport's first period of substantial growth—the 1960s. Richard's bright smile came naturally, he was a hit with fans, and he understood that his job didn't end at the checkered flag. On many nights, he sat and signed autographs until the last fan had been satisfied. Working on cars and driving them well wasn't enough.

If there was a singular force behind NASCAR's acceleration as the 1950s turned into the 1960s, it was Petty. He was front and center as Daytona International Speedway became a national racing capital and other big tracks followed near Charlotte, North Carolina; Atlanta, Georgia; Rockingham, North Carolina; and beyond. NASCAR was running its races in front of more faces and at new places, and Petty's piano-key smile could be seen everywhere.

While Petty aimed toward bigger things, Pearson seemed comfortable, at least for the moment, stacking win after win in Late Model Sportsman races. Even in those early years on dirt, Pearson had started working on his driving style, making his approach more of a thinking man's game than a wild dash through every lap. He wanted to race smarter, not necessarily faster.

"I was always thinking ahead and seeing who I had to outrun," he said. "I spent the first half of a race judging everybody. I'd drop back and run with one and then the other, seeing if I could beat them through the corners. If the car wasn't right, you changed your style to make it work."

In a future that wasn't that far away, Pearson would carry that strategy to the faster tracks of the big time. He and Petty were almost there—one waiting on a twenty-first birthday and for the family stamp of approval, the other much more under the radar, his name not yet

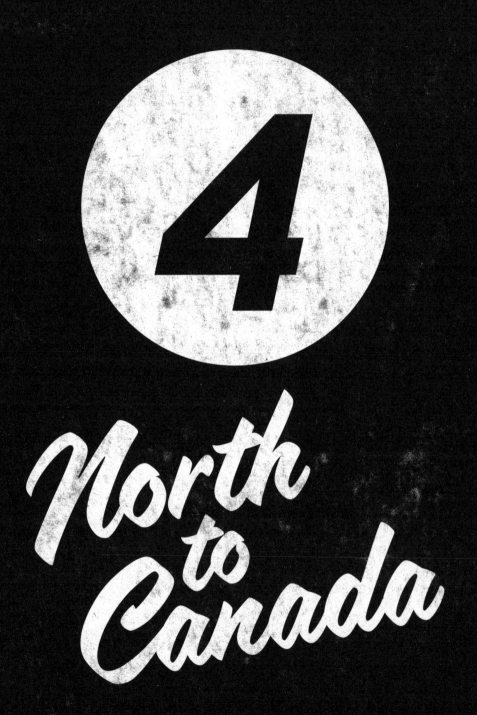

*T*he irony would not become evident for many years.

The first of Richard Petty's 1,184 Cup Series starts came not at Martinsville or Charlotte or Daytona or any other of dozens of NASCAR mainstay tracks. His initial laps in the sport weren't even recorded in the United States. No, the driver who would come to define the sport for millions of fans cranked a Cup engine for the first time in, of all places, Toronto, Ontario, Canada.

The date was July 18, 1958, and there was no grand scheme behind the decision. This was no attempt to hide Petty's inexperience by sending him across the border to race in relative anonymity. It was simply the next race on the Cup schedule, and Lee Petty determined that his boy was ready to make the jump from the Convertible Division to the top series. Off the Petty team went, north of the border, a pair of 1957 Oldsmobiles prepared for Lee and raw rookie Richard.

"Daddy handled everything about when we raced and where we raced," Richard said. "It was the next race on the schedule, so we went."

Their target was the grounds of the Canadian National Exposition (CNE). The stadium at CNE contained a 0.3-mile (483-m) paved racing oval, a rather nondescript track that hosted weekly racing for various area series in the 1950s and 1960s. It was far from the best of venues, and NASCAR's top series would not return there after the 1958 race. The place is better known as the original home of the Toronto Blue Jays of Major League Baseball and the Toronto Argonauts of the Canadian Football League.

Richard had raced for the first time only six days earlier, finishing sixth in a NASCAR Convertible Division race at Columbia Speedway in South Carolina. He had at least a rudimentary understanding of what to do and when to do it from that experience, so he was tossed into the fire less than a week later in NASCAR's featured series. Lee Petty, the family "Papa" and the Petty team boss, figured his son would advance more quickly if he raced against the best, not drivers from a lower division.

"I didn't feel I had to prove anything," Richard said. "I wasn't trying to show anybody that I was the son of Lee Petty. In fact, it was probably just the opposite. If I made it in racing, I wanted to do it on my own, as I tried to develop my own style."

And he had "space" to work on that.

"The big deal with me when I came along is there wasn't enough public relations about it to put me under a microscope," Petty said. "There were just a few people covering racing. We didn't have TV. We didn't have commercials to do. We were more in the racing business and not in show business. I was never really compared that much to what my dad had done because there wasn't that much PR to do."

Racing against the "best" that Friday for Richard involved racing against the old man. Lee Petty, an established NASCAR star by this point, put car No. 42 in victory lane; Richard finished seventeenth (of nineteen entries) in car No. 142, a tired Oldsmobile that had accumulated many laps in the service of Lee Petty. It was the definition of a hand-me-down. The race lasted only forty-six minutes.

Richard didn't finish the race because another car crashed into him fifty-five laps into the 100-lap event. The driver of that car? Lee Petty.

Lee's car was strong, and Richard was feeling his way around in his rookie run. Holding the lead, Lee, hounded for first place by Cotton Owens, approached his son's car, planning to lap him. Richard was in the way, so Lee punted him. Simple as that.

"Richard was all over the track," said Ross Kennedy, a Toronto resident who flagged the race. "Lee was leading and he came around and there was Richard in the way. Whomp! That was the end of Richard."

Richard said he doesn't have many solid memories of his Cup debut.

"I remember Daddy and Cotton Owens [who finished second] racing together," he said. "I was all over the place. I know Daddy hit me. He spun me out. He wound up winning the race. We just had to find a great big Oldsmobile bumper to put back on the car. I soon found out that racing is a tough business, but I knew it was what I wanted to do."

Was there a father-son fuss after the race? "Nah, he didn't talk about it," Richard said. "He was doing good because he won the race. If he hadn't won, I probably would have gotten chewed out pretty good. It wasn't a totally bad night for the Pettys. At least Daddy won."

One of Petty's memories of that day didn't involve the track.

"The thing that sticks out the most is that I remember they sold gas by the liter," he said. "That just blew my mind. It's funny how you'll pick out something that's not important and remember it. When they tore the track down, somebody sent me a steel pole that the fence went on. So, I have a souvenir of my first Cup race—a 4-foot-high [1-m-high] beam."

Among the drivers who finished in front of Petty that day were Peck Peckham, Neil Haight, Howard Phillippi, and Bill Poor. None would drive on to major racing careers, but they always could say they outraced a future king one day on the shores of Lake Ontario.

The race wasn't a barnburner. There were only two leaders all day: Lee Petty, who was in front for twenty-nine laps, and Rex White, who led seventy-one laps from the pole position.

The Oldsmobile Richard Petty drove on that historic day didn't survive to be considered later as a museum piece. "I think I 'eliminated' it at Trenton [New Jersey]," Richard said. "I crashed it so bad it couldn't be fixed."

The Toronto track's weekly (sometimes twice-weekly) racing program shared the bill that day with the Cup race. Former racers in the Toronto area said the Cup race didn't attract as much attention as the parts of the program that included the drivers who raced regularly at the track.

"The spectators, enthusiastic about the regular stock-car races, seemed bored by the late model cars," reported the next day's *Toronto Daily Star* newspaper. Many in the crowd of about 10,000 had left before the race ended, the paper said. Its eleven-paragraph story included only two sentences about Lee Petty's victory. His son was called Dick Petty, a name Richard's mother despised and Richard avoided.

"The NASCAR cars were much slower," said Nate Salter, who attended the race. "The Supermodifieds were quicker, and there was a lot more passing. The fans were used to them and to the guys who were driving."

In the not-too-distant future, those fans would know much more about this kid named Richard Petty.

A fter his racing days were over, Lee Petty took up golf on a whim. He bought a few clubs and started chipping balls around the front lawn of his house. His confidence in the game grew, and soon he was scoring in the 70s.

In the 1970s and 1980s, anxious to test himself against other players and retaining the competitive edge he had in racing, Petty often signed up to play in invitation-only tournaments hosted by speedways or race sponsors on the Wednesday or Thursday before NASCAR races.

At one such event, in Florence, South Carolina, before the weekend's racing activities began at nearby Darlington Raceway, Petty was standing in a buffet line waiting for lunch prior to the tournament. Someone walked up and asked him, "Lee, whatever happened to that trophy that Johnny Beauchamp got at the first Daytona 500?" Petty, always ready with a gruff response, even when one wasn't necessarily needed, huffed, "I guess he took it to hell with him."

The Petty family's long and wildly fruitful but sometimes dramatically dangerous relationship with Daytona International Speedway (DIS) began in 1959, the mammoth raceway's first season and the year that Lee Petty scored a controversial Daytona 500 win over Beauchamp. Over the following decades, the track, which became NASCAR's showcase facility and an international racing capital, saw Richard Petty win the Daytona 500 over and over again, finish first in a tight last-lap fight with Cale Yarborough while a US president looked on, and lose two tense showdowns with David Pearson. Father and son, Lee and Richard, would also cheat death on the track's fast asphalt and just outside its walls.

David Pearson had a mixed relationship with Daytona, too, winning its biggest race, the Daytona 500, in a fascinating last-lap encounter with Petty in 1976 and outfoxing Petty in the 1974 summer race but seeing other potential Daytona wins disappear.

A tri-oval (D-shaped), 2.5-mile (4-km), high-banked monster of a racetrack that would redefine the concept of stock car racing, Daytona International Speedway rose from the swampy ground of Daytona Beach, Florida, because of the stubbornness of one man, Bill France Sr., and the relentlessness of time and tide on the shores of the Atlantic.

France, the driving force in the formation of NASCAR in the late 1940s, began promoting stock car races on the hard-packed sand of the Daytona beachfront in the 1930s. France paired the Daytona beach sand flats and the parallel asphalt ribbon of Highway A1A to form one of the strangest laps in the history of automobile racing. Drivers raced down the beach, made a hard left turn through rutted sand onto the highway, ran side by side on the narrow beach road, and then made another left to return to the beach. It was barely controlled chaos with a definite "end" time. Once the Atlantic tide rolled in, even the most talented drivers couldn't race through the surf, although they occasionally ran their tires into the water to cool them.

Those wild races on the beach-road course reverberate to this day. Every February, in the week before the Daytona 500, hundreds gather on the beachfront to celebrate what was a unique form of racing, bringing restored race cars and their memories. Russ Truelove, whose spectacular crash in a 1956 beach race resulted in a sequence of dramatic photographs in *Life* magazine, was among the old beach racers who attended the reunion virtually every year until his death in 2018. "I'm not a young man anymore," Truelove said in a 2010 interview. "Yesterday is still important to me. I want to relive yesterday. I'm so thankful there is this to come home to. It's a high."

Racing on the beach, as popular as it was for the competitors and fans watching from the sand dunes, ended in the late 1950s for two reasons. First, development along the increasingly popular beachfront was making it more and more difficult to stage an event with dozens of race cars and thousands of fans. Second, it was dangerous. Drivers and those supporting their cars could take the risks, but if a calamity resulted in spectator injuries or deaths, there would be hell to pay.

France, who often thought years ahead of his contemporaries, realized the issues earlier than most and began planning an audacious alternative: a giant speedway several miles (11 km) to the west of the oceanfront, a track that would be the equivalent of—no, better than—an Indianapolis Motor Speedway for stock car racers. Designs, contracts, government approvals, and money (the last being the most difficult) came together after years of planning, and France opened his palace of speed in 1959.

Overnight, racing changed for the good ol' boys and self-taught mechanics who were hauling fast cars all over the country in pursuit of dollars and glory. They didn't know what "fast" was until they hit the high banks of Daytona.

They drove into the speedway's twin tunnels, dipping deep into the Florida sand and under the track, emerging on the other side into what, at that time, was a bizarre wonderland like nothing any of them had seen, even in their dreams.

"It was a whole different world," Richard Petty said. "We came through the tunnel in the truck with a race car on the trailer behind us. There was nothing in the infield, no buildings. There was a lake out there somewhere, but you couldn't see it. The first and second turns looked like they were 2 to 3 miles [3 to 5 km] away.

"Even though most of the boys on the racing teams were smalltown Southern folk, we thought we'd been around a spell and nothing much could impress us. But when we showed up at Daytona for the first time, even though most of us wouldn't admit it, we were pretty awestruck. It was then, and still is, one gosh-awful big place. Those steep grades in the turns were like something from another world to us until we got used to them."

It was the edge of morning in what would amount to a new era.

Cars soon rolled onto the track for practice laps. Drivers found the speeds exhilarating but the physics of going so fast on a high-banked track puzzling.

"We ran 130 miles per hour [209 km per hour], so it wasn't a big deal," Petty said. "Pace cars run faster now than the race cars did then. But the fastest place we'd ever been was Darlington, so it was unreal to run around a racetrack and never think about taking your foot off the gas. That was the big surprise to the whole deal. But, once you did it, it was pretty dang easy.

"The cars lifted under the front end because of the air, and nobody knew what they were doing. We learned to deal with whatever the circumstances were. You didn't know what to expect, so you just adapted. The deal that was really different was when the wind was blowing. You'd come down the frontstretch and, at the end of the grandstand, there was an open area there, and the wind would come across the track and move the car over half-a-car-length. That was different."

Mechanic and team owner Bud Moore said drivers showed no fear in a radically new environment. That perspective wasn't shared by everyone, however.

"A race driver—if you didn't tell him how fast he was running, he didn't know anyway," Moore said. "If the car feels good and it sticks, it didn't matter how fast you were running. I rode around the track with Fireball Roberts. He ran 157 [253 km per hour]. It didn't really scare me."

Buddy Baker, who would become a master of NASCAR's fastest tracks, said he was rattled by his first look at the track. "You could put five racetracks together and not make this place," he said. "I hadn't ever been on anything even close. The first time I went through the corner wide open, I was thinking, 'What have I done?' But it's kind of like soloing in an airplane for the first time. You don't go back to the ground. You're already committed."

Fireball Roberts, who would become one of the best on NASCAR's new, faster tracks, said circling Daytona was so easy that "Even a gorilla can drive here." Cale Yarborough later offered the opinion that even sports writers could drive at Daytona. "You don't drive here, you aim," he said.

Not that the track didn't have a dark side. There was a driver death at the speedway even before its first race. Marshall Teague, a Daytona Beach resident and one of the best of the first wave of stock car drivers, was killed February 11, 1959, while trying to set a closed-course speed record at the track. Teague, who won the AAA national stock car championship in 1952 and 1954 and had raced in the Indianapolis 500, was driving a modified Indy car in an attempt to better the 177.038-mile-per-hour (284.915-km-per-hour) run Tony Bettenhausen had recorded in 1958 on a track in Monza, Italy. Only a few days after DIS officially opened on February 1, Teague, driving alone on the track, turned a lap at 171 miles per hour (275 km per hour), later telling reporters the car hadn't been finetuned and that he expected faster speeds in the days ahead.

On Teague's second lap on February 11, he lost control of the car and it began flipping when its wheels reached the area where the track banking meets the flat asphalt of the apron. The car tore apart as it flipped, ejecting the cockpit seat. Teague died instantly.

Over the years, dozens of drivers would die at Daytona, forming a grim line that ultimately would include superstar Dale Earnhardt, who, in 2001, became the first driver killed in the Daytona 500.

There was a sense of danger in 1959 as drivers began figuring out the new track. Most said the driving was easy, but the outside guardrails loomed large at the high speeds. "There wasn't a man there who wasn't scared to death of the place," Lee Petty said.

CALE YARBOROUGH OFFERED THE OPINION THAT EVEN SPORTS WRITERS COULD DRIVE AT DAYTONA. "YOU DON'T DRIVE HERE, YOU AIM," HE SAID.

Still, there was work to do and a trophy to pursue.

South Carolinian Lester Hunter was among the mechanics dealing with the new challenges of preparing race cars for this great unknown.

"We tried to talk to the driver about what worked best, but he didn't know, either, because everything was so new," Hunter said. "I found out one of the best ways to figure things out was to ride a motorcycle in the infield down near the corners and watch the cars slip through there. I'd change the chassis based on that. I had a lot of fun down there on the beach course, but the new track was nice. I walked in there and told Bill [France], 'Hey, I really like this.'"

NASCAR had arrived in the big time in a shiny new facility that would start a wave of new and faster tracks and move the sport to a new level of professionalism.

Bud Moore, who jumped into racing after decorated service in the US Army in World War II, remembered the bad old times.

"We had reservations in Darlington for the first race down there [in 1950]," he said. "Me and [driver] Joe Eubanks went down to check into the hotel. We got a room, went upstairs. I pulled the cover back on the bed. They had a bunch of big old cockroaches. They were all over the place. I told Joe, 'I ain't staying here.' I went back downstairs; told the guy I can't sleep in here with all them damn cockroaches and bugs. He said, 'Well, they got to have some place to sleep, too.' So, we slept out at the racetrack on the ground, blankets rolled up underneath the race car.

"It was all different then. We went to a lot of races where they didn't have cars to fill the field. France would go down and get some rental cars and put numbers on them and tape up the headlights and put anybody in them to start the race. They did that many times."

Daytona International Speedway opened the door to bigger and better—and certainly faster—things.

On the first Daytona 500 race day, sunshine welcomed a crowd of more than 41,000, many showing up simply because of the novelty of the moment and wonder about the place. Remarkably, the race rolled along without a yellow flag, most of the drivers perhaps using a bit more caution than normal because of the new frontier they were attacking.

Lee Petty, in a showroom-new Oldsmobile, and Beauchamp, driving a Ford, battled for the lead in the closing laps. At the end of 500 miles (805 km), they crossed the line side by side, with the lapped car of Joe Weatherly making it a three-wide finish.

NASCAR flagged Beauchamp as the winner, and he rolled into victory lane to receive flowers, the trophy, and a hug from trophy queen Scottie McCormick. But as the celebration was taking place, there were doubters as to the accuracy of the finish order. Chief among them was Lee Petty, who was certain he had won.

T. Taylor Warren, who would build a distinguished career as a racing photographer, was standing in the pits as the race ended. Using his German-made Rolleiflex camera, he snapped what would become an iconic photo showing the three cars crossing the stripe. In that photo and other still shots, plus film footage, it appeared that Petty had gotten to the line a few feet (1 m) in front of Beauchamp. Some in the Beauchamp camp thought none of that mattered and that Petty was a lap down to Beauchamp at the finish.

"I was standing just past the finish line," Warren said forty-eight years later. "Nobody had thought about the finish being that close. I had one chance to get the shot. You just shoot and don't think about it."

In his darkroom, Warren looked at the print from his 2¼ x 2¼ inch negative and immediately determined that Petty had won the race. "I looked at it and it wasn't what Bill had called," Warren said. "I carried the print to [NASCAR official] Pat Purcell and said, 'We have a problem.'"

Although Warren's photo showed Petty in front, it was shot at somewhat of an angle, giving those who thought Beauchamp had won an opening for their argument. "People were telling Bill that the angle affected it," Warren said. "That's why it took so long for him to change his mind. He was trying to get all available pictures and make sure the angle didn't distort it."

Three days later, France changed gears and awarded the win to Petty, who happily accepted the first-place check without the trophy. There are two schools of thought concerning why France took so long to decide on the finish. It took a while to gather any photos or film that might be relevant, but France also benefited from the publicity that accompanied the three-day wait. The reports that flew out of Daytona Beach that weekend gave NASCAR national exposure and made the new speedway's debut even more of a story.

France was happy.

Among those who were impressed was a future president of the United States named Jimmy Carter, who later sent a note to France: "I'll always remember being there for the inaugural race, when Petty and Beauchamp almost tied!"

That win would be Lee Petty's only Daytona 500 victory. Injuries would soon end his career. Richard also drove in that first 500, but he was a spectator at the finish, having dropped out of the race after only eight laps because of a sour engine. He finished fifty-seventh in a fifty-nine-car field. In later years, he would more than make up for that dismal start, winning the 500 a record seven times and putting the Petty stamp firmly on the track.

"Daytona just sort of fit in with my career," Richard said. "I grew up in the superspeedway as it grew up. It made it very fortunate for me because people like my dad, Junior [Johnson], and all that, they had to relearn tracks like Daytona. I didn't have to relearn. I didn't know anything. So, I just started with nothing and then learned."

Richard drove in the second 500 in 1960. Also at Daytona Beach for that race was David Pearson, making his Cup Series debut at what then was the series' fastest track. The drivers who were destined to become two of NASCAR's best raced against each other for the first time on February 12 in one of two 100-mile (161-km) qualifying races for the 500. In that year, unlike now, the qualifying races counted as Cup Series point events, making the 100-lapper Pearson's first official start. Petty had run nine times in 1958 and twenty-one times in 1959, all without a win.

RICHARD DROVE IN THE SECOND 500 IN 1960. ALSO AT DAYTONA BEACH FOR THAT RACE WAS DAVID PEARSON, MAKING HIS CUP SERIES DEBUT.

Pearson had had so much success in Carolina short-track racing that his friends in Spartanburg launched a fundraising effort to help Pearson buy a car to go Cup racing. He did it almost reluctantly.

Pearson worked at Edmund Rogers' Spartanburg service station. Rogers and Ralph Sawyer, a city policeman and a friend of Pearson's, had been urging Pearson to make a run at NASCAR's top level.

"I was having fun on the half-mile [0.8-km] and quarter-mile [0.4-km] tracks," Pearson told writer Joe Whitlock. "I didn't want to kill myself. I guess I sort of told those two that the main reason I couldn't go Grand National racing was because I didn't have the money."

Sawyer had a response. On a Spartanburg radio station broadcast, he announced the formation of a "David Pearson Fan Club" and urged Pearson's friends and fans to donate money so the driver could race on bigger and faster tracks.

Spartanburg responded with nickels and dimes and quarters and some folding money here and there.

"I didn't even know who to give the money back to, so I was hooked," Pearson said.

Using the donations and a loan from his father (which he eventually would pay back), Pearson bought a 1959 Chevrolet from Spartanburg Cup driver Jack Smith and was on the road to Daytona Beach. Rogers gave him a credit card to buy gasoline for the drive to Daytona Beach and for the trip home.

Pearson finished seventeenth in the 100-miler (161 km), two laps behind winner Fireball Roberts and seven positions behind Richard Petty, who was one lap down to the leader. There is no mention in race reports concerning whether the two future superstars competed for position on track.

Pearson had a "moment" as he slowed to avoid a wreck. "I stuck my arm out the window . . . to slow the car down [like he had done on short tracks]," he said in a *NASCAR Images* interview years later. "I like to broke my arm. [It] flew back, hit the side of the quarter panel. I never did stick my arm out the window no more."

Junior Johnson won the 500 that year, finishing in front of Bobby Johns, Richard Petty (a surprising third), and fourth-place Lee Petty. The day wasn't good for Pearson, who finished twenty-eighth, fifteen laps behind the winner in a car that was something less than competitive.

At the end of the 1960 season, however, Pearson was named Cup Rookie of the Year, an award Petty had won the previous season. Pearson had three top fives and seven top tens in twenty-two races. He remembered being awarded $250, a set of shock absorbers, and a leather coat.

The 1961 *NASCAR Record Book*, in the Rookie of the Year section for the previous season, described Pearson as "hard-driving. He made a fine impression with his driving in a car that was virtually worn-out."

For a few minutes on June 14, 1959, at Lakewood Speedway near Atlanta, Richard Petty thought he was floating in the rarefied air of his first Cup Series victory. He ran under the checkered flag at the end of the 150-lap race, the last Cup event held on the tough one-mile (1.6-km) dirt track where some of NASCAR's pioneer drivers had learned the art. Petty's victory was immediately protested, however, and a check of the scorecards resulted in the win being awarded to the driver who'd filed the complaint.

His name was Lee Petty.

Lee Petty, an advocate of tough love, wasn't the sort of man who would "give away" a race win, even to his son. And especially not in the circumstances of the day. The race was what NASCAR called a Sweepstakes event, meaning both hardtops and cars from the Convertible Division were eligible to compete. For hardtop drivers, including Lee, the first-place prize included a new car. The car wasn't part of the prize package for convertible drivers, a list that included Richard. Thus, Lee's protest. The Petty team went home with a new car. Lee won $2,200. Richard won $1,400 and left Atlanta still winless.

"He didn't win the race; I did," Lee told *The Atlanta Constitution* after the race. "Richard puts his feet under my table, and when he wins, it's going to be fair and square. . . . I would have protested my mother if I needed to."

Lee Petty was the boss. His words were almost scriptural.

Richard understood. He stayed at the track after the race, sitting on top of his convertible and signing autographs for all comers, visibly happy despite the day's odd turn of events.

"Second was the best I'd ever run, so I was tickled," he said. "I was out of the car jumping around 'cause I'd just won for the first time. Then somebody came over and said Daddy had protested. Later, he explained that we'd make more money with him winning, and we needed every little bit we could get. It didn't matter that much to me. All I cared about was that we had enough cars and money so I could keep racing.

It didn't make that much difference as long as the company came out ahead. In the end, I think the scorers got it right."

As on so many other occasions for the Pettys, it was about business—about the money.

Richard would have to wait eight months to taste the goodness of victory lane. And this time he got an assist—not a protest—from Dad, a man who already had forty-eight wins.

The scene was the Southern States Fairgrounds track near Charlotte on February 28, 1960. The half-mile (0.8-km) dirt track was far from pristine, its ragged surface pockmarked by holes and ruts. The track had been on the Cup schedule since 1954. It was miles away from the Charlotte Speedway that had hosted the first Cup Series race in 1949.

Richard qualified seventh and was strong from the start. Lee dropped out only thirty-eight laps into the 200-lap race but would return to the track to relief-drive for Doug Yates. That put Lee, now in a lapped car, in position to be a wingman for his son. While Richard battled Rex White, who would win the Cup championship that year, for the lead, Lee nosed his car into the picture, bumping White and sending his Chevrolet into a slide. That enabled Richard to take the lead for good, although he said later that White's progress was hampered by a huge hole in the track.

"Honestly, I don't remember much about that race," Petty said in a 2023 interview with writer Al Pearce. "It was a long time ago. I do remember the track was unbearably rough, but not much else about what went on. There were potholes and bumps and ruts all over the place. Rex got into one of them, and I went by him. I got through the rough spots better than he did."

Richard did admit later that "Daddy bumped Rex a little bit and sort of ran interference for me."

Many years after the race, White, who ultimately would join both Pettys in the NASCAR Hall of Fame, said he probably could have won the race if there had not been contact from Lee. "As much as I raced with Richard through the years, I never had any confrontation or disagreement with him," White said. "He didn't do a thing to me that afternoon. But I didn't get along with Lee, not one bit. And I wasn't the only one. No, sir."

White finished second, six car lengths behind. Only seven of twenty

-one starters finished the race on a day when cars decided they didn't want to take the punishment on a rough track. David Pearson was one of those missing at the end, having parked his car with radiator issues near the halfway point.

Richard, whose wife Lynda was four months from giving birth to their first child, Kyle, won $800. He picked up the check at the pay window before leaving the track. In a circumstance that wasn't necessarily unusual for that time, the victory did not come with a trophy. That error was corrected thirty-two years later during Petty's final Cup season (1992) when John Moose, who had co-promoted races at the fairgrounds track, presented Petty with a trophy commemorating win No. 1.

The headline in *The Charlotte Observer* the day after the race read, "Dick Petty Wins Fairgrounds Race." None of the Pettys cared for Richard's rarely used nickname. Speculation is that the *Observer* used it because "Richard" wouldn't fit in the headline space.

That newspaper, and many others, would have a multitude of chances to use Petty's real name.

The first important clue that David Pearson would not approach Cup Series racing with any measure of anxiety came as the green flag waved on the World 600 at Charlotte Motor Speedway (CMS) May 28, 1961.

Pearson started the race in the third position. At the moment the race began, he swerved low on the CMS tri-oval, put his car's left-side wheels on the bare ground adjacent to the asphalt, kicked up some dirt, and roared into first place.

It was a rather audacious move for a second-year driver making his first start in a competitive car. Eyebrows were raised along pit road.

Chris Economaki, who would become one of auto racing's most prominent journalists, both in print and on television, did a voiceover for film of the race after the fact. "The green flag is out," Economaki said. "The race is on. And what is this? David Pearson, a brash young rookie [he was still a newcomer but not technically a rookie] whose 1961 Pontiac was fastest in qualifying in the field, has thrown caution to the wind and cut inside to beat the leaders to the first turn."

Economaki would be talking about David Pearson for many years to come.

This was Pearson's first big chance to score a Cup Series win, and it was clear from that bold beginning that he was going to take advantage of the opportunity. It was a wild start, and there was a wilder ending. After a grueling five hours and twenty-two minutes of racing, Pearson chugged into victory lane, his car running on three tires and a rim that previously held the fourth tire.

Petty had scored his first win on a fading dirt track that was about to disappear from big-league racing. Pearson's first victory was also logged near Charlotte, but it arrived in more dramatic, almost-storybook fashion on the nearly new 1.5-mile (2.4-km) CMS oval.

Pearson had struggled racing his own equipment in the 1960 and 1961 Cup seasons and was leaning toward returning full-time to Late Model Sportsman racing on Carolina short tracks. Fate intervened in the person of Ray Fox, whose respected Pontiac team had a driver vacancy entering the Charlotte race. There are numerous versions of what happened between Fox and Pearson in the days before the season's longest race, and several individuals have been mentioned as key to Pearson getting the ride of his life. Joe Littlejohn, a mover and shaker in the NASCAR world, was among Pearson's long-time boosters, and Spartanburg mechanic and team owner Bud Moore also is said to have recommended him. NASCAR chief technical inspector Norris Friel also apparently signed in with a vote. Whatever the circumstances, Fox contacted Pearson, offering him a seat in the race and Pearson bolted for Charlotte, no questions asked.

Pearson had been working odd jobs around Spartanburg to support his family and his racing.

Never would he have a "real" job again.

"So, Bud Moore and Joe Littlejohn and maybe Cotton [Owens], I don't know who all, talked to Ray and told him that he ought to give me a chance and let me drive the car," Pearson said. "They told him they thought I could drive the car and do a good job, so they called me and asked me about it. I said, 'Lord God!' and I just threw everything down and quit right then. I said, 'Yeah, I'll drive Ray's car!' because I knew it was a good car."

The white Pontiac was numbered 3, a digit Dale Earnhardt would ride to glory years later. Junior Johnson had qualified the car in a preliminary sprint race, but he had another commitment for the 600, leaving Fox with an empty driver's seat.

Pearson arrived at the track and soon was wheeling the car in his first practice, reaching a speed of 138 miles per hour (222 km per hour) and marveling at his sudden good fortune. Other teams and drivers took note, their stopwatches showing numbers few expected from a driver who previously had been mostly in the shadows. "When I got back in, Ray asked me how the car felt," Pearson said. "I told him, 'I don't know how it's supposed to feel; I've never run this fast.'"

Along with others along pit road, Fox was impressed. "Pearson's a damn good driver, and I have a lot of confidence in him," he said. "I've noted our tire wear is at a minimum because of his ability to handle the car. He just had a natural instinct on what to do."

Pearson ran the race, a marathon that tests the strength of cars and the patience and persistence of drivers, like a seasoned veteran. Perhaps as a harbinger of things to come, he took the lead for good on lap 272, passing another young driver named Richard Petty. Pearson led 225 of the race's 400 laps and had a comfortable lead with two laps to go. Then trouble arrived.

As Pearson sped down the backstretch approaching the white flag, his right rear tire blew. He retained control of the car, determined to finish the race despite sparks flying from the wheel. Fireball Roberts, who was in second place several laps behind, gunned his car hoping to overtake the ailing Pontiac, but Pearson nursed the car to a slow-rolling finish, winning by two laps over Roberts.

The air crackled with trouble and distress, but Pearson didn't panic.

"Coming off four, I saw the guy waving the white flag, but I didn't know how far ahead I was," Pearson said. "But I figured I'd finish pretty good anyway if I stayed on the track. When I got there and I got the checkered flag, that was the biggest thrill I've ever had in my life. I was running on three tires, a rim, and a prayer."

In victory lane, Pearson's Pure Oil T-shirt, one that had been given to him five minutes before the start of the race, was soaked. He ran the race in jeans. The T-shirt, and Pearson, one day would make the NASCAR Hall of Fame.

Pearson's share of the winner's purse was $12,000. A few days later, he used the cash to buy a house on Ash Street near his childhood home in Spartanburg. The idea of owning his home debt-free was one he could only have imagined days before the Charlotte breakthrough. He also won a new Pontiac convertible. "I stayed in Charlotte that night and waited until the next morning to get my money," Pearson said. "I don't know how to explain how I felt. I had never even dreamed about winning something like that. I always thought it would be nice, but when it actually happened—winning that much money and a new car. I was just a mill-town boy, but, man, I was 'uptown' after that win."

Pearson's unlikely win gained much attention. "I guess the first thing I ever heard tell of Pearson is when he won in Charlotte," Richard Petty said. Petty finished thirtieth in the race, the engine in his Plymouth expiring in the final 100 laps.

The Pontiac Pearson rode to that landmark win began its life along the Halifax River in Daytona Beach, Florida. Ray Fox maintained a garage there in the Fish Carburetor building where he both built race cars and repaired passenger cars.

Mechanic Olin Hopes helped build the Pontiac. A longtime resident of Daytona Beach who, as a kid, swept the garage floor at Bill France Sr.'s shop, Hopes was the jackman for the Fox team. He was working for $60 a week.

"I didn't even know who David Pearson was, and I don't think Ray did," Hopes, eighty-eight years old, said in a 2024 interview. "But Ray didn't care. He just wanted somebody who could race. Pearson was full of piss and vinegar. He was a lot of fun to be around."

There was tension in the Fox pit, Hopes said, over the race's final laps. Crew members were burning through cigarettes, smoking like Pittsburgh. "But we were so excited that he was out front," he said. "He made it across the finish line and everybody went crazy. I'd never seen Ray so happy. Everybody ran up to victory circle. I stayed back in the pit packing stuff up to go back home."

It would be a nice return ride to Daytona Beach.

The breakthrough wins by Petty and Pearson lifted them to a new plateau. Petty would become a stronger force within the family team, running forty of forty-four races in 1960 and winning three times. Pearson would ride the Charlotte success and the Fox-built cars to equally powerful moments, winning superspeedway races at Daytona Beach and Atlanta in the 1961 season and firmly establishing himself as a driver on the rise.

In Level Cross, the Petty Enterprises compound grew. The original reaper-shed space that served as the team's launching pad had been expanded in 1956 and again in 1957. A room that doubled the team's space was tacked on in the early 1960s, continuing the Petty trend of adding work areas as money allowed. Over the decades, the compound would grow in haphazard leaps and bounds, expanding without a master plan. Buildings would rise where space allowed, the area eventually looking more or less like a misshapen outdoor mall. But wins came out of those spaces.

THERE WAS TENSION IN THE FOX PIT OVER THE RACE'S FINAL LAPS. CREW MEMBERS WERE BURNING THROUGH CIGARETTES, SMOKING LIKE PITTSBURGH.

Just when things were trending upward for the Pettys after Lee and Richard combined for eight wins in 1960, everything came crashing down, literally, in 1961.

Daytona International Speedway, which had hosted Lee's biggest win in 1959's inaugural Daytona 500, turned into a house of horrors for father and son in the days before the 1961 Daytona 500.

The starting lineups for the two 100-mile (161-km) qualifying races had Richard in the first race and Lee in the second. Neither would finish. Both would leave the speedway—in their race cars, over the guardrail.

On the last lap of race one, Richard, trying to avoid Junior Johnson's spinning car, rolled up the track banking and onto the outside guardrail. His car sailed out of the speedway and down a 40-foot (12-m) bank. The wreck looked gruesome from the infield, where Petty family members were watching. Oddly, Petty wasn't hurt in the crash but suffered a twisted ankle climbing out of the wrecked car. After he left the infield medical center, Petty's eyes started hurting. He returned to revisit the doctors, and they discovered that tiny glass particles had flown into Petty's eyes during the wreck.

As Petty later described it, "That ol' Plymouth got airborne and went sailing four stories down into the parking lot and splattered itself all over the Florida landscape."

Worse was yet to come—far worse.

As Richard was returning to the Petty pit area, Lee was involved in a spectacular crash on the opposite end of the track near the end of the second race. Lee and Johnny Beauchamp, his nemesis from the inaugural Daytona 500 two years earlier, had locked horns in the fourth turn, a wreck that sent both cars over the wall. When Petty was finally removed from the car and examined at a nearby hospital, he had a mangled leg, numerous cuts, internal bleeding, and a damaged lung.

Richard ran to the crash scene, his progress hampered by his sore ankle. He was stunned by the sight. His father's car had been pounded by the impact, pieces of the vehicle scattered about the crash site. There was blood inside what remained of the cockpit, and Lee was unconscious as safety workers loaded him into an ambulance. Richard rode to the hospital in another ambulance and walked to the operating room by following the trail of his father's blood in the hallway.

He arrived to find his father on the narrow line between life and death.

Lee Petty had two surgeries and faced a long rehabilitation. It was the closest he came to losing his life in all his racing years.

The sport's all-time leading race winner would never win again. Although Lee Petty expected to leave the hospital within a few days of his accident, he was there four months. He eventually returned to the driver's seat for a few races but was never a serious threat again before retiring in 1964.

Beyond the near-death experience for the team patriarch, the Pettys faced other huge problems. Lee had run the team with an iron hand since the very beginning and knew the ins and outs of every part of the operation, from bending metal to counting dollars. Suddenly, he could not drive and, more seriously, would be absent from his management role for months.

"When he got hurt, we didn't have no money," Maurice Petty said years later. "I mean, we were flat broke as far as when we came back from Daytona. We tore up two race cars. He told us—he was laying there all beat up and banged up—to go home and get the race car ready, go on to the next race."

Kyle Petty, who eventually followed his father and grandfather into the driver's seat, was four months old when the twin crashes occurred. He heard the stories over and over as he grew up in the Petty shop. "My dad and Uncle Maurice went back to Level Cross busted, broke, and out of business," Kyle said. "They had no cars, and my granddad was in the hospital. It was a hard time."

Lynda Petty, Richard's wife, sat in the track's scoring stand for both races alongside Lee's wife, Elizabeth. "We were at the hospital all night, not knowing if Lee would live or not," Lynda said in a 1982 interview with *Grand National Illustrated* magazine. "As far as the cars were concerned, all we had to take home was two piles of junk."

Instead of becoming unmoored, Richard and Maurice returned to the Petty shop determined to keep rolling. The next race was a week after the 500 at the Piedmont Interstate Fairgrounds track in Spartanburg, South Carolina, and Richard Petty finished second to hometown driver Cotton Owens. As the team rebuilt, Petty ran forty-two of fifty-two races that season, winning at Richmond and Charlotte.

"You see, the Pettys ain't through in this business 'til they take us outta here toes up in a pine box," Richard Petty had told *The Atlanta Constitution* after the wrecks at Daytona.

Across the decade of the 1960s, despite troubles, Petty and Pearson would finish one-two thirty-nine times, Petty winning twenty, Pearson nineteen. They were entrenched as victory threats, and championships awaited.

The first thing visitors noticed when entering Raymond Parks' small office on Northside Drive in Atlanta in the early 1990s was a somewhat tarnished trophy.

More than forty years old at that point, the trophy had lost much of its shine. What it represented was a moment in time that seemed of another age. Cars owned by Parks, one of stock car racing's pioneers, and driven by Red Byron, who raced with a leg mangled in World War II, won the first championship in what would become the NASCAR Cup Series. That 1949 championship trophy, along with a few others, were prized possessions for Parks, although he made no grand attempts to showcase them. The rare visitor to his office, located next to one of two Atlanta liquor stores he owned, almost accidentally stumbled onto a big piece of motorsports history.

Over the years that followed the Parks-Byron triumph, the chase for the Cup trophy would involve some of the best race car drivers in the world, the best engineers and innovators Detroit's car industry could produce, millionaires who bought into the sport and sought its glory, and homegrown mechanics who turned wrenches and heads in pursuit of faster laps.

After the victory lane photos are finished and the winner's money is spent, it is the trophy that remains, the ultimate prize for drivers and teams, symbolizing consistent success across a long season and across a big country.

Despite a limited ten-year career in the sport, Parks held his trophy close, the memories of those times perhaps as important as the successful business empire he built. In those early days of NASCAR's sputtering growth, his strong, polished race cars and his financial input were keys to lifting stock car racing from its scraggly roots.

Parks died in 2010. The first championship trophy was donated to the NASCAR Hall of Fame and is now part of its permanent collection.

Richard Petty and David Pearson would pursue—and claim—some of its descendants.

The 1960s became the Petty-Pearson decade as both drivers grew in stature and prominence, and both started stacking wins and versions of the big trophy. Half of the decade's titles went to the duo, Petty winning in 1964 and 1967, Pearson driving to the championship in 1966, 1968, and 1969. Across the decade, they combined for 158 race wins and led 39,166 laps.

The first one-two finish recorded by Petty and Pearson occurred on August 8, 1963, at Columbia Speedway in South Carolina. It was an appropriate spot for such a historic result. The Columbia track was a classroom for young drivers, its layout a good test and its cast of regulars always providing good competition. Strangely enough, or perhaps as somewhat predictive of the future, in a field of twenty-two cars, Petty and Pearson were the only leaders, Petty leading 138 laps, Pearson sixty-two. Petty, who won by nine seconds and pocketed $1,140, took the lead for good on lap 166 of 200.

There would be sixty-two more Petty-Pearson (or Pearson-Petty) finishes at the top of race results sheets over the next fourteen years. On many Sundays, they were the show. Fans usually favored one or the other, almost never both.

Even as successes were recorded, the middle years of the 1960s held periods of trial for Pearson and Petty and for auto racing in general. Death visited tracks. Two NASCAR greats—Joe Weatherly and Fireball Roberts—died of injuries sustained in on-track accidents in 1964, and drivers Dave McDonald and Eddie Sachs were killed in a fiery crash in the 1964 Indianapolis 500, a race always run under the shadow of sudden danger. In September 1964, NASCAR driver Jimmy Pardue died while tire-testing at Charlotte Motor Speedway, his car blowing a tire and sailing out of the track between turns three and four. A gruesome wreck in a January 1965 tire test at Daytona International Speedway killed Billy Wade. Buren Skeen (Darlington) and Harold Kite (Charlotte) died in crashes later that year.

The fatal wrecks accelerated efforts to improve safety at most of the top levels of motorsports, but the hard realities remained. There were risks every time out. Wives didn't see their husbands come home. Children were suddenly without fathers.

Calamity would alter plans at Petty Enterprises. Lee Petty, walking with a limp caused by his wild sky-riding crash in 1961 at Daytona, raced only six times after that day—once in 1962, three times in 1963, and twice in 1964. In what became his finale, he ran only nine laps on the road course at Watkins Glen International in New York. The injuries and his failure to run competitively after the big wreck made his decision an easy one. He had no desire to make laps with no real chance at success, and the new dangers associated with faster speeds were real indeed.

That put the family torch firmly in Richard Petty's hands, and he ran with it. Over the course of the decade, Petty Enterprises became the Tiffany team, a leviathan crushing all in its path and a model for success.

Richard won three races in 1960, two in 1961, eight in 1962, and fourteen in 1963 before a nine-win season in 1964 gave him his first Cup championship. He was honing the style and racing smarts that would carry him to an unmatched career, and he had the backing of the sport's best team, one that reached new levels of professionalism while leaving the competition lagging. It was a potent combination.

"There were people who were drivers," said Bobby Allison, who became one of Petty's main competitors. "Cale [Yarborough] was a driver. David Pearson was a driver. They were really good at what they did, but Richard Petty—he really went into the workings of what it took to go to a race and win it, whether it was a quarter-mile [0.4 km] or half-mile [0.8 km] or Daytona or a road course or a dirt track. He knew what it took to go to that place and win a race. I admired that. That was always my target.

"Richard had the family deal, and it was orchestrated really well. He was the living, breathing, operating model of what every race driver would really want to be—to have the best of equipment and best crew and drive good and win races and do all those things."

Long-time mechanic and team owner Bud Moore said all the elements were in place to make Richard Petty a star. "He had a great teacher in his daddy, Lee," Moore said. "Richard was a heck of a competitor. He liked to race. Most of us only ran eighteen or twenty races a year for quite a while. The Pettys ran them all. If there were fifty races, Richard ran them. And his daddy taught him quite a bit about what to do and what not to do."

Richard's success and his attitude toward accommodating fans put a new shine on the sport.

"Richard really had an awful lot to do with giving the sport a quality name and respect," said Johnny Allen, who raced against Petty in the 1950s and 1960s. "When I first came in, it was all pretty much roughnecks. There was a lot of stuff going on—a lot of fights at the track. NASCAR did a good job of controlling it, but it could get rough. Richard helped to change some of that. I always admired him for the way he handled himself. All the drivers liked and respected him. He was never big-headed or a smart aleck. I've seen him leading a race with three laps to go and blow a tire and finish far back. Then he'd still sit in the back of his truck and sign autographs, all the while smiling."

That Petty attitude—the fan is all-important—persisted throughout his career and beyond. "People would ask what Richard was like behind the scenes," said Steve Tucker, one of the many public relations representatives who worked with Petty over the years. "I would tell them that he's exactly what you see on television. Many times, we were some of the last people to leave a racetrack. He was not one of those who tried to sneak out of tracks after a race. He valued the fans and his relationship with them. He was the best at giving people their 'hero' moment. I've seen people just melt down when they finally got to meet him. He would give everybody time and not make them feel rushed. He treated them like they were gold."

While Petty was pushing his win total into double digits in the early 1960s, Pearson was getting his footing after his unexpected win in the 1961 World 600 at Charlotte. After two more superspeedway wins that season, he wouldn't win again until 1964, but he excelled that year, falling only one short of Petty's nine-win total.

All the while, Pearson and Petty were traveling across the country from big tracks to little cow towns, racing packed schedules that gave little time for relaxation—or recovery. Both drivers ran sixty-one races—the full schedule—in 1964. (There were sixty-two races that year, but drivers ran in only one of the two Daytona 500 qualifying events). "I remember one night we ran at Nashville, and the next night we had to go to Maryville [Tennessee]," Petty said. "It was hot. We were whipped. I got in the back of my truck and started taking some oxygen, and then David and Bobby Isaac came in. I passed the oxygen over to Pearson and to Isaac. We thought it helped." It must have been quite a sight, three men who would win NASCAR championship trophies getting fresh breath in the back of a truck.

The race cars of those years, still very stock in many ways, didn't have the creature comforts of the purpose-built racers of the 2000s. With no power steering and none of the cooling apparatus current drivers enjoy, plowing the car through 500 miles (805 km) on a hot day could be a brutal experience.

"These guys run a 500-mile [805-km] race now and jump out of the car and jump up on it and all," driver Donnie Allison said. "In those days, they had to get us out of the car with a damn crane, especially at places like Rockingham, Darlington, Bristol, and Dover. Everything has gotten better."

"YOU DO WHATEVER YOU HAVE TO DO TO STAY WITH THEM OR OUTRUN THEM, AND IF YOU DON'T YOU FIGURE OUT WHAT YOU'RE DOING WRONG."

Things were much more casual in the early 1960s, even as the battles for wins became more stressful. Petty family and team members ate sandwiches prepared by Richard's mother, Elizabeth, in the back of the team truck. Drivers would wander from one truck to another, sometimes sitting together and as Petty put it, "talking politics or racing or girls." Food was shared from team to team, even crossing manufacturer lines. Ford drivers were not opposed to eating Plymouth sandwiches.

Petty and Pearson were establishing the styles they would carry for many seasons to come. The fastest speeds weren't always the best speeds, a fact they learned from repetition and experimentation. Although Pearson raced to lead every lap in his early years, he soon modified his approach to be able to be around at the finish.

"None of it comes natural," Pearson said. "You've got to figure it out. You do whatever you have to do to stay with them or outrun them, and if you don't you figure out what you're doing wrong. It's all part of the game. You go to a racetrack for the first practice and you find the quickest way around."

Pearson quickly discovered that what worked on one end of a track might not produce the same results on the other.

"You might beat them bad in one place, and they beat you in another," he said. "It's a thinking game. You're trying to outsmart the other guys. You don't just go out there and run wide open. You've got to figure out how to get around the racetrack fast. They're not necessarily the same thing."

In 1964, Pearson got a lesson of sorts from team owner Cotton Owens, who signed Pearson full-time the previous year. Even as Petty won the title in 1964, the year was also Pearson's big breakout season. He got a nudge along the way in September at Richmond Raceway in Virginia. Owens, who had hauled two cars to the race, decided to emerge temporarily from retirement as a driver to show Pearson a thing or two after they had disagreed about one thing or another.

He succeeded. Owens, who was forty years old and hadn't run a Cup race in more than a year, won. Pearson, twenty-nine, was second. It's easy to imagine the humorous exchanges that followed.

"He always kidded me about teaching me to drive," Pearson told *Grand National Illustrated* in an interview years later. "He did win, and I was second, but it wasn't because he outran me. I lost some time in the pits. I know I lapped him in the last fifty laps. However, I was already a couple of laps down. It was a good race, a good one for him to talk about. It tickled him to beat me, but I told him the crew deliberately held me up in the pits, that he had the race rigged against me."

Owens said later the race helped Pearson better understand how to work with the team. "Racetracks would get so rough that it was hard to keep a car together for a hundred miles [161 km]," Owens said. "I learned that before David ever came into it. You have to let the pit crew help you. He just wouldn't listen. He would just ignore us on that part of it. We went to Richmond. I beat him on account of pit stops. It was right comical."

One of Pearson's wins in the 1964 season came after a heated battle with Junior Johnson, one of the sport's stars and a driver racing toward retirement. At Hickory Motor Speedway in North Carolina, Pearson led the first twenty-one laps before Johnson, a relentless charger who typically either won or ran his equipment into the ground (or a fence), powered his way in front for the next forty-three. Johnson ran his car so hard that it overheated, and Pearson passed him on lap sixty-five for the lead. He won the 250-lap race by three laps over Larry Thomas.

"To outrun Junior there was something," Pearson said. "After lap after lap, I finally got around him. He followed me real close, hounding me, trying to get me to overdrive and get in the wall. I just kept cutting across coming off the second turn and slinging mud in his radiator. Got his old car running hot."

Pearson was running so well during most of that season that his lap times kept stopwatches spinning along pit road. "You had to watch Pearson," said Dale Inman, Petty's crew chief. "You couldn't predict what he was doing. You watched him practice. You used those old stopwatches. When it got time to qualify, he could step it up unbelievably."

Petty has spoken often of the pair's approaches to racing, emphasizing they were generally different.

"David's racing strategy was not to race," Petty said. "'If I don't have to race,' he thought, 'I'm not going to. If I can keep up, that's good enough.' And it proved to be the right strategy. He had confidence in himself to be able to take care of his car. He won a bunch of races by doing that and not racing people."

Although Petty was famously cool and calm during races, he said Pearson "probably was more laidback than I was. I liked to race people, but you have to be around at the end to do any good."

"Being around" at the end, for both Petty and Pearson, often meant gritting one's teeth and avoiding midrace conflict. "Richard Petty's like everybody else, he gets mad from time to time," Petty said. "I try to keep my temper under wraps as much as possible. There was never a situation where it was just a vengeful deal that, 'Hey, that car hit me; I'm going to hit him in spite of heck.' Because my whole philosophy of running . . . is to win the race. And whatever it takes to win the race, then that's what we try to do. So, a lot of times you'd like to do something during the race, but you know if you do, you're not going to win the thing. So, we still tried to keep winning as the priority of things and aim from that standpoint."

With his aim set directly on winning the championship in 1964, Petty had his own challenges that season, especially from fellow North Carolinian and established star Ned Jarrett, his key foe in the race for the title. "He got into it one night with Ned Jarrett in Asheville," Inman said. "Richard was leading the race, and his right rear hub went out. It cost him some time, slowed the car down. Ned came up and passed us late in the race and hit us. Richard went up afterward and was talking to him. Maurice was there. Somebody pulled a knife out. Maurice said, 'I ain't scared of that damn knife.'"

They never invented the thing that might scare Maurice Petty. No one was cut. They raced on.

That season also marked the beginnings of one of the most controversial periods in the history of stock car racing. Car manufacturers had realized the benefits of NASCAR success back in the 1950s, employing the advertising pages of national magazines and big-city newspapers to publicize Cup victories. In the 1960s, Detroit became increasingly involved—either above board or under the table—in giving its NASCAR teams the best opportunities to win, and that rush included throwing cubic dollars at the sport. Deep inside the huge manufacturing plants in Michigan, there arose what might be called black ops units—teams of engineers and other developers targeting faster speeds and more reliable race car components.

One result was the Hemi. It was one of the biggest, boldest, bad-assed engines ("Hemi" was short for hemispherical, the shape of the combustion chambers) ever to appear on the racing scene, a 426 cubic inch (7 L) powerhouse described by Maurice Petty, the team's engine builder and a man not known for hyperbole, as "a monster of a motor." Inman also chimed in: "Lord, have mercy, what an eye-opener that was. Richard was head and shoulders above everybody else at Daytona. We had to work on the car to make it drive safe. He was going so fast he felt like he would fall out of the car in the turns. We took a 2x4 piece of wood and wrapped it with an Army blanket and bolted it to the seat [the car had a bench seat, as opposed to a single driver's seat] so he could lay his ribs against it to help with the increased G forces. Hey, we had Richard Petty as a driver. When we built a car, we built it around him."

Prior to the development of the Hemi, racing engines were extremely modified versions of the powerplants used in passenger cars. The Hemi was designed and built with racing in mind. A new, more powerful version of a 1950s model, it was a game- and rule-changer in NASCAR. It arrived in 1964 and had an impact that was as loud as it sounded down the long Daytona backstretch.

Two weeks before NASCAR teams assembled in Daytona Beach for the 1964 Daytona 500, scheduled for February 23, Chrysler engineers were running final tests on the Hemi. Team owner Ray Nichels and driver Paul Goldsmith ran the first on-track test with the new engine at a test track in San Angelo, Texas. Goldsmith ran 180 miles per hour (290 km per hour), going airborne at several spots on the rough track. It was obvious that the engine was a bear.

At Daytona, Chrysler officials urged drivers to hold back and not show the new engine's full potential, in part to avoid a NASCAR crackdown. "During the weeks of qualifying and getting the cars ready, we never, during that time, did a wide-open lap," Chrysler's Troy Simonsen told writer Anthony Young. "Going down the backstretches, they would lay their foot in it and feel what it did, and they would feel what it did in the corners, but they never, ever made a complete lap wide open because they didn't want somebody in the stands timing them and finding out they were 8 or 10 miles an hour [13 to 16 km per hour] faster than Ford" (this was many years before sophisticated timing devices recorded exact times and speeds).

Still, the Chryslers rang up big numbers. Goldsmith qualified at 174.910 miles per hour (281.490 km per hour), and Richard Petty ran 174.418 (280.699 km per hour), almost 20 miles per hour (32 km per hour) faster than his time-trial speed at the track a year earlier. It was a quantum leap. In a sport in which full-throated engines eventually would be choked because of the fear of faster and faster race cars flying into grandstands, the Hemi, at least for a while, made motormen jump with joy. It was power set free on a new frontier.

Chrysler shipped engines for the 500 to its teams in Daytona Beach via truck, hesitant to risk the millions of dollars it had spent on engine development by using a plane.

Chrysler products dominated the race, and Petty took the checkered flag for his initial 500 victory, leading 184 of the 200 laps and winning by more than a lap. It was a beatdown of major proportions. He won $33,000, a king's ransom in that era. In prerace ads, Ford had emphasized its "Total Performance" slogan. After Chrysler placed its cars one-two-three in the 500, operations personnel donned buttons that asked, "Total What?"

Petty later called that Daytona 500 "the closest thing to a dream race that I've ever driven. . . . It was almost like going for a Sunday spin, things went so smoothly." He admitted, however, that the engine boost meant he "had to stay right with the car every second at the speeds we're going now." He had no thought of the dramatic rise in speeds still to come.

The Plymouth Belvedere Petty drove in that 1964 Daytona 500 was not too many days removed from the showroom. It ran the race with the price sticker still glued to a window.

The victory was Petty's first on a superspeedway. He had sprinkled his early driving years with dominant performances on short tracks, but he was 0-for-32 on the tour's big ovals prior to that 500 win.

That day marked the start of Petty's love affair with Daytona International Speedway, a track that would grow in importance even as Petty became the sport's headliner. More so than any other track, the Pettys would look forward to the tour's two annual events at Daytona Beach, treating both trips as family vacations of a sort.

Kyle Petty, born in 1960, remembers going to the track as a child. "The scoring stand was in the infield then, and my grandmother and mother would score our cars," he said. "Under the scoreboard was a playground with swing sets and sliding boards and stuff. The wives would drop off the kids under the scoreboard. One of them would bring us sandwiches. I thought it was the coolest place in the world—a racetrack with a playground. And a beach and an ocean."

The Hemi made news across that season, dominating the big tracks and rattling competitors. Ford, involved in a sort of Wild West battle with Chrysler for the lead role in NASCAR, issued protest after protest about the outsized engine. Late in the year, NASCAR issued rules for the 1965 season, including banishment of the Hemi. Infuriated Chrysler officials announced the manufacturer would not participate in Cup racing in 1965.

This was cataclysmic news at Petty Enterprises, which had become synonymous with the Plymouth brand and was clearly on the upswing as Richard Petty was gathering more and more wins and more and more fans. The team's march toward world domination was abruptly halted, the garage door slammed in its face. After tinkering with the idea of racing Plymouths despite the rules changes, the Petty team decided to follow Chrysler's call and abandon NASCAR.

The 1965 Daytona 500, already the sport's showcase, was run without top Chrysler teams, and that meant Petty, David Pearson, Jim Paschal, Bobby Isaac, and Paul Goldsmith were absentees. Fred Lorenzen won the 500 as Ford products finished in the top thirteen positions, a Daytona sweep for the ages. Neil Castles, in seventeenth place, drove the only Plymouth finishing in the top twenty. In one year, Chrysler had gone from Daytona glory to an afterthought.

AFTER TINKERING WITH THE IDEA OF RACING PLYMOUTHS, THE PETTY TEAM DECIDED TO FOLLOW CHRYSLER'S CALL AND ABANDON NASCAR.

Ford teams won forty-eight of the season's fifty-five races, and Ford's Ned Jarrett won the championship, the first Cup title for the Blue Oval. Chrysler returned late in the year (much to the glee of track promoters, who had seen attendance numbers plummet) after NASCAR modified the rules again, allowing limited use of the Hemi.

The battle to see which manufacturer could build the boldest engine was on.

Ford developed a huge engine of its own late in 1965, submitting a 427 cubic inch (7 L) powerplant for NASCAR approval. Officials frowned at this latest escalation, ruling that the new Ford engine could be used only if Blue Oval products carried extra weight. Early in 1966, Ford announced its own boycott of NASCAR. Defending series champion Jarrett, a Ford stalwart, was testing tires at Darlington Raceway when he was called to a pay phone in the garage. He was told to park his race cars immediately, beginning with the next night's Cup race at Columbia, South Carolina.

These sorts of rules brouhahas would pepper NASCAR over the years, irritating drivers, teams, and not incidentally, fans. Sometimes, there was as much bitching and moaning about rules in the garage as there was beer in grandstand coolers.

What next? Oddly enough, the Pettys detoured to the alien sport of drag racing. As did David Pearson, whose Cotton Owens–owned Dodges were also victims of the NASCAR rules changes. Petty and Pearson ran exhibition drag races against a variety of opponents, padding their wallets during the break from NASCAR.

SOMETIMES, THERE WAS AS MUCH BITCHING AND MOANING ABOUT RULES IN THE GARAGE AS THERE WAS BEER IN GRANDSTAND COOLERS.

Owens turned a Dodge Dart station wagon into a drag car (nicknamed The Cotton Picker), and suddenly Pearson was racing in a straight line at dragstrips far from the NASCAR spotlight. "We went down to Augusta, Georgia, one time," Pearson said in a *NASCAR Images* interview, "and I was running Fred Lorenzen, and I beat him the first time. It was best two of three. So, they came to me and . . . said, 'We got to make this look good. You got to let him win this next one.' I didn't say I would or I didn't say I wouldn't, but I knew if I messed up and he beat me on that second, in the third one he would win, so I said there was no way I'm going to try to let him win the second one. So, there wasn't going to be a third one."

Pearson was ultracompetitive even in the short run.

Petty's brief foray into drag racing occurred in a Plymouth Barracuda numbered 43/Jr., labeled Outlawed, and carrying the Hemi engine. It wasn't a great fit for a team used to running in circles, and the weird adventure ended in tragedy. In February 1965, Petty lost control of his car on a backwoods dragstrip in Dallas, Georgia. An overflow crowd estimated at 10,000 had turned out to see the NASCAR star race in their town, and spectators were closer to the track than on normal race days, when the track attracted about 2,000.

The Plymouth ran into a bank, jumped a fence, and went into the crowd. An eight-year-old boy was killed and several other spectators were injured. Newspaper reports said the boy was hit by a wheel that flew off the car.

Petty, described as being in a state of shock after the accident, later speculated that a suspension piece broke but said the car was so badly damaged that it was difficult to determine an exact cause of the crash. It was one of the darkest days of Petty's long career.

Both Petty and Pearson soon left the drag racing scene.

Pearson had signed on to drive for Owens' team in 1963, and they scored eight wins in 1964 and two in 1965 before posting fifteen victories and Pearson's first Cup championship in 1966. Pearson ran forty-two races in that season, finishing in the top five twenty-six times and recording a remarkable average finish of 6.4.

Owens, a wiry and tough short-track racer, had a successful career as a driver before deciding to concentrate on car building. He probably would have competed on-track longer, but his vision was hampered by injuries suffered in a nightmarish race crash in 1951. Owens swerved trying to avoid a wrecked car and slammed into the track's bandstand. His face hit the steering wheel. "My face was knocked sideways, and half of my teeth were out," Owens said. He was hospitalized for about two months. "They wired up some bones in my cheek," he said. "They did the best they knew how back then." Later, he raced with double vision after four operations failed to correct problems with his left eye.

Owens repeated the success of his driving years as a team owner, his cigarette smoke floating in his Spartanburg shop as he and team members labored over their Dodges. He and Pearson brought the championship trophy home to Spartanburg in 1966. Long after that championship season, Owens called Pearson the best driver he had seen. "He could drive anything, anywhere, any time," Owens said. "Dale Earnhardt is good, but I don't know if he could drive other type vehicles like Pearson. He got in an Indy car during a tire test at Atlanta in the 1960s and was running a second faster than the other guys on his third lap. Then he got out and said he didn't like it. Pearson could get out of one car and get in another and run it faster than the guy who had been in it. I saw him do things in a race car that I knew just weren't possible. He once won a race even though the car he was driving had no brakes. He would turn the engine off entering the turn and fire it back up as he exited. I wouldn't have believed it if I hadn't seen it myself."

Pearson later left Owens and scored back-to-back Cup championships with the Holman-Moody (H-M) team in 1968 and 1969, winning twenty-seven races over the two seasons. H-M was Ford's power team over a long stretch of years, sending fire-breathing race cars out of its shop near the Charlotte airport.

Robert Yates, who later would become one of NASCAR's most successful team owners, worked in H-M's engine shop in 1968 and 1969. "That was a big house and it had it going on," Yates said. "That was a serious place as far as manufacturer racing—Ford against Chrysler—and it was an honor just to get to work on them."

Richie Barsz holds an unusual place in NASCAR history in that he worked with both Pearson and Petty during their championship years. He was a fabricator and crew member at Holman-Moody during Pearson's championship runs and then he was a key player in the successful Petty Enterprises seasons.

Barsz said Pearson "had no ego; he was just a guy. You might think he wasn't running well in practice at Darlington, and you'd ask him what was wrong. He'd say, 'Just make sure the cigarette lighter in the car is working and that I got some chewing gum taped to the dash. I'll take care of the rest.' He wasn't lying. He did. He just knew when to go and when not to go.

"He was as cool as you could be on the track. I remember him going out to practice for the first time at Martinsville. He got on the radio and said, 'Hey, look up in the stands about the fifth row. Look at the one with the red shorts on.'

"When it came time to race, he was ready. He was so good that a lot of the normal stuff just didn't matter. He never showed anything until the last fifty laps of the race."

Pearson was known to light a cigarette during caution periods, and he used the chewing gum—always Wrigley's spearmint flavor, nothing else would work—to keep his mouth moist.

He chewed through a lot of gum in two brilliant seasons. "Holman-Moody was a great team, a team with everything you needed," Barsz said. "You were supposed to win with that kind of money behind you."

Long-time NASCAR crew chief Tim Brewer said Pearson was the best driver ever. "He had talent, pure-ass talent," Brewer said. "He was there to win the race and to make money. There was nobody smarter or tougher. When it came time to run for the win, he was there. He would race for 100 miles [161 km], ride for 300 [483 km], and race for the last 100 [161 km]. And he was going to kick your ass."

And he did in 1966, easily outrunning second-place James Hylton and third-place Richard Petty for his first championship. More would follow.

Mother's Day in 1971 might as well have been Father's Day in the Parsons home near North Wilkesboro, North Carolina. The Cup Series raced that day at South Boston Speedway in Virginia in a relatively short event known as the Halifax County 100. Benny Parsons, then in his second full-time season in the series, started from the second position in a Ford owned by North Carolina businessman L.G. DeWitt, and there was a bit of hope in the Parsons house about how things might go. The family had stayed home, it being Mother's Day and all.

Late in the afternoon the phone rang. Benny was calling to let the family know he had won the race, crossing the finish line in front for the first time since he left a successful career in the Automobile Racing Club of America (ARCA) series to fish the bigger pond of NASCAR. This was big news for a driver still trying to find his place in a new racing world and a financial boost for a growing family.

Kevin, Parsons' five-year-old son, grabbed the phone and listened to his father describe the win. Kevin was happy, but he wanted to know: "Was Richard Petty there?"

It was a good question.

Didn't Richard Petty win every race at every track on every Sunday? Was he even there, Dad? Did he call in sick?

Turned out Petty raced that day. In fact, he finished second to Parsons, a full lap behind. That was so unusual as to be a bit ridiculous.

By 1971, Petty had won 119 races and could reasonably be expected to challenge for victory at every stop. He had won eighteen times the previous season and ten times in 1969, and the 1971 season would produce twenty-one victories.

Drivers who had starred on their home tracks and looked to NASCAR's highest level as a shiny goal knew they would run into the brick wall that was Richard Petty when they tried to make the move to the big time. He was the colossus at the gate and a target for all comers, the big guy with the big stick. The gold standard, draped in Petty blue.

His statistics were off the charts.

All of Petty's other numbers paled in the bright glare of 1967, however, for it was that year that Petty was bestowed the regal nickname that would ride with him the rest of his days, far beyond his driving years.

King Richard.

The car is innocent enough, in its way. It rests on one side of the Petty Museum in Level Cross, North Carolina, engine silent, cockpit empty. It has no great presence, shows no great threat as might the wildly designed Plymouth Superbird to come or the big hulking Plymouths of the past.

No, the 1967 Plymouth Belvedere was a relatively nondescript race car, distinctive only because it carried the Petty blue color that the team already had made famous. In fact, it really wasn't even a 1967 model. Petty mechanics had retooled and rebooted the Belvedere model from the previous year.

The car's history, though, is that of a behemoth. You didn't want to mess with it.

In 1967, Petty ran forty-eight Cup races (most in the refined version of the Belvedere), winning twenty-seven—yes, twenty-seven—and finishing in the top ten forty times. Even more remarkably, he did something drivers of the current era view as simply ludicrous: he won ten consecutive races.

Ten. Consecutive. Races.

It was a year of magic and wonder, and it carried Petty's name outside the often-insular boundaries of auto racing into the wider world, a world he was helping NASCAR invade.

Perhaps as early as 1965, somebody labeled him King Richard. Some evidence indicates that the nickname originated with *Atlanta Journal* sportswriter Bill Robinson, who traveled the NASCAR circuit for years.

"I figure some writers were sitting around a bar one night after being at the track, had maybe too many drinks and came up with that," Petty said. "It's been around a long time."

In 1967, Petty's best year ever, the nickname became a permanent part of the lexicon surrounding him. Decidedly, he was king. They might as well have given him a crown (in fact, he did get a championship). He has admitted that the title can be a bit embarrassing, however, particularly when people ask him to sign his autograph as "King Richard." "I've never signed that," he said. "I said, 'My name's Richard,' and that's what I put down. It's something that somebody else calls you, and you don't pay that much attention to it. A lot of people just call me the king. I answer to that, but it's not a deal that I meant for it to happen."

Even in years when Petty didn't occupy the throne, the title fit comfortably.

The 1967 season didn't start with a flourish for Petty. There was no evidence of the grandeur to come. The team's brand-new 1967 Plymouth wasn't fast out of the gate. There were issues, and the King wasn't happy.

"We ran it four times and had trouble with it every time," Petty said. "I told Dale [Inman], 'That car ain't got no personality. Put it in a corner.'"

It was the timeout the team needed.

Inman and his mechanics refurbished the Belvedere the team had run with success late in 1966 (the car earned the nickname *Ol' Blue*) and returned it to the fray. It worked again. Petty won the sixth race of the year at Asheville-Weaverville Speedway in the shadow of the North Carolina mountains, leading 150 of the 300 laps. Later came wins at Columbia Speedway, South Carolina, and Hickory Motor Speedway, North Carolina, and Petty was on his way to a great year. But no one could have imagined how crazily successful it would be.

"It was phenomenal the way it worked," Petty said. "Unbelievable."

Even Inman, low-key and never one to get overly excited, was impressed with the car. "The remarkable thing was we had the same car all along," he said. "To keep the car under him for ten races in a row and win them, I thought that was a feat."

A feat it was.

A rundown of Rapid Richard's Rampage of 1967:

Win 1—Winston-Salem, North Carolina, August 12. Margin of victory—three laps over Jim Paschal. Petty led all 250 laps in a caution-free race at Bowman Gray Stadium. It was Petty's eighteenth win of the year, tying him for most in a Cup season with Tim Flock. "A nicer guy couldn't have tied the record," Flock said. "Richard has been in racing practically all his life, and I'm sure that he'll win a lot more before he gets through." That was an understatement.

Win 2—Columbia, South Carolina, August 17. Margin of victory—one lap over John Sears. Petty and Bobby Allison swapped the lead late in the race, but Allison tagged the wall with nine laps remaining and finished fourth. Columbia Speedway was also the scene of Petty's first start in 1958.

Win 3—Savannah, Georgia, August 25. Margin of victory—five laps over Elmo Langley. Petty led all 200 laps in one of his easiest wins of the season. In qualifying, he set a track record of 71.942 miles per hour (115.779 km per hour).

Win 4—Darlington, South Carolina, September 4. Margin of victory—five laps over David Pearson. Petty had very little success at Darlington across his career, but this was his day. He led 345 of the 364 laps and left Pearson five laps in his wake, claiming the Southern 500 for the first time. The victory marked the first time a driver had won four straight races from the pole position. Petty won eighteen poles during the season.

Win 5—Hickory, North Carolina, September 8. Margin of victory—one lap over Jack Ingram. Not even a late-race flat tire could stop the King. He ran the final two laps on a flat, beating rookie Cup driver and short-track ace Ingram to the finish. The win gave Petty an unusual Hickory sweep. He won the Hickory spring race on a dirt surface. The track was paved before the tour returned in September, giving Petty victories on two very different surfaces at the same track in the same year.

Win 6—Richmond, Virginia, September 10. Margin of victory—one-half lap. Petty took the lead on lap 138 (of 300) and led the rest of the way. His $2,450 check for the win put his seasonal total at $113,570, a record.

Win 7—Beltsville, Maryland, September 15. Margin of victory—two laps over Bobby Allison. Allison's pursuit of Petty was hindered when he was black-flagged because of a loose gas cap. Petty set a record in qualifying with a lap of 81.044 miles per hour (130.428 km per hour).

Win 8—Hillsborough, North Carolina, September 17. Margin of victory—Dick Hutcherson was the only other driver on the lead lap. Petty's run on the fast and challenging 0.9-mile (1.4-km) dirt track included an unscheduled pit stop to wipe mud from his windshield.

Win 9—Martinsville, Virginia, September 24. Margin of victory—four laps over Dick Hutcherson. Paul Goldsmith had a strong car and led most of the first half of the race, but he eventually parked with engine trouble. Petty dominated from that point.

Win 10—North Wilkesboro, North Carolina, October 1. Margin of victory—two laps over Dick Hutcherson. Petty won in front of Ford motorsports czar Jacque Passino, the point man in the Blue Oval's difficult pursuit of victory in what clearly was a Petty year.

In eight of the ten victories, Petty finished in a lap by himself. Hutcherson, driving a Bondy Long Ford, finished second in four of the races.

The season would produce an avalanche of statistics as officials and journalists scrambled to keep up with Petty's march through the schedule. General Sherman would have been proud.

OFFICIALS AND JOURNALISTS SCRAMBLED TO KEEP UP WITH PETTY'S MARCH THROUGH THE SCHEDULE. GENERAL SHERMAN WOULD HAVE BEEN PROUD.

Petty's twenty-seven wins that year are more than some NASCAR Hall of Fame drivers, including Dale Earnhardt Jr., Joe Weatherly, Terry Labonte, and Fred Lorenzen, scored in their entire careers.

Petty led 5,553 laps during the season, including at least one lap in forty-one races. Oddly, he didn't lead a lap in either race at Daytona International Speedway, one of his best tracks. No other driver won more than six races in that Petty-perfect year. He was as brash as a Baptist driving a beer truck.

How did all this happen? How could one driver and team be so dominant?

"The difference was between the seat and the steering wheel," Maurice Petty said. "We've got the best driver."

Of course, the answer went deeper than that. Obviously, Richard Petty was among the top drivers of the era (and all eras), but it's worth mentioning that the race fields that season were often uneven, with only a handful of drivers capable of winning. Additionally, eleven of Petty's wins came in races of 100 miles (161 km) or less, not exactly marathon tests of driver and machine.

Still, the accomplishments shouldn't be diminished. Ten wins in a row? No one else has won more than five straight in the history of the sport.

"EVEN WHEN WE WIN, TALK OF THAT DAY'S RACE ENDS AT MIDNIGHT. THE NEXT DAY WE START WORK ON THE NEXT ONE."

Never one to get too emotionally high or low, Petty looks back on the streak as more or less normal, considering how well the No. 43 team was functioning during the time and how strong and consistent most of its cars were. Typical of the Petty operation for virtually its entire existence, there wasn't a lot of postrace pondering and analysis. A standard rule around the shop: "Even when we win, talk of that day's race ends at midnight. The next day we start work on the next one."

Petty said the streak built on itself.

"The first six or seven races in a row weren't that big of a deal because we were just winning races and going to the next one," Petty said. "We were all about winning races, so we just looked at things as normal."

Chrysler executives loved the normal, even as rivals in the Ford camp squirmed. After the ninth win, Chrysler flew Petty to New York City for a public relations tour, a sort of stick-it-in-your-eye moment emphasizing the success of Chrysler products. It was another important event for the driver, team, and NASCAR. "That was a really big deal," Petty said. "Other than that, we were just busy racing. We weren't thinking much about records. We just won a race, so we said, 'OK, we've got to get home and get the car ready for the next one.'"

Inman didn't make the trip to New York. "I guess I was working," he said, smiling.

Inman and his crew reworked much of the car between races. Some of the changes were more extensive than others, simply because the team had more time. For example, there were eight days between the wins at Columbia and Savannah, giving mechanics time to rework every important piece on the car. But the turnaround time between the races at Beltsville and Hillsborough was only two days, so the work was almost like running a car through a car wash.

"We had to do good maintenance to keep a good car under Richard," Inman said. "The wheel bearings, the grease, the motor oils just weren't as good as they are today. We did everything to the car that we had time to do."

In those days, each race winner went to the press box overlooking the track after victory lane ceremonies to be interviewed by journalists (a similar process occurs now, but interviews typically are conducted in a media center in the track infield). After the ninth win—at North Wilkesboro Speedway, one of NASCAR's oldest tracks—Petty sat down in the front of the press box and looked at many of the same writers who had followed him through the long run of victories. "How about me interviewing you guys today," he said. "I don't have much to say that I haven't already said."

He came. He saw. He conquered.

Although the Pettys saw the constant winning as par for the course, news media outlets across the country and even elsewhere in the hemisphere saw the streak for what it was: big news. Petty remembers receiving a clipping from a Canadian newspaper late in the season. The headline read "Petty Runs Second." The editor considered the fact that Petty failed more important than penning a headline about the race winner.

Publicity about the streak helped NASCAR reach new territory. Petty told reporter Ben Blake that the unprecedented run "broke us out of the South. Those people in Canada, California were paying attention to this because it was out of the ordinary, beyond the call of duty."

That season is even more impressive considering Petty had some bad luck during the year and had to rally to score some of the twenty-seven wins. For example, Petty won at Nashville in July despite blowing a tire and hitting the wall early in the race. He lost seven laps during repairs but returned to the track and watched the other leaders fall out one by one. By race's end, Petty had a two-lap lead.

It's good to be great—it's also great to be lucky.

"Dale [Inman] used to tell me when I'd say, 'Hey, we won twenty-seven races,' he'd tell me, 'Well, you lost twenty-one,'" Petty said. "If we had had exceptionally good luck that year, we would have won two-thirds of the races."

The ten-race streak and the publicity it generated pushed the sport along at a time when NASCAR was mainly a curiosity for many Americans. Petty's visibility that season helped remold the sport for many, taking it beyond its reputation as a pastime strictly for old bootleggers and yahooing rednecks. There were miles still to go, but it was a big step. To those who might complain that Petty was too dominant, NASCAR founder Bill France Sr. countered that the team earned every win and carried the entire NASCAR family along for the ride.

"It took a lot of people to get me to the point where it was even possible to win twenty-seven races in one year," Petty said in his 1971 autobiography. "It has never been just Richard Petty out there in a stock car. I've had a lot of company."

As the streak and Petty's reputation grew, so did his fan base. "Petty for President" bumper stickers began appearing in speedway parking lots, and membership in his fan club pushed toward 15,000.

"As we had got so much into winning, I said I wonder what it will feel like to lose," Inman said.

Where was David Pearson, Petty's top rival, during this remarkable streak? It was another of his abbreviated seasons. Pearson, who had won the championship in 1966, won twice early in 1967 for team owner Cotton Owens then finished the year with Holman-Moody. He drove in only twenty-two of the year's forty-eight races.

Pearson's 1967 schedule included only three of the ten races in Petty's streak. He was second to Petty at Darlington and third at Martinsville but dropped out of the North Wilkesboro race with a blown engine. It was one year in which the duo's rivalry was barely a whimper.

The Petty streak ended with a thud in the National 500 on October 15 at Charlotte Motor Speedway. Ford, desperate to end Petty's run, entered nine factory-supported cars in the race. Among the Ford hotshots on hand was superstar Mario Andretti.

"They were certainly sending the best they had at us, throwing everything in to try to beat us," Inman said.

Oddly, though, it was a fellow Plymouth driver who stopped Petty's long march. Paul Goldsmith lost an engine and slid early in the race, making contact with Petty and damaging both cars. Petty stayed in the race but later dropped out with a blown engine. The driver who had finished first ten consecutive times was in the garage at the end of the day, settling for eighteenth-place money ($1,225). The day's winner, Buddy Baker, scored his first Cup victory.

"It was just another race that we didn't win," said Petty. "You have to figure that, in a couple of the races we won, we got far behind and made up the laps. Some of the races just came to us. That one didn't."

However, Petty picked up big trophies and wads of cash at the end of the season after breezing to his second championship. And the big numbers he rang up during the best season of his career would impress the NASCAR world for decades to come.

"What happened was we started getting the breaks," Petty said. "Wrecks would happen either ahead of us or behind us. We stopped having so many flat tires. It was just fantastic what was happening to us during the ten-race streak. A lot of it was due to luck, but we were always in position to be lucky."

It was a Petty–blue streak for the ages.

"I have lost all of my respect for you. I hope that you never win a nickel driving a Ford and if you fail to qualify at all the big races, it would please me no end."

"I just want you to know that you're not my favorite driver anymore. You're a stinking Ford driver!!!"

"We wish you luck in your Ford—all bad."

On November 25, 1968, Richard Petty announced that his team would end its long and fruitful association with Chrysler and Plymouth to race Fords in the 1969 NASCAR season. After some back and forth, the Petty organization could not come to an agreement with Chrysler officials to extend their contract, so Petty signed on with rival Ford.

It was as if the world had ended for fans dedicated to the Plymouth insignia and to the driver who had driven it to greatness. The vitriol spewed forth from all corners of the country in letters and telegrams to Petty. People were not happy.

"There will be one less Petty fan in 1969."

"TRAITOR. You are no hero now—just another 'damn' Ford driver. You have sold your soul brother."

"We use [sic] to be raceing [sic] fans. We did't [sic] know you would stoop that low!"

"We feel that you have done Crysler [sic] wrong and we have went to our last race. I hope you lose every race with that race hungry bunch of nuts."

"DON'T DO IT!!!"

There was even a poet in the bunch:

> "I Like PLYMOUTH,
> I Like Blue.
> I Like 43, and
> I Like you.
> But when you went FORD,
> Which you shouldn't do,
> You lost me, and
> I hate you."

This was predictable (well, maybe not the poetry). In that era (and, to a smaller extent, in today's racing), many fans were devoted to car makes. Petty's splendid partnership with Chrysler and its Plymouth brand was perfect for fans who both admired Petty and drove Plymouths on the street. A Petty win was also a win for them, as they saw it. They were in this together.

Until they weren't.

To have Petty abandon Plymouths for the hated Fords was a slap in the face—an unforgivable sin—to many in his fan base. It was as if a Yankee player suddenly signed with the Red Sox or an Auburn football booster contributed to Alabama's recruiting budget.

"The rivalry was as much about Ford and Chrysler as it was about Petty and Pearson," Kyle Petty said. "You don't have that any more. At that time, one led one camp, one led the other camp. By God, that's the way it was. There was no in-between."

Petty's stunning move was one major news item in a 1969 season that was full of them. And Petty and David Pearson were in the middle of, or around, most of the big moments.

Pearson won eleven races and the championship in 1969, backing up his 1968 title season, in which he won sixteen times. Pearson had left the Cotton Owens team in the middle of the 1967 season after a minor dispute and joined Holman-Moody, Ford's flagship operation.

So Pearson and Petty were teammates under the Blue Oval banner in 1969. Petty won ten races that season and scored his landmark one hundredth victory at, of all places, tiny Bowman Gray Stadium in Winston-Salem, North Carolina. A lot of people in the racing community had problems accepting that he did it in a Ford.

Petty later said his team considered proposals for the 1969 season from both Chrysler and Ford before deciding to make the dramatic switch. He said the team's long relationship with Chrysler had led officials there to consider the Pettys like family, along with the assumption that families never break up. But Ford made an attractive offer and the Pettys signed a one-year contract with an option for a two-year renewal. It would be a successful but short partnership.

The team built a pair of Ford Torinos to haul to the first race of the year, the road course at Riverside International Raceway in California.

Operating in a new environment, Petty lost control of his car twice but recovered each time, eventually moved into first place, and held off a late-race charge by A.J. Foyt to win. The King had scored in his first outing in a Ford, and the folks in Dearborn were ecstatic. The win was Petty's first in a car not in the Chrysler family.

Meanwhile, Pearson was trucking along in his second full season with Holman-Moody, a polished team that carried much weight in the Ford camp.

Despite success, including winning the 1966 championship with good friend and team owner Cotton Owens, Pearson left the Dodge team in the spring of 1967 after winning a pair of races that season. In retrospect, the reason for the breakup was silly.

The team was scheduled to race at Columbia Speedway in Columbia, South Carolina, about a hundred miles (161 km) southeast of Owens' Spartanburg shop. The race car was outside the garage when team members arrived. While waiting for Owens to return from home, they drove nearby to buy some ice for their drink coolers. When they came back, the car was gone. They apparently thought Owens had left for Columbia with it, so they drove to the track. When Owens arrived at the shop, no one was around. Not wanting to drive the tow truck, he pulled the car back into the garage and decided to skip the race. Owens was upset and talked of firing team members, Pearson said in a 1997 interview. "I said if you're going to fire one you might as well fire them all," he said. "He fired off at me, too, and said, 'If you don't like it you can go, too,' or something like that. So, I said alright, and that's the way it happened."

Owens later said he and Pearson probably "got too close. In racing, a lot of times things happen that you think are going to happen, and it upsets you. It works on your nerve system, and it was beginning to work on my nerves."

There were other issues. Owens, one of the most safety-conscious car builders in those years, would sacrifice a bit of speed to put more weight and protection inside his cars. Pearson favored lighter—and thus faster—cars. But their ultimate breakup was mostly a case of two stubborn men letting a minor misunderstanding upend one of the sport's top teams. Pearson and Owens healed the rift quickly and remained friends the rest of their lives. They shared lunches, along with local team owner Bud Moore, at the Peach Blossom Diner, a popular "meat-and-three" spot in Spartanburg, and in later years, Pearson drove Owens to church services.

So, after running ten races that season with Owens, Pearson accepted an offer to drive for Holman-Moody, replacing Fred Lorenzen in one of the tour's hottest cars. Lorenzen, one of the sport's most popular drivers, suddenly decided to retire, a choice he later regretted. He returned to run a few races for other teams but never added to his twenty-six wins.

Pearson wasted no time proving his worth at Holman-Moody, winning the pole for the May 13 race at Darlington Raceway and finishing second (to Petty) in the race.

Pearson failed to win the rest of that season, but he had four second-place runs and two third-place finishes in the H-M Fords.

Pearson's adventures with two teams in one season were mostly back-of-the-book material in 1967 because of the brilliant season Petty was enjoying. He won twenty-seven races, including ten in a row, and rolled to his second championship.

PEARSON ACCEPTED AN OFFER TO DRIVE FOR HOLMAN-MOODY, REPLACING FRED LORENZEN IN ONE OF THE TOUR'S HOTTEST CARS.

The 1968 and 1969 seasons were golden for Pearson and Holman-Moody. After a sort of "get-acquainted" period over the second half of 1967, they were ready to make noise in the blue-and-gold No. 17 Fords. Pearson had walked through the doors of Holman-Moody's Charlotte shop and marveled at the number of people and extent of the inventory. It was an assembly line for powerful race cars.

Kyle Petty, who took some of his first steps as a toddler inside Petty Enterprises, surrounded by brilliant blue race cars, remembers walking into the Holman-Moody shop with his father when he was eight years old. "You have to remember that I grew up in this shop [Petty Enterprises]," he said. "Everything I saw was Petty blue. I rode with my dad to Holman-Moody. We went in that place, and it was like, 'How would you race against these guys?' It was like walking in Hendrick Motorsports today. They had everything. And that blue and gold 17 was the most beautiful race car I'd ever seen in my life. It was. That Torino. And all of a sudden, those colors were everywhere."

Those comments are on the edge of blasphemy for a Petty, but the striking colors of the No. 17 Fords indeed were royal. And the team was stacked with talent and the best of equipment and racing with the full power of Ford behind it.

"We had it right there," Pearson said. "We had engines galore . . . and [highly respected engine builders] Robert Yates and Waddell Wilson." At one point, H-M had about two dozen employees building chassis, both for in-house cars and to sell to other racers. And H-M's reach stretched beyond NASCAR to drag racing, sports car racing, and off-road racing.

Pearson also had legendary NASCAR mechanic J.C. "Jake" Elder, who had made Holman-Moody one of many stops in his long career of bouncing from team to team. Along the way, because of his tendency to pack his toolbox and leave at a moment's notice, Elder picked up the nickname "Suitcase Jake." Because of his talents, he had no trouble landing the next spot.

Elder, who might have been a teacher if there had been an "old school" for mechanics, was known to bend a rule now and then. He got results.

"I always thought a lot of old Jake," Pearson said. "He couldn't read or write, but he could remember. He could tell you what springs, what shocks he used at every racetrack we went to. And he never took a note. He was good with me. A lot of people he would argue with. You just had to kind of argue back with him."

Richie Barsz was another mechanic at Holman-Moody during that period. "I worked with Jake," he said. "The reason they put me to working with him was because nobody else could work with him. He was a true racer. He didn't have much formal education, but he was great." Barsz later would work with Elder at Petty Enterprises. "Jake got mad at Lee Petty one day," Barsz said. "He told Lee, 'The next time I come back here I'll have enough money to buy this place.'"

With Elder slinging wrenches and former driver Dick Hutcherson newly named to manage the No. 17 team, Pearson was in one of the best spots of his career as he rolled through 1968. Ford Motor Co. had doubled down on its commitment to win championships, and Pearson and Petty were atop the mountain. They won sixteen races each in a season in which no other driver won more than six.

In the middle of that season, the tour made its annual swing through the Northeast, racing at Islip, New York; Oxford, Maine; Fonda, New York; and Trenton, New Jersey—four races in eight days. Waiting anxiously for teams to arrive in the area was an eleven-year-old boy named Robin Pemberton, who rode his bicycle to area tracks. Later, he would be a race-winning crew chief, a leader of Ford's NASCAR operations, and a vice president of NASCAR. In the summer of 1968, he was a young fan with a camera.

Pemberton's family lived in Malta in upstate New York, about 45 miles (72 km) from the Vermont border. He and his friends attended area short-track races and followed the stars of Cup racing through occasional clips on television and in weekly racing newspapers, which they bought trackside. "We got news then however we could get it," Pemberton said. "We learned as much as we could about the guys running in NASCAR. I met Richard in 1968 when their team stayed at the motel across from the restaurant my family ran. We made friends with the team, so I kept track of Richard. You always had a feeling for him and Pearson. You'd have thought there was nobody else on the track."

One of Pemberton's cherished photos is one he shot of Petty's No. 43 on a trailer on the side of the road in front of Bosley's Motel in 1968. That Plymouth would win two of the four races in the Northern Tour that year.

Pearson scored four straight wins in May and three straight in August and outran Bobby Isaac, his closest friend in the garage, for the championship. From June 22 to September 8, Pearson ran eighteen races with no finishes outside the top five. It was a stretch that reminded fans of Petty's charge through the 1967 schedule.

Among Pearson's wins that year was a victory in the May 11, 1968, Rebel 400 at Darlington Raceway, a cranky old track that had befuddled

NASCAR racers since its opening in 1950. It was Pearson's first superspeedway win in almost seven years. (In 1970, he would win the Rebel race again, leading 117 of 291 laps and winning by a three-lap margin. He called it one of his "happiest" victories.)

Pearson became famous for solving the mysteries of the egg-shaped, 1.3-mile (2.1-km) oval. The track was narrow, fast, and unforgiving, with some drivers content to simply finish 500 miles (805 km) there. Pearson became its master, scoring a record ten wins, a number unmatched by other Darlington stars, including Dale Earnhardt (nine wins) and Jeff Gordon (seven). For years after, drivers looking toward making their first starts at the track would contact him asking for a bit of the magic, a hint of advice that might help.

"Every time I've been to Darlington, there will be four or five who come up and talk to me about getting around the racetrack," Pearson said. "The biggest problem is that most of them are trying too hard. They run into the corner too hard. Some of them you can explain it to, and they'll try it. And it works for a while, but they'll run up on somebody in a corner and that will be it."

Among the drivers who had difficulties at Darlington was Petty, who won there only three times—one Southern 500 and two spring races. His last win there occurred in 1967, meaning he would race twenty-five more years without visiting Darlington's victory lane again. In sixty-five races at the old track, Petty finished in the top five twenty-five times.

Pearson remained hot in 1969, winning eleven races (to Petty's ten) and outlasting Petty for the title. That season marked the only time Pearson and Petty finished one-two in the point standings. In one of Pearson's wins—July at Bristol Motor Speedway—Petty drove in relief for Pearson after David was sidelined by a case of the flu. Although Pearson returned to the cockpit before the end of the race, Petty would tease him that he deserved credit for half of the victory.

The championship was Pearson's third, making him only the second driver (after Lee Petty) to win three titles. He won a series record $229,760 that season. His fan base and his résumé were growing. His dark skin, handsome face, and wavy black hair fired female hearts from Richmond to Riverside. He was a star.

There was trouble ahead, however. The Pearson partnership with Holman-Moody soured after the 1969 championship. With Ford backing away from a full-season commitment after two straight titles, Pearson scored only one win in 1970 and decided to leave the team in the middle of the 1971 season. His last race with the team was at Darlington on May 2, 1971. He qualified second and led early in the race but parked the car after thirty laps, angry about steering problems.

"What happened that day was, the crew changed a whole bunch of suspension stuff on the car Sunday morning, and he came off the fourth corner and slid along the wall," team co-owner Ralph Moody told writer Tom Cotter. "He pulled in and stopped and got out and said, 'The hell with the sumbitch . . . I quit.' I went over and asked him if he really meant it, and he said, 'Yeah, I quit.'"

In the previous three races, Pearson had scored three second-place finishes.

But money matters also impacted Pearson's departure. Team co-owner John Holman asked Pearson to take a pay cut after Ford trimmed its support to the team. "I actually left the team because John Holman wanted me to take a cut in my percentage [from fifty percent of the race purse to forty]," Pearson told writer Bob Myers. "As a matter of principle, I just didn't think I should drive for any less than what I'd been getting."

Pearson talked about the parting during his NASCAR Hall of Fame acceptance speech in May 2011: "I said, 'John, I ain't never drove for anybody for forty percent. I always got half of whatever you win. Another dime ain't going to keep you in business.' Anyway, he said, 'Well, that's what we're going to have to do.' I said, 'I can't drive for you no more. If I can't get that, I might as well go somewhere else.' So that ended that. I left there."

Moody had lost confidence in Pearson, then thirty-six years old. "For a couple of years, he'd said he wanted to retire," Moody said. "The year he finally quit he'd gotten to where he wasn't aggressive any more. He just didn't have it like he used to."

That claim soon would be proven very wrong. Indeed, Pearson's best years were ahead of him.

"I didn't try to explain why I left Holman-Moody at the time because I didn't want people to think I was just making excuses," Pearson said. "I don't really care what people who bad-mouth me think so long as I know the truth. I knew I wasn't washed up."

The 1969 season included one of the most bizarre scheduling situations in NASCAR history. The Firecracker 400 at Daytona International Speedway was run on its traditional date of July 4. Two days later, NASCAR scheduled a 300-mile (483-km) race at the new Dover International Speedway in Delaware, 900 miles (1,448 km) from Daytona Beach.

LeeRoy Yarbrough won the Daytona race, and the teams who had decided to run at Dover immediately hit the road, traveling north along the East Coast to run on a fast one-mile (1.6-km) track that was hosting its first race. Many of the circuit's established drivers skipped the Dover event, primarily because of the travel issues, but Yarbrough, Petty, and Pearson were among those who made the trip. Petty drove with his family, rolling into Dover Saturday afternoon after an overnight stay in

"I DON'T REALLY CARE WHAT PEOPLE WHO BAD-MOUTH ME THINK SO LONG AS I KNOW THE TRUTH. I KNEW I WASN'T WASHED UP."

Myrtle Beach, South Carolina.

When team members arrived at the speedway Sunday, some climbed onto workbenches in the garage and slept before track activities began. Some drivers had to be awakened when the track opened for practice. "I remember crew guys sleeping on the tables in the garage," said Dale Inman, Petty's crew chief. "We were tired. We went in there never having seen the place. I tell guys today that it ain't always been this easy."

Pearson won the pole with a speed of 130.430 miles per hour (209.907 km per hour). The event became a test of tires. With proper setups mostly a mystery, teams didn't know how long tires would last. Petty led 150 laps and won the race by a whopping six laps over Sonny Hutchins. Pearson and Yarbrough, the only other leaders, crashed out. Practice, qualifying, and the race all took place on Sunday.

"Everybody's tongues were hanging out," Petty said. "We had driven a long way from Daytona, and there was no time for anything. Nobody knew anything about setups or anything. We hadn't even seen a picture of the place."

Some teams used the same car they had raced in Daytona Beach two days before. Others stopped at shops in North Carolina and picked up another car.

The 1969 season also saw the opening of the giant Talladega Superspeedway (then called Alabama International Motor Speedway) in eastern Alabama. The 2.66-mile (4.28-km), high-banked track was NASCAR founder Bill France Sr.'s last big project, and it became one of his most controversial. Its arrival also put Petty in one of the most uncomfortable positions of his racing career.

No one was surprised when, in test runs by numerous drivers, the track produced speeds faster than its sister track in Daytona Beach, Florida. That was among France's goals. Stopwatches clocked cars approaching 200 miles per hour (322 km per hour). There was concern when the racing tires of the day, supplied by Goodyear and Firestone, couldn't handle the fresh asphalt and the alarming speeds.

Teams arrived for the first race weekend in mid-September with tensions high. The stage for trouble had been set earlier in the summer when a group of drivers met to form the Professional Drivers Association (PDA). The PDA was intended to give drivers a voice in numerous matters, including the size of race purses and the condition of driver facilities at speedways. But the main topic was Talladega and the scary reports that were coming out of testing there. During the meeting, Petty was elected PDA president, and he would be a focal point of the trouble to come at Talladega. Within a few weeks after the organizational meeting, most Cup Series regulars had become PDA members.

Dodge showed up at Talladega with its new Dodge Charger Daytona, a unique race car design. It had a long, pointed nose and a high wing atop the rear deck, and it created a buzz across the garage area and among fans arriving at the huge track for the first time. Spectators saw the winged, futuristic cars flash by and immediately wanted to buy one.

Unfortunately, the biggest word of the weekend was a little one: tires.

When cars crossed the 190-miles-per-hour (306-km-per-hour) mark (easily reached on the wide, superfast track) in the week's first practice, tires often failed or shredded into pieces. Driver meetings popped up in the garage area as concern grew, and the PDA soon suggested to France that the race be postponed until the tire companies could develop a new compound that could handle the Talladega speeds. With tens of thousands of tickets already sold for the track's debut race, France had no intentions of calling for an embarrassing postponement in what should have been one of the biggest weeks in his career. He suggested that drivers adapt to the conditions, trimming their speeds to numbers the tires could handle.

As might be imagined, this idea was about as attractive to the drivers

WHEN CARS CROSSED THE 190-MILES-PER-HOUR MARK IN THE WEEK'S FIRST PRACTICE, TIRES OFTEN FAILED OR SHREDDED INTO PIECES.

as spoiled meat.

After more tire compounds were quickly tested at the track, Firestone decided to pull out of the race. That left Goodyear as the only tire supplier for the race.

Discussions continued and France held his ground. With talk of a boycott growing, he jumped in a race car and turned laps at about 175 miles per hour (282 km per hour) in an attempt to prove that there could be safe competition on the speedway. This performance, viewed by many as a publicity stunt, had little or no impact on drivers. Late Saturday afternoon, the day before the scheduled race, more than thirty drivers and teams loaded their cars and tools and left the speedway. It was a bizarre and unprecedented sight, team trucks pulling out of a speedway within twenty-four hours of a scheduled race start, most of them heading home to North Carolina shops. An Atlanta reporter, driving to the track Saturday to assist in coverage of the race, met the trucks heading in the other direction and later told friends he thought he was in some sort of drug trance and had awakened too late for the race.

France, never one to back off in a confrontation, was not moved. The Talladega 500 was held as scheduled on Sunday and he filled the rest of the field with drivers and cars from a lower series. Well-spaced caution flags gave the teams chances to change tires repeatedly. The race was completed without an accident, and the win went to unheralded North Carolinian Richard Brickhouse, who had resigned his PDA membership, calling it "a mighty hard decision to make," to drive a Ray Nichels Dodge. Brickhouse admitted that he feathered the throttle in his car, hoping to protect the tires.

Six drivers parked their cars before the completion of the tenth lap. Only fifteen cars finished, and Brickhouse won by seven seconds. He never won another race and soon disappeared from the scene (although he returned years later to run a few races). The PDA also faded into vapors.

Although the drivers who refused to participate in the race made their point about unsafe conditions, some look back on the day with more than a bit of sadness. There was a race, and they weren't in it.

Bobby Allison, who would have been racing at his "hometown track" in front of thousands of cheering Alabamians, was among those who left the track. "I was hurt, disappointed, and maybe even a little bit mad," he said in a 1997 interview. "I felt that I had tried to adjust and to help find a solution. I wanted to run. I sat in the backyard in Hueytown and listened to the race. Had a long, agonizing day. Didn't want to do anything else—eat, drink, or didn't even want to feel merry."

Both Petty and Pearson boycotted the Talladega race. Better tires were ready in time for the track's two 1970 races, and both were won by Pete Hamilton in Petty Enterprises Plymouths. Pearson finished third in the first race of 1970 and fourth in the second. Petty was seventh in both races.

The Talladega track eventually prospered despite the controversy that clouded the first race, becoming one of NASCAR's most popular destinations. Pearson, who admitted that the track was far from his favorite, would win there three times, Petty twice.

It took a while for the issues swirling around the first Talladega race to fade into the background. Petty, who had led the boycott, was a target of disgruntled fans. Two weeks later, at Martinsville Speedway, a fan hurled a beer can and hit Petty's car. Petty won anyway.

No reason to think a beer can might stop the King.

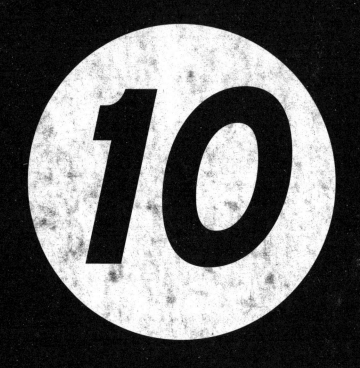

"**I** thought, 'Hell, he's dead.'"

The speaker was Dale Inman. He was not alone. Thousands in the frontstretch grandstand at Darlington Raceway, and many more watching on television, likely had the same unthinkable thought: Richard Petty was dead.

The NASCAR careers of Richard Petty and David Pearson were dramatically different in at least one way: Petty broke virtually every bone in his body in a long list of brutal crashes, while Pearson was never significantly hurt in a race car.

From NASCAR's early days, the specter of death hung over every racetrack, from the biggest to the smallest. Larry Mann was the first driver to perish in a Cup Series race, September 14, 1952. He hit the outside guardrail at infamously dangerous Langhorne Speedway in Pennsylvania and was pronounced dead from head injuries that night at Nazareth Hospital. In the first ten years after the 1959 opening of Daytona International Speedway, six drivers were killed in accidents. Over the decades, the Daytona death list would grow past forty, including motorcycle racers, sports car drivers, and a go-kart racer. In 1994, Daytona claimed popular Alabama driver Neil Bonnett in a crash in practice. On the day of Bonnett's funeral in Alabama, Rodney Orr died, also in Daytona practice. Other tracks had their own dark days. In 1995, drivers Gary Batson and Russell Phillips died in gruesome crashes in Late Model Sportsman races at Charlotte Motor Speedway. Also lost to accidents: Adam Petty (grandson of Richard), John Nemechek, Tony Roper, Kenny Irwin, and, for many the unkindest cut of all, Dale Earnhardt.

Legendary motorsports journalist Chris Economaki often said that automobile racing mattered only if it had two things: speed and danger. NASCAR had both, sometimes too much of both. Across much of the 1990s and into 2001, with the death of Earnhardt, whose fan base rivaled that of Petty, the danger seemed omnipresent, like a midnight rider dropping in for a kill.

"A young driver I know went to the [NASCAR] Hall of Fame recently and told me that the cars we drove—you guys had to be idiots," three-time Cup champion Darrell Waltrip said. "He said we had to be out of our minds to get in those cars with no more safety equipment than we had. He said, 'I wouldn't do it. Those cars weren't safe.' The cars that I drove—and this is blunt, they would kill you. If you hit a concrete wall at 180 miles per hour [290 km per hour], you certainly weren't going to walk away."

Even for bold, brave race car drivers who often talked of ignoring the threat of death because it was impossible to race with that thought lodged in the head, the reality was there.

"You start this race, and basically you've got a chill," Waltrip said of racing at Talladega Superspeedway. "From the time it starts to the time it's over with, you've got a chill, wondering if this is going to be the day they're going to put you up in the catchfence. Somebody is going in the catchfence."

For too many years, although there were sporadic safety advances, the possibility of death or severe injury in NASCAR races generally was accepted as part of the game. Funerals were held, families grieved, a departed driver was replaced by the next one in line, and the sport raced on. A familiar phrase—he died doing what he loved—was uttered far too often. But Earnhardt's death changed the landscape dramatically. If the Intimidator, Ol' Ironhead, the Man in Black, a man seemingly indestructible, could be killed on a racetrack, no one was safe. Critics claimed NASCAR was too insular and too slow in its safety initiatives, but a popular view in the garage area was that there were enough smart people in-house to solve every dilemma. The stretch of deaths in the 1990s and early 2000s challenged that line of thinking, and the two most important safety advances—head-and-neck restraints and so-called "soft walls"—were developed outside NASCAR. After Earnhardt's death, efforts to protect drivers from serious head injuries accelerated. The wall barriers dramatically reduced the possibility of serious injury or death when cars collided head-on with concrete walls, generally the most serious kind of wreck, and head-and-neck restraints lessened the possibility of often-fatal neck snaps in high-speed crashes.

Those revolutionary changes were decades in the future when Richard Petty experienced the worst wreck of his career. Petty survived a string of dangerous crashes, none more violent than his stunning wreck in the Rebel 400 at Darlington Raceway, May 9, 1970. Petty veered right into the fourth-turn wall on the race's 176th lap, and the contact sent his car across the track and into the concrete pit wall. Petty's car destroyed that portion of the wall and continued down the frontstretch, flipping several times before stopping on its roof. Petty's arm could be seen flopping from the driver's window during the tumble. He looked like a rag doll.

The ABC television network had joined the race in progress a few minutes before Petty's crash. "There's been a crash on the homestretch!" announcer Jim McKay said. "A car upside-down. A blue car."

Retired driver Ned Jarrett, also working the broadcast, said, "That's Richard Petty."

A television camera showed the shocking scene. Petty was on his back in the car, motionless. As is often standard practice in life-threatening race crashes, the camera operator didn't zoom in for a closer view, but it was clear that Petty was hurt. The red shop rag that Petty usually kept in his mouth to keep it moist during races had fallen out, and a quick look at the crash scene gave the mistaken appearance that there was blood on Petty.

"I ran with a rag in my mouth," Petty said. "It looked terrible. I think the TV people said to move away from it. He looks like he's coming apart."

McKay said, "He certainly looks to be unconscious. The pit crew is running out. This could be a very bad accident to one of the best-known race drivers in the world."

Members of Petty's crew, including Dale Inman and Richie Barsz, and members of several other teams jumped the pit wall and ran to the car, even as other drivers were swerving to avoid the wreck. Petty was hanging upside-down in his seat harness. While the crewmen worked to free him, conscious of the danger of a possible fire erupting, Petty, stirring awake, said, "I hurt my danged shoulder."

A track safety worker, noticing smoke around the car, ran up and turned on a fire extinguisher. It clouded the wreck scene, making rescue more difficult. "Maurice [Petty] like to killed him," Inman said.

Petty blacked out as they removed him from the car and loaded him into a waiting ambulance.

"He was hanging upside-down in the car," Inman said. "We unhooked the seatbelt and kind of dropped him. He said, 'Ohhhh,' so I knew he was alive."

Buck Brigance, then a member of Paul Goldsmith's team, was among those who ran to the car to help. "Cars were going by right and left," Brigance said. "The car was smoking from under the hood, and it was so red hot you couldn't touch it. A fireman was also there and started spraying foam all over the car and everybody. Maurice just sort of picked him up and carried him off away from the car."

"I HAD A DISLOCATED SHOULDER, OUR ONLY THREE RACE CARS WERE TOTALED, AND PETE AND I MADE A TOTAL OF $2,050 IN THE RACE."

Petty was checked at the infield hospital and then placed in an ambulance for transport to a hospital in nearby Florence. "They got me out and rolled me through the doors into the emergency room," Petty recalled years later. "Here came a big ol' nurse. She said, 'You can't take him in there! He's got to sign all these papers. Who's going to be responsible for him?' There was a boy with me who was a doctor friend of mine. He said, 'Take him on in there and fix him up. I'll sign all the papers.'"

Doctors repaired Petty's dislocated shoulder, and he spent that night in the hospital. He left the next morning despite the protests of nurses. With his arm in a sling, he missed the next five races. That long without driving a race car? It was a punishment worse than the crash itself for a man who practically lived at speed.

The entire Darlington week had been dismal for the Pettys. Richard and teammate Pete Hamilton arrived at the track ready to practice and qualify a pair of winged Plymouth Superbirds. Petty crashed in practice, mangling his car. The team drove back to Level Cross to pick up a replacement, one of Petty's short-track cars. In the race itself, Hamilton crashed before Petty, destroying his Superbird.

"I had a dislocated shoulder, our only three race cars were totaled, and Pete and I made a total of $2,050 in the race," Petty said. "I made $50 more than he did."

Petty's wife, Lynda, said she was as frightened that day "as I have ever been in my life."

Hamilton, out of the race because of his crash, had seen Petty's accident. Lynda approached him in the chaos of the following minutes. She wasn't sure what had happened and asked Hamilton. Hamilton had been told by a team owner who had been at the infield hospital that the accident was bad. Shaken, he couldn't talk to Lynda.

This was life at the top level of auto racing when everything goes wrong. The fact that such accidents happened occasionally didn't make the trials of it all easier for anyone involved.

Watching races in which husbands, fathers, sons, and grandsons had tense moments, either in wrecks or riding on the edge of failure, tested the nerves of the extended Petty family, year after year, generation after generation. "I watched my mom watch my dad drive for years," said Rebecca Petty Moffitt, Richard and Lynda's youngest daughter. "Then I literally got on my knees with her watching Kyle. He was in the duals [qualifying races for the Daytona 500] at Daytona, and he was the guy on the bubble, racing to get in the 500. My mom and I were literally on the floor in our motorhome, praying, 'God, please let him get in the race.' When Kyle was racing somewhere else, somebody wrecked him, and I was not very nice about it. That's why I watch races by myself or with my family, not somewhere where I might show my butt. I probably cussed or hit something."

Other than the five races he missed, Richard Petty experienced little lasting impact from the wicked Darlington crash. He won fourteen more races that season. It can be argued (and Petty has) that the races he missed cost him the 1970 championship. He finished in fourth place despite the absence, running forty races. Champion Bobby Isaac ran forty-seven.

The wreck and the fact that Petty's head and arm dangled outside the window during the crash sequence led NASCAR to mandate strong window nets for its race cars. The first unofficial window net was sewn by Elizabeth Petty, Richard's mother, who used pieces of an old driver's uniform and her sewing machine after seeing her son's wreck.

David Pearson won the Rebel race that day. "Is Richard all right?" was his first question upon reaching victory lane.

Petty returned to the circuit June 7 for a race at Michigan International Speedway. "Richard was sitting in the car at Michigan getting ready to race that day," crew member Richie Barsz remembered. "[Mechanic] Jake Elder walked up and said, 'Are you sure you're ready?' Richard moved his arm around and said, 'Yeah, see?' It was the arm that wasn't hurt."

Petty lasted halfway through the Michigan race before parking with ignition problems. He won the next two races—at Riverside, California, and Kingsport, Tennessee.

At Pocono Raceway, one of the NASCAR tour's fastest tracks, Petty broke a wheel going into the second turn in a 1980 race and smashed into the wall. His car slid down the track and was hit near the driver-side door by Darrell Waltrip. The impact broke Petty's neck—for the second time, as X-rays showed. "The doctor, after seeing the X-rays, asked me when I had broken my neck before," Petty said. "I didn't know until then."

The next race was at superfast Talladega Superspeedway. A few days before the race, Petty climbed out of a car in a motel parking lot in Anniston, Alabama, near the speedway. He was wearing a neck brace and seemed a bit surprised to run into a reporter a few parking spots away. Seemingly upbeat, he revealed his intention to start the race despite the obvious dangers of racing with a broken neck. He rolled off with the rest of the field in the No. 43, thus collecting the race points awarded to the driver who started the race, but soon turned the car over to relief driver Joe Millikan. "Richard looked like warmed-over death," Dale Inman said.

Later, Petty said NASCAR probably wouldn't have allowed him to start the race if officials had known the severity of his condition. That certainly would be the case today, as NASCAR has strict health protocols, especially relating to head and neck injuries.

Petty escaped serious injury in another spectacular crash in the 1988 Daytona 500. Near the race's halfway point, Petty's red-and-blue Pontiac turned sideways after contact with another car. Petty's car lifted into the air and began a series of rolls, spinning on its nose, ballet-style. The car tagged the frontstretch catchfence, sending car parts flying into the grandstand area. The car finally came to rest, but the accident wasn't over. Brett Bodine hit Petty's car in the left-front fender, and the impact of that crash injured Petty's right ankle.

It looked bad. Very bad. Many in the crowded frontstretch grandstand turned away from the scene. There were echoes of the 1970 Darlington wreck. Many thought Petty was seriously hurt—or worse.

Steve Tucker, Petty's PR representative, saw the wreck from a suite high above the grandstand. His heart skipped a beat, too, but he knew something that many others who saw the accident didn't. Petty was alive. "People were freaking out," Tucker said. "They were assuming he was dead. But I was on the team radio, and I heard Dale Inman ask if he was okay, and Richard said, 'Just let me get my breath.'"

Speculation about Petty retiring from driving had popped around the sport for years, and Chris Economaki, on the television broadcast, speculated that the violence of the wreck might lead to Petty parking for good. Much earlier, Petty had told his wife Lynda that he wanted to keep driving as long as it was fun for him.

"Lynda and the kids walked into the hospital, and she said, 'Are we having fun?'" Petty said. "I had always said I would quit when I stopped having fun. That was probably the beginning of it [thinking about retirement]. It was in the back of my mind for a year or so."

The wild nature of the Daytona accident, combined with the fact that Petty wasn't seriously hurt, got the attention of television talk-show host David Letterman and his staff. A Letterman representative contacted the team about a possible Petty appearance on the show, and Petty was on his way to New York City a few days later to explain it all to Letterman and his viewers. "Letterman came into the green room for two or three minutes and chatted with Richard," said Steve Tucker, who accompanied Petty. "He was amazed that Richard could be in that kind of accident and talking to him a few days later." Petty appeared on the show wearing a white "STP Racing Team" sweater, without his trademark cowboy hat and sunglasses.

Although the Daytona wreck fueled Petty's thinking about possible retirement, he would drive four more years, including the following week at Richmond Raceway, where he finished third. He eventually would leave the driver's seat with a list of injuries that would have kept a medical school professor busy: broken shoulders, broken ribs, dislocated shoulder, dislocated back, both knees broken, both feet broken, broken neck (twice), and concussions.

Oddly enough, Petty missed driving time in the 1966 season because of a football injury. He and some crew members were playing touch football during lunchtime outside the Petty shop and he broke the ring finger on his left hand. He drove with the painful finger for a while but eventually visited a doctor, who told him without surgery the finger would be essentially immobile. He decided on the operation.

Petty was an advocate of the "mind over matter" approach to life. If he could convince himself that he wasn't hurting enough to move to the sidelines, he would drive on, blotting out the pain.

"It was all mental to me to go out and prove the point," he said. "I never looked at it as if I had a bad accident and that I had to be careful and build back up. That never crossed my mind. You have to look at the drivers' mentality. They look at it differently from the average guy. Most don't blink an eye. It's just part of the territory. You just go on with it."

Petty tried to pass along that way of thinking to his four children—Kyle, Sharon, Lisa, and Rebecca. "He deals with emotions in a different way," Rebecca said. "When we were little, he used to try to teach us mind over matter. Like if you tell yourself it doesn't hurt, it doesn't hurt. He did it by way of tickling us and we couldn't laugh. I think he truly tries to use it. He can mentally block out stuff. If something's really bothering him, he'll go off by himself and lie down. He thinks if he closes his eyes and wakes up, the problem will be gone. I remember going to the funeral of Wade Thornburg [a former Petty crew member] with him.

I kind of teared up. He said, 'That's the last thing they need to see. Tell yourself you have to control that.'"

Petty did slam the door, however, on one particular race series after a hard crash at Daytona in February 1978. He was competing in the International Race of Champions (IROC), a made-for-television series that matched drivers from different racing series in identically prepared cars. Competition in the IROC events typically was close, and Petty tangled with open-wheel winners Al Unser and Johnny Rutherford on the Daytona backstretch and wound up in the hospital.

Petty later said he didn't know where he was or who he was for about forty-five minutes after regaining consciousness. He probably had suffered a concussion. In the hospital, Petty asked what had happened. "They told me I'd wrecked in the IROC," he said. "I asked, 'What's an IROC?'" He decided to abandon IROC racing, mainly, he said, because he didn't want an injury to threaten his ability to race in the Cup Series. Unlike several other top NASCAR drivers, including Bobby and Donnie Allison, Cale Yarborough, and LeeRoy Yarbrough, Petty showed no interest in driving in other forms of racing, preferring to concentrate on the thing that he did well and that kept the money flowing into Level Cross.

IN THE HOSPITAL, PETTY ASKED WHAT HAD HAPPENED. "THEY TOLD ME I'D WRECKED IN THE IROC... I ASKED, 'WHAT'S AN IROC?'"

In addition to injuries, Petty has had other health issues across the years. He had surgery to remove almost half of his stomach because of ulcers. ("The ulcers were named Dale and Lynda," Dale Inman joked). He recovered from prostate cancer. His gall bladder was removed. "Ain't much left in there," he said. "I must have really good DNA."

Hard wrecks ran in the Petty family. In 1955, Lee Petty soared out of the track at the dangerous Memphis-Arkansas Speedway, a fast and unforgiving 1.5-mile (2.4-km) dirt track that lasted only four years on the Cup schedule. Petty's car landed in a pond outside the track.

In 1961, Lee and Richard left the Daytona track in separate qualifying races for the Daytona 500. Richard had only minor injuries, but Lee was hospitalized for four months, his driving career essentially at an end. Kyle Petty suffered a broken leg in a twenty-car crash at Talladega Superspeedway in May 1991.

Although he had a few close calls, Pearson was proud of the fact that he never had a hospital stay related to a race accident. He was involved in crashes, of course, but team owners and crew chiefs who raced with him said he was among the best at anticipating accidents and maneuvering to avoid them.

"I've heard people say if you see a car spin out, head toward it and it'll be gone by the time you get there," Pearson said. "That's a bunch of bull. I never did head for it. You see a bunch of people when there's a wreck spin out a long time before they get to the wreck. That's crazy. I'd just start slowing down and slow it as slow as I could get it until I got to where the wreck was and then make my decision when I got there whether I was going right or left. You keep your car as straight as you can keep it."

ALTHOUGH HE HAD A FEW CLOSE CALLS, PEARSON WAS PROUD OF THE FACT THAT HE NEVER HAD A HOSPITAL STAY RELATED TO A RACE ACCIDENT. HE WAS INVOLVED IN CRASHES, OF COURSE, BUT TEAM OWNERS AND CREW CHIEFS WHO RACED WITH HIM SAID HE WAS AMONG THE BEST AT ANTICIPATING ACCIDENTS AND MANEUVERING TO AVOID THEM.

Pearson's worst wreck occurred at Bristol Motor Speedway, one of racing's fastest half-miles (0.8 km), in July 1965. Pearson, then driving for Cotton Owens, was involved in a crash with Marvin Panch, who was in the No. 21 Wood Brothers Racing car Pearson would drive in later years.

"Wheels got locked up with Marvin Panch," Pearson said. "I hit the wall the hardest I've ever hit anything. I hit it so hard my shoes came off. I'd always heard when people were killed in a car wreck it knocked their shoes off. My shoes were just laying there like I had placed them there, side by side. I couldn't wait until somebody came and talked to me so I could answer them and see if they'd talk back to me. I didn't know if I was dead or not."

He wasn't hurt. He raced on.

11
Smokin'

Bud Moore, a NASCAR lifer, had one eye on engines and the other on dollars when he fielded cars in the Cup Series. Racing ate money, a reality that Moore often discussed with NASCAR founder Bill France Sr. The two were friends, often enjoying deep-sea fishing trips, but they also had some animated discussions.

"In the early 1960s, we were running forty-five to fifty races a year, on dirt, quarter-miles [0.4 km], everywhere," Moore said. "Elmo Langley, Ed Negre, some of those guys, the ones we called the backmarkers—they had a meeting with Bill France. Told me they were going to try to get their prize money up. The next morning, I saw France in the garage area. I said, 'Well, how did the meeting come out last night?' He said, 'Bud, we're going to have to help them boys. They've got a good beef about that.' I said, 'Well, France, while you're helping them you need to help the front a little bit, too.' He looked at me kind of funny and poked me right in the chest and said, 'Bud, let me tell you one thing. Your asses have got to have somebody to pass.'"

Bigger bags of money appeared in the 1970s—for the asses and the backmarkers. In fact, cubic dollars arrived—both in the sport in general and for Petty Enterprises and David Pearson, in particular.

Some of the money showed up quite by accident. The process involved not a smoke-filled room but a smoke-filled garage area. The R.J. Reynolds Tobacco Company (RJR) had millions of extra dollars to spend in advertising after federal government restrictions eliminated television as an avenue for tobacco company pitches. NASCAR team owner Junior Johnson, in search of a sponsor for his cars, talked to RJR executives at their offices in Winston-Salem, North Carolina. Johnson probably was looking for something in the six-figure range. RJR's cup overflowed. "Country smart" with numbers and such, Johnson quickly understood that the company was playing with much more money than he originally thought, and he suggested that a broader sponsorship involving NASCAR might be the best idea for RJR.

Word traveled quickly, and talks resulted in RJR announcing its sponsorship of NASCAR's top series for the 1971 season, a move that would change everything for almost everybody connected with stock car racing. Benefits at the Cup level would include a $100,000 check to the season point fund, and $40,000 of that total would go to the champion.

This was only the beginning of a cash train that would carry NASCAR for the next three decades. It was nothing short of a financial revolution for drivers and teams, and David Pearson and Richard Petty would be among the beneficiaries. Reynolds added more and more money to the point fund every year. It created the Winston All-Star Race, a non-points sprint race with a huge purse. It added the Winston Million, a million-dollar bonus available to any driver who could win three of the season's top four races. It was almost too much for teams to comprehend. Money didn't grow on trees, but it was stuffed into every cigarette carton. Winston filters never smelled finer. Even drivers who didn't smoke welcomed the aroma.

RJR's largesse extended beyond hard cash and outside stock car racing's top level. The company pumped support to weekly short tracks across the country, improving infrastructure and splashing red and white paint (Winston's colors) on virtually everything that didn't move. Reynolds also brought a higher level of public relations to NASCAR, expanding and fine-tuning communications operations and helping push the sport into bigger media markets. Men and women wearing the bright red colors of Winston cigarettes roamed NASCAR garages and infields, taking every opportunity to lift the profile of the sport—and thus RJR products. This was a perfect match (pun intended) for NASCAR tracks, where it seemed at least one of every two spectators smoked, some religiously.

In addition to the cubic dollars RJR pumped into NASCAR, it took on a significant role in forging the sport's direction, joining the France family as an active partner. The Frances rarely opened the doors of their business quite so willingly. As historian Dan Pierce wrote in a 2001 article, "Perhaps the most glaring example of NASCAR's deep regional roots is its unique form of management and the lack of union representation for its drivers and mechanics: NASCAR's style of management is more typical of a cotton mill than a modern, billion-dollar, professional sporting enterprise." Among the changes sparked by RJR was a severe reduction in the Cup Series schedule—from forty-eight races in 1971 to thirty-one races in 1972. Among tracks booted from the schedule were legendary speedways in Hickory, North Carolina; Columbia, South Carolina; Greenville, South Carolina; and Maryville, Tennessee. Instead of racing two or three times a week in short events, teams had more time to work on their cars for longer and higher-profile races, and there was new emphasis placed on winning the championship. RJR money talked.

Two years earlier, on September 30, 1970, NASCAR had run its final Cup Series race on a real dirt surface (Bristol Motor Speedway covered its concrete surface with dirt for three races from 2021 to 2023, a bold experiment that wasn't wildly successful). The 1970 race was held at the North Carolina State Fairgrounds track, a half-mile (0.8-km) facility in Raleigh, North Carolina. To no one's particular surprise, Richard Petty won the race. In addition to being the series' final dirt-track race, the event sparked another oddity. Petty won the race in a car not owned by Petty Enterprises. The team had sold a car specifically built for dirt-track racing to team owner Don Robertson. The Pettys borrowed the car from Robertson, put in a new engine, won the race, and returned the car to Robertson and his driver, Jabe Thomas, with the powerful engine as payment for the rental. Pearson did not compete that day but had won at the track the previous year, beating Petty in one of their one-two finishes.

The dramatic 1972 schedule change and the abandonment of small-town short tracks that had been reliable winners for Petty had almost no impact on his success. He won the championship in both 1971 and 1972. "The cut in the schedule was definitely the way to go," Petty said. "They were cutting out the 100-mile [161-km] races, and the purses quadrupled. And Winston was advertising all over the country. Then we got STP."

Petty opened the 1972 season with a bold new design on his No. 43 cars. After some tough negotiations with auto racing entrepreneur and showman Andy Granatelli, who had an oversized presence in motorsports and who was anxious to put his name in lights alongside that of Richard Petty, the Petty team signed a $250,000 sponsor agreement with STP oil treatment. That contract would change the Petty racing dynamic for the rest of his driving career—and beyond.

From his early racing days, Petty's cars had been painted in a color that became known as Petty blue, a combination of white and blue paint. The distinctive color was an accident of sorts. Late in the 1950s, in a hurry to prepare a car for the next race, the Pettys mixed blue paint and white paint—there wasn't enough of either color in the shop to cover the whole car—and came up with the light blue that would become a Petty trademark. Granatelli, a raconteur in the larger motorsports world, wanted the shocking bright red associated with STP on the Petty cars. Finally, a compromise was reached. The red and blue colors would share space on Petty's cars, a design that would become as familiar as any in the history of the sport, one easily spotted from the grandstands and on television.

What did Petty do in his first race for STP, the 1972 season-opener on the road course at Riverside International Raceway in California? He won, of course.

Petty's popularity continued to mushroom as he tacked on wins. More and more fans got in line to request the Petty autograph, a looping, swirling signature that Petty had learned in a business school handwriting class. Both at tracks and at his shop, to which fans would mail autograph requests, Petty signed and signed and signed. Sometimes, the total would reach 500 a day. In 2017, a Petty public relations representative used a nonscientific method to estimate that the King had signed more than two million autographs since he signed the first. That number was hardly an exaggeration. And it grows daily.

He signs photographs, race tickets, diecast cars, souvenir program covers, various body parts, dollar bills, hundred-dollar bills, and virtually anything else a fan can thrust toward him. The weirdest? "A duck," Petty said. "It was at a state fair promotion for Pepsi."

Fellow driver and sometimes teammate Buddy Baker said Petty's signature had so many swirls and loops that it resembled the rigging on a sailing ship. There is a method to the madness. Petty signs by moving his hand, arm, and shoulder in unison, thus avoiding finger cramping during long autograph sessions.

Did Petty, an autograph machine, ever ask for one himself? Only once, he said. "Bart Starr [NFL Hall of Fame quarterback] and I were staying in the same hotel in Dallas," Petty said. "Kyle was a big Green Bay Packers fan. We got to talking, and I said, 'Hey, give me an autograph for my son.'"

After racing a year in Fords in 1969, Petty returned to the Chrysler camp in 1970, lured in part by the car builder's decision to develop an exotic race car—the Plymouth Superbird. The car had a sharp nose and a high (almost 2 feet [61 cm]) wing mounted on the rear deck, and it looked fast sitting still. Longtime crew chief Harry Hyde, who knew a thing or two about the subject, called it "the perfect race car." Tilting the huge rear wing enabled mechanics to dramatically impact the balance of the car.

THE CAR HAD A SHARP NOSE AND A HIGH WING MOUNTED ON THE REAR DECK, AND IT LOOKED FAST SITTING STILL. TILTING THE HUGE REAR WING ENABLED MECHANICS TO DRAMATICALLY IMPACT THE BALANCE OF THE CAR.

The winged-car concept had debuted the previous season at Talladega Superspeedway with the Dodge Daytona, Richard Brickhouse driving that car to a win in the track's controversial first race. The Superbird was Chrysler's modified version of the Dodge Daytona. Plymouth built 1,920 Superbirds. The street car sold for $4,298. A pristine model can bring ten times that total today, and its futuristic design can still send shivers down the back of a car enthusiast.

Pete Hamilton drove a Petty team car to a win in the 1970 Daytona 500, proving that Petty Enterprises' brief departure from Chrysler was barely a bump in the road.

The Petty/STP partnership opened doors for other major companies to get involved in team sponsorship. The days of sponsors like Joe's Car

Wash, Leake's Amoco, the Excuse Lounge, and the Velvet Touch Health Clinic massage parlor (which was more about touch and less about health) were fading.

Darrell Waltrip, who eventually would become a major challenger to Petty and Pearson in NASCAR fast lanes, broke into Cup racing in 1972, the same year Petty signed with STP. Waltrip offered some perspective on the difficulties involved in starting from scratch at the top level of NASCAR in those days: "There was nobody wanting to get into Winston Cup racing to sponsor cars. There were four or five well-supported teams and then a bunch of what we call independents. You went around and scraped up all the money you could and put together a car, and part-time help would come on the weekend and help you out." Waltrip drove an old delivery truck with "Maxwell House Coffee" painted on the side to Talladega, Alabama, to make his Cup debut. Along the way, he and his wife, Stevie, and their dog, Charlie Brown, stopped at a Western Auto to buy jackstands and tools to go racing. "It looked like I was going fishing," Waltrip said.

Cup purses were growing. The total payout for the 1959 Daytona 500 was $53,050. Five years later, the 500 paid $100,750. In 1985, the race purse reached $1 million for the first time.

New money in the sport changed both the bottom line and the top dollar. Crew members jumped from one team to another as salaries increased.

"As time went along and the money got bigger and bigger and bigger, everybody started trying to cutthroat each other," team owner Junior Johnson said. "It didn't really get that bad until somewhere in the late 1960s and the mid-1970s. It started getting real bad. I'd train the guys and get them up to where you'd not have to stay with them all the time, and that's something like ten years you've got in a guy. Then somebody would come along and hire him away from you just to find out what you're doing. They can get everything you've worked on for the last five or six years to get to the front, and they can get it overnight by just paying the guy two or three hundred a week more."

The arrival of RJR and its satchel of dollars coincided with the naming of Bill France Jr. as NASCAR president. On January 12, 1972, Bill France Sr. handed the keys to the organization he had founded

Top: Richard Petty built an excellent record at Daytona International Speedway over his long career, but that relationship started with a bust. Petty, standing in front of the Oldsmobile convertible he ran in the 1959 Daytona 500, finished 57th in that race after falling out with engine failure. His father, Lee, was the winner. *ISC Archives/CQ-Roll Call Group via Getty Images*; *Bottom:* Although Richard Petty used the number 43 for most of his career, Petty team cars also carried 42, a number made famous by his father, Lee. *RacingOne/ISC Archive/Getty Images*

Top: David Pearson stands in victory lane after his unlikely win in the 1961 World 600 at Charlotte Motor Speedway. The victory was the first in the Cup Series for Pearson. The Pure Oil shirt he is wearing eventually wound up in the NASCAR Hall of Fame, as did Pearson. *ISC Archives/ CQ-Roll Call Group via Getty Images*; ***Bottom:*** As happened so many times during their careers, David Pearson (No. 6) and Richard Petty (No. 43) are bumper-to-bumper before the start of a race. They are shown here before the start of an April 1964 race at Columbia Speedway. *ISC Images & Archives via Getty Images*

Above: In 1966 David Pearson won his first of three Cup championships driving for team owner Cotton Owens. Both were from Spartanburg, South Carolina. *ISC Images & Archives via Getty Images;* ***Next page, top:*** Richard Petty (No. 43) and David Pearson (No. 17) are side by side in a 1967 race at Asheville-Weaverville Speedway in North Carolina. Petty finished second and Pearson third in a race won by Bobby Allison. *ISC Archives/CQ-Roll Call Group via Getty Images*

Below, left: This crash in the 1967 National 500 at Charlotte Motor Speedway damaged the cars of three auto racing giants: Richard Petty (No. 43), David Pearson (No. 17), and Mario Andretti (No. 11). *Bettmann via Getty Imagess;* **Below, right:** Sharing secrets? Not likely. David Pearson and Richard Petty look over some notes during a test session at North Carolina Motor Speedway in Rockingham several weeks prior to the Inaugural 1965 American 500. *Smyle Media*

PETTY VS. PEARSON

Top: Petty blue, a brilliant color shade, rode on virtually every car raced by the King. Here, Dale Inman leans in to talk with Petty during the 1967 season. *Smyle Media;* **Bottom:** Man at work—Richard Petty prepares to make a qualifying run for the 1964 Rebel 300 at Darlington Raceway. *Smyle Media*

Top: Richard Petty gets service from his Petty Enterprises crew, including brother Maurice (wearing hat), during the 1968 Carolina 500 at North Carolina Motor Speedway. Maurice was the team's chief engine builder and a valued pit crew member. *Smyle Media;* ***Bottom:*** Richard Petty and David Pearson talk on pit road during qualifying for the 1964 Southern 500 at Darlington Raceway. *Smyle Media*

Previous page, top: David Pearson races his No. 17 Holman-Moody Ford during the 1968 Dixie 500 at Atlanta Motor Speedway. Pearson won a pair of Cup championships with the team. *Smyle Media*; ***Previous page, middle:*** With rare exceptions, Richard Petty and David Pearson felt comfortable racing each other across NASCAR's varied landscape. This was Charlotte Motor Speedway in October 1977. *Smyle Media*; ***Previous page, bottom:*** David Pearson pits in his Wood Brothers Mercury at the 1972 Daytona International Speedway Firecracker 400. The Wood Brothers revolutionized the NASCAR pit stop and gave Pearson solid race cars every weekend. *Smyle Media*; ***Above:*** A feathered cowboy hat and wrap-around sunglasses built the defining image of Richard Petty. *Smyle Media*

Above: David Pearson and Richard Petty, dressed in the Purolator and STP colors they would carry for much of their careers, were rivals on track but close friends in the garage. *Smyle Media;* ***Below:*** David Pearson's sons Larry (center) and Ricky share victory lane with their dad at Darlington Raceway after he won the 1968 Rebel 400. *Smyle Media*

Top: David Pearson wasn't a big talker, but he had to get used to explaining his wins in victory lane. *Smyle Media*; **Bottom:** David Pearson and Richard Petty thrilled crowds from coast to coast with side-by-side racing. This shot was taken during the 1975 Atlanta 500 at Atlanta Motor Speedway. *Smyle Media*

Top: David Pearson sits in the Daytona garage in front of the famous Wood Brothers No. 21. *Dick Conway*; **Bottom:** Richard Petty, dressed for driving, shakes hands with David Pearson, in civilian clothes, at Charlotte Motor Speedway in May 1979, weeks after Pearson lost his ride with the Wood Brothers team because of a pit miscommunication at Darlington Raceway. *Dick Conway*

Top left: Father to son—Lee Petty offers Richard a little advice at Daytona International Speedway in 1977. *Dick Conway;* ***Top right:*** Richard Petty failed to qualify for a Cup race at Richmond Raceway in March 1989, ending a streak of 513 consecutive starts. He hit the wall on his second qualifying attempt. *Dick Conway;* ***Above:*** Cars driven by Richard Petty (No. 43) and David Pearson (No. 21) spin and crash in front of the Daytona International Speedway grandstand on the final lap of the 1976 Daytona 500. Pearson kept his engine fired despite the wreck and won the race by limping across the finish line. *ISC Archives/CQ-Roll Call Group via Getty Images*

PETTY VS. PEARSON

Top: David Pearson leads Richard Petty during another tense battle on Daytona International Speedway's high banks during the 1972 Firecracker 400. *Smyle Media;* ***Bottom:*** David Pearson, buckled in and ready to race, won 105 Cup events, second only to Richard Petty's 200. *ISC Images & Archives via Getty Images*

Above: David Pearson stands in the middle of a wild victory lane celebration after winning the 1976 Daytona 500. Pearson's No. 21 Mercury shows the damage resulting from a last-lap, last-turn crash with Richard Petty's car. *ISC Archives/CQ-Roll Call Group via Getty Images*

PETTY VS. PEARSON

Top: The bright red and blue colors of Richard Petty's Dodges were a familiar sight in NASCAR circles. *ISC Archives/CQ-Roll Call Group via Getty Images; Bottom:* A great ride: David Pearson poses with the Wood Brothers' No. 21 Mercury, a car that would dominate NASCAR's superspeedways. *ISC Images & Archives via Getty Images;* **Next page, top:** Wood Brothers Racing crew chief Leonard Wood and David Pearson formed one of the most formidable combinations in NASCAR history. *ISC Images & Archives via Getty Images;* **Next page, bottom:** Richard Petty's Pontiac appears to stand on its nose as Petty took a wild ride in the 1988 Daytona 500. His car went airborne along the frontstretch, twirled several times and then was hit by Brett Bodine near the end of the wreck. Petty was not seriously injured. *ISC Archives/CQ-Roll Call Group via Getty Images*

to his 38-year-old son. Bill Sr. remained involved and still carried a big stick over the next several years, but the sport clearly was in the hands of his son and understudy, who would expand NASCAR's horizons and more closely tie racing's future to television, a critical move in the sport's growth.

France Jr. had Richard Petty riding alongside, giving the sport a marquee face and a hero to draw others' fire. Over a five-year period (1971–75), Petty won four championships and became the first Cup driver to total $1 million in career winnings. "I've never even seen a million dollars," Petty said. "For certain, I don't have a million dollars, know what I mean? It would really be something if they had a big pile of it here on this table so I'd know what it looked like. Heck, we've probably spent about all we've made just to make it. This is nice and all that, but winning a million dollars in my career doesn't mean a whole lot right now."

While Petty was busy collecting dollars and wins, Pearson was adjusting to new realities. After leaving Holman-Moody near the middle of the 1971 season, he teamed with car builder Ray Nichels and investor Chris Vallo, a newcomer to the sport, to run seven races in the second half of the year. That pairing produced all zeroes—Pearson failing to finish six of the seven races, and it ended in frustration. "I just wrote 1971 off as a bad year," Pearson said.

Times were about to improve for Pearson—and in a major way. Although most should have known better, there was talk around NASCAR garages that Pearson's best days were over, that, at thirty-seven years old, he no longer had the patience or persistence to win races on a consistent basis.

Then came the call from Virginian Glen Wood. He offered Pearson a ride in the team's No. 21 cars in what originally was a part-time deal. Pearson drove two races for fellow Spartanburg resident Bud Moore at the beginning of the 1972 season but moved along to the Woods' team. IndyCar great A.J. Foyt also drove for the Stuart, Virginia–based Ford team.

The notion that Pearson could no longer drive a race car at competitive levels vanished immediately. He won in his first time with the Woods, finishing first at Darlington. He followed with five more superspeedway wins that season and became the Woods' only driver in 1973 when Foyt moved on to concentrate on IndyCar.

The 1973 season was Pearson's glory year. He ran only eighteen races (he would never run a "full" schedule after the 1969 championship year) and, stunningly, won eleven. He won four superspeedway races in a row early in the year, including a victory at North Carolina Speedway in which he led 491 of the race's 492 laps. By the 19th race of the season, he had totaled nine wins. Competitors up and down pit road were busy trying to figure out how the Woods-Pearson combination was embarrassing everyone else. Pearson ruled the tour's big tracks.

The car Pearson ran with so much success that season was a 1971 Mercury, chosen over newer models because, Leonard Wood said, "It had a different shape and better aero. We could look at the two cars and know immediately that was the one we wanted. The back end would hang out, and it wouldn't be loose. You had a better feel for the car. That's the one that stands out in my mind as THE car."

Pearson ran it to its limits—but only when necessary.

"When I went out and practiced, I wouldn't run like I would run during the race," Pearson said. "I'd run different places on the racetrack and do anything else to keep anybody else from knowing where I did run."

Glen Wood said Pearson simply "drove his own race. If somebody was up front and outrunning him, he would settle back and run behind them for a little while. Sometimes, he could run behind a car and keep up fairly well compared with the effort you have to put into it to be ahead. He understood he wasn't getting away. He'd just let him run up there. He could see him. Then, of course, cautions would fall. He rarely ever got lapped running his own race. Later in the race when the chips were down, he could run with anybody."

In the middle of that splendid 1973 season, numerous Spartanburg residents organized David Pearson Appreciation Day. Pearson's accomplishments that year—and from the beginnings of his career—were celebrated with a parade, a luncheon, a dinner, and other festivities. More than 1,000 attended the banquet honoring Pearson. Among the guests were South Carolina Governor John West and numerous Cup Series drivers and team members, including Richard Petty, Glen and Leonard Wood, Bobby Isaac, and Wendell Scott. Spartanburg musician Joe Bennett wrote a song, "Little David," for the occasion (Sample lyric: "Times ain't hard, they call him Big David now. He's got meat to put in the gravy. Sock it to 'em, Davy. You're driving them crazy."). Pearson, who had told event organizers that they wouldn't be able to get 20 people to attend, called it "the greatest day of my life."

Later that year, Pearson traveled to New York City to accept the American Driver of the Year Award, a trophy presented to the top United States racer across all series.

"David was so good on the mile-and-half [2.4-km] tracks and superspeedways," Dale Inman said. "I don't think he liked the short tracks. He would say, 'Damn, I'm going to be good today because this little track is hot and slick.' He was kidding."

Pearson's deal with the Woods meant he rarely had to address driving on short tracks. For many years, the Woods ran in only the big-money, big-track events, cherry-picking the schedule for the best opportunities. This matched Pearson's plan exactly. It was his best life.

Although he had made the move to the Woods, Pearson still rolled around his hometown in a Ford Torino GT painted in Holman-Moody's blue and gold colors—no need to abandon a free vehicle.

"You always thought David enjoyed life," Inman said. "It was no big deal for him to get in a race car and go race. It was like he was going to the grocery store. When you raced him, you might think you had him beat, and he'd step it up another notch. Cale [Yarborough] ran hard as he could every lap. Bobby [Allison] was probably his own worst enemy. Richard drove hard. But he wanted the car to do all the work. I told him once, 'Damn, Richard, if the car gets any better, I'll drive it.'"

Pearson needed only a few days to mesh with Leonard Wood. Pearson's patient and alert driving style matched perfectly with Wood's innovative work in the pits.

"Pearson is one of the best there's ever been," Wood said. "He took care of his car. If you think about it, you're driving it wide open as hard as you can go and floating the valves and all, so that thing is not going to be too good at the end of the race. But he'd take care of it. In the last part of the race, he'd begin coming on.

"He didn't over-rev the motor. When times got tough near the end, he's got a good car to race you with. He didn't really show all he had until it counted. He always said he couldn't do something, and then he did. He never wanted to tell you he could and then not be able to. I loved racing with him in our car."

Pearson called Wood "a master of racing. He would have the car ready, and we would hardly ever have to change that thing. And, if we did, we would sit down and talk about it before we ever changed it, and I think that's why we were so successful. Everything clicked right together."

It was about this time that Pearson picked up a nickname—the Silver Fox—that would stay with him the rest of his career. "It was a two-sided deal, I guess," Pearson said. "My hair was turning gray. In fact, I had some gray in it when I was in high school. And there was the way I raced, I guess. But it didn't really matter, as long as they talk about you."

The pairing of the Silver Fox and the Woods was golden. The Wood Brothers team had been in existence since 1950. The brothers Wood totaled five—Glen, Leonard, Delano, Ray Lee, and Clay. Glen, the team's first driver and the organizational leader, and Leonard, universally admired as one of the best mechanical minds in the history of motor racing, were the mainstays.

The family racing history began in the front yard of a small, white-clapboard farmhouse in Stuart, Virginia. The Wood boys were attracted to fast cars, and they joined hands to work on a 1938 Ford coupe, using some shade-tree mechanical knowledge to make it go fast. How fast? There wasn't a racetrack nearby, so Glen ran the car much faster than he should have on Highway 8, a twisting mountain road that ran in front of the Wood house and down along Buffalo Ridge. There was big noise in the night.

"I came down through there wide open with that thing," Wood said many years later. "If you had a good car, you could run 95 [mph] [153 km per hour] down through there." He ran at night, when meeting another car was unlikely.

Of course, there was tinkering on the toy. The boys decided to remove the engine for service. They had no shop, no lift, and no stationary hook. What they had, in the front yard beside a small creek, was an 80-foot (24-m) American Beech tree with a big, strong limb. "We hung a chain over the limb and hoisted it," Wood said. "It was the only way we had to get the engine out. We didn't have a skyhook or anything. You did what you had to do."

From that strong tree, rooted in Virginia soil, grew one of the greatest racing teams in America. It had the bough that did not break.

Glen, who operated a sawmill to bring in money, began racing on area short tracks. Leonard and the other brothers pitched in, and wins came quickly. Like Lee Petty in North Carolina, Glen saw racing as a primary way to make money, and he soon was out of the lumber business. "I was racing and sawing at the same time," he said. "It got to where timber was a right good ways away. You had to go somewhere to find it. I was doing pretty good racing."

Glen won four times in sixty-two Cup starts. As speeds accelerated on giant new tracks in the 1960s, he decided to devote his time to running the team, leaving the driving to others. Thus began a long string of superstar drivers sitting in Wood Brothers cars. The list would include A.J. Foyt, Cale Yarborough, Curtis Turner, Dan Gurney, Dale Jarrett, Parnelli Jones, Neil Bonnett—and David Pearson. It is a remarkable group of driver talent, and when the Woods were asked who was the best, they always began with Pearson.

The Woods were a mainstay in Ford's racing operations, and their reputation as innovators and speed demons on pit row resulted in the team making an unusual one-time-only detour into IndyCar racing in 1965. Ford official John Cowley asked the team to pit driver Jimmy Clark in the Indianapolis 500 that year, and the Woods jumped into an unknown environment with the best sort of success. Clark won the race.

"On race day I guess you could say we hit a home run," Leonard Wood said. "We got the most publicity for doing less work than we ever had during a race, but everything went like clockwork. We made only two pit stops and didn't have to change tires. We checked them, but never had to make a change, and we won the race."

Under the direction of Leonard Wood, the team's pit crew worked daily to trim time from pit stops during Cup races, becoming one of the first teams to put so much emphasis on gaining positions while in the pits. "Leonard, especially, he was so focused on trimming every move that a guy had to make, whether he started with the right foot or the left foot," Ford racing engineer Mose Nowland said. "He was an expert at shortening the pitting efforts. They had clearly become pit stop strategists and were outshining everybody in NASCAR at that time."

From 1972 through 1979, Pearson won forty-three races for the Woods. Among the impressive records he posted during those years was an eleven-race pole-winning streak at Charlotte Motor Speedway. As Pearson added to that qualifying success at CMS, the track tried various incentives, including bonus money, to encourage other drivers to beat Pearson. No one did. For the 1978 World 600, the track posted a record purse of $15,000 for the pole winner. Pearson collected, running a four-lap average speed of 160.551 miles per hour (258.382 km per hour) to outrun second-place Cale Yarborough at 159.736 miles per hour (257.070 km per hour). The continuation of the qualifying streak, which became a public relations bonus for CMS, was one of Pearson's great racing pleasures.

"Humpy [track president H. A. 'Humpy' Wheeler] did everything he could to stop us or, shall we say, make it tougher," Pearson said. "We were stinking up his show. He changed the qualifying format from two to four laps, but that didn't work. The track had some 'Humpy Bumps' in it, and he rearranged a bump in the first turn, saying I was getting over it better than anybody. When that failed, I gave him a clue by telling him he had worked on the wrong end of the track."

Joe Kennedy, who was Pearson's public relations director during several of his peak years, said Pearson had "some secret at Charlotte. Maybe it was the bump in the first turn. I think it was just Pearson."

In an unusual pairing in the post-Pearson years, the Woods also built cars for Kyle Petty, who drove for his family team's greatest rival.

"I think Leonard Wood is the smartest man in the garage area, bar none," said Kyle Petty, who raced for the Woods from 1985 to 1988. "I've said it before, and I'll say it again, and I'll go to my grave saying that he's the smartest man I've ever met who knows cars and motors and front-end settings and chassis and tires and racetracks—the total package. I learned more in the three or four years I was there than I've learned everywhere else. I probably should have stayed there and let him teach me a lot more."

It has been said that Wood, who continued to make magic for the family team well into his 80s, could build an engine from a paper clip. A bit of an exaggeration, of course, but his mechanical abilities were respected by everyone who drove for the team—and virtually everyone who tried to beat it.

Charlie Gray, a former director of Ford's stock car racing program, remembered a race day in which Wood turned a probable failure into victory. Cale Yarborough was driving for the team in the first race at Michigan International Speedway in 1969. "We were using the 429 engine then, and we didn't have that many of them," Gray said. "The morning of the race, Leonard Wood was warming up the car and noticed a leak by a spark plug. Ford had a working trailer there that we had used at the race at Le Mans—it was the first of the really big trailers that people started bringing to tracks, and Leonard went in there and machined a valve cover to accept a spacer he made so the oil couldn't leak out."

Cale Yarborough edged LeeRoy Yarbrough for the race win that day in Michigan. There was no leak.

Leonard Wood was a wizard. Like all the best mechanics of his time, he knew how to play the gray areas of the rule book.

"Everybody kept their secrets to themselves," Bud Moore said. "Leonard and them did their little tricks. Ford didn't tell Leonard he had to do so-and-so. They got by with a lot of stuff. We all did. We all cheated every way we could.

"I remember a race at Daytona. The Woods had put a tarp over their car. Leonard had some turnbuckles under the hood. He'd get under there and pull those turnbuckles and pull the front end closer to the ground to make it run faster. Joe Gazaway [NASCAR official] happened to see his feet sticking out from under there. He picked up the tarp and smiled. He said, 'Lenny, what do you think you're doing?' That was the biggest laugh."

Throughout NASCAR history, teams that put together long streaks of success drew added scrutiny, both from officials and competitors. Pearson's superspeedway dominance in the 1973 season was no exception.

"Yeah, everybody thought we were cheating," Pearson said. "It was like when Jeff Gordon won so much. They said he was cheating. They said the same thing about me. But you got to win them while you can and do what you can to win them. We went to a lot of trouble to win all those poles at Charlotte. We had a special set of hubs we used. They used graphite in them. You could spin that wheel, and it would keep turning. It was real free. If something would happen and I had to hit the brakes, that wouldn't have worked because I didn't have any brakes. They had all the brakes backed off so there wouldn't be any drag. It was all completely legal. There was just no drag on that car at all. We had everything as loose as we could get it. And we fooled with tire air pressure a long time ago. We were changing cars with air pressure way before anybody had heard about it. The Woods were so slick. They were measuring tires before I even knew about it myself. I would tell them if it was a little too tight or too loose, and they'd say, 'We'll get it on the next pit stop.' They hardly even raised the hood.

"Leonard made a lot of stuff with his hands. He'd make the parking light areas and bend them in a little, just for aerodynamics. I got on to him one time when I was driving for Holman-Moody. His car was behind me, and I told him the front bumper looked like a nail coming at me the way he had it pointed right in the center. They would do things like that—anything to get the air to flow a little better."

While Pearson and the Woods parachuted in to run occasional races, the Pettys remained road warriors, showing up at every event and continuing pursuit of the championship. Even though RJR's sponsorship had trimmed the schedule dramatically, there were still many miles to run—both on track and on the interstates of America.

Along for the ride in two of those years, from 1970 to 1972, was a young mechanic from Springfield, Missouri. Roger Wasson, a racing fan, was in North Carolina on vacation and stopped by the Petty shop. He met Richard and was encouraged to send his résumé to Maurice.

Wasson wound up working in the engine room, a dream job for a street-car mechanic. Dozens of employees moved through the Petty shop in those years, some staying for a while, others becoming lifers. Some called it Petty University, as top mechanics often moved on to crew chief jobs at other teams. "It was the best two years of my life," Wasson said. "I got to work for my hero. But it was a grind."

Yet the NASCAR road wasn't all work. Bud Moore remembered an incident that highlighted his team's return trip from a race at Richmond, Virginia.

"Junior Johnson's team was in front of us," Moore said. "Henry [Benfield] was driving the truck, and Junior was riding with him. They saw us coming and got out in the middle of the road. They wouldn't let us by. We were running 65 to 70 miles an hour [105 to 121 km an hour]. They finally pulled over in the left lane to let us by. We got up by their side. I was shaking my fist at them. Junior stuck his big rump out the window. Mooned us. I couldn't believe it."

Nothing to see here. Just two future Hall of Famers sharing an unfortunate and not-so-intimate moment.

The NASCAR garage was abuzz in the weeks leading to the May 29, 1977, World 600 at Charlotte Motor Speedway. The track had announced that actress Elizabeth Taylor would be the grand marshal for the race, and that news attracted the interest of more than a few drivers. Taylor, then 45, was still a Hollywood icon, but she wasn't quite the same actress as the one who had starred with Paul Newman in *Cat on a Hot Tin Roof* in 1958. Taylor was introduced during that day's drivers meeting. Driver Buddy Baker was sitting near the back of the room. He leaned over to someone sitting beside him and said, "That woman has a lot of miles on her." A man traveling in Taylor's entourage overheard Baker's comment. "I don't think Ms. Taylor would appreciate what you said about her," he said. "What's your name?" Without skipping a beat, Baker said, "Darrell Waltrip."

The presence of a movie star, one of track official Humpy Wheeler's many public relations stunts over the years, had no impact on the race, although Petty and Pearson might have been inspired to a degree. They were the only drivers on the lead lap at the finish, Petty beating Pearson by 30 seconds. Baker finished fifth, and the driver Baker said he was, Waltrip, was sixth.

NASCAR garage areas were hotbeds of trickery, merriment, and goofing around in those days. Drivers were known to throw artificial snakes in the cockpits of cars. A particularly pungent trick involved placing an open can of sardines under a driver's seat before the start of the Southern 500 on a particularly hot afternoon. Petty typically wasn't known for hijinks, but Pearson was a different story. He was an accomplished practical joker, and he was so sharp and alert that he rarely was a victim of others' attempts. During his time with the Woods, Pearson often would find a place in the garage area to hide as qualifying time approached. Leonard Wood, ever nervous, would send Eddie or Len Wood, team owner Glen Wood's sons, to search for Pearson. Every time, he would show up at the car just in time to qualify. And he'd typically win the pole or qualify in the top five.

On a visit to a Florence, South Carolina, restaurant for dinner during a Darlington race week, Pearson spotted fellow driver and best friend Bobby Isaac in line waiting for a seat. He gave a young boy a five-dollar bill and some instructions. The boy walked over to Isaac, hugged him around a leg, and called him Daddy.

Petty mechanic Richie Barsz was on board for much on-the-road zaniness. Some stories, he said, are best left untold. "But we were in Atlanta one time at a beer joint," he said. "Kyle was in there with us. He was on his back on the floor, and we'd spin him around like he was break-dancing. We had fun." Kyle claimed that Barsz, a mainstay for decades at the Petty shop, "fixed the handles on my bicycle, taught me how to weld, and babysat me."

Pearson, a pilot, owned a helicopter for several years. In addition to making travel a bit easier for him, the helicopter was a vehicle for Pearson's sense of humor. Danny Pearson, David's cousin, remembered a helicopter ride: "If he was going to trick you, he'd set it up. He told me all the way on the trip to not let him forget to stop to get fuel. I reminded him. He said, 'I think we can make it.' He started pecking around on the gauges. I said, 'What's wrong ... the gauge shows it half full.' He said, 'It doesn't work half the time.' So, I really started getting anxious. He flipped some kind of breaker, and the fuel light started blinking. I couldn't speak. He scared me to death."

Pearson delighted in such antics.

While the Petty-Pearson rivalry remained fierce, Petty also met another challenger in the person of bold newcomer Bobby Allison, who roared into the sport bringing along a fierce independent streak, superb mechanical skills, and driving talents that few were able to match. Allison targeted Petty from the very beginning, concluding that to be a star he had to go after the reigning star. It was a troubling brew.

The Petty-Allison feud—and it was that and more—began in July 1968 when Allison used some aggressive racing to bump past Petty to win at Islip, New York. Tempers flared on pit road after the race, and the bumper-into-bumper action carried over to other tracks and other months. Short tracks provided the perfect opportunity for the two to tangle, and they took advantage of most of them. The rivalry reached a tipping point at North Wilkesboro Speedway (North Carolina) in October 1972 as Petty and Allison slammed into each other repeatedly over the final laps. Petty won by two car lengths. "Allison was playing with my life out there today, and I don't like it," Petty told the media after the race. "The other competitor had to wreck me to win, and that's what he did," Allison said. "I had so much smoke in my car I could hardly see."

In the post-race confusion, a fan attacked Richard Petty, and Maurice Petty reacted by hitting the intruder on the head with Richard's driving helmet.

The feud had reached the point of no return.

"It just grew and grew and grew until it got out of hand," Petty told *The Charlotte Observer*. "We essentially destroyed each other's car at North Wilkesboro Speedway in 1972, and there was almost a riot among our fans. We knew we had to end it, and we did by sitting together at the Sunday morning chapel service at North Carolina Motor Speedway a couple weeks later.

"You meet and say, 'We've got to stop this before we hurt ourselves or somebody else.' That's what we did. We sat down one day and said, 'Man, we're tearing up too much equipment.' . . . We were fortunate we just crashed each other. But you're going to get other people involved that are innocent. We called it to a halt and went on down the road.

"The rivalry with Pearson was strictly trying to beat each other. There were no confrontations or anything. With Allison, it got to be more personal. We got into personal arguments. You didn't need to with Pearson. I liked Pearson. I liked Allison. . . . If I had a little argument with Pearson, in fifteen minutes we might get in the car and drive off. You couldn't do that with Allison."

Auto racing stories about Daytona Beach, Florida, sometimes begin with a tale of two saloons.

One is the venerable Boot Hill Saloon on East Main Street, a beer-bottle toss from the Atlantic. It's a typical beach bar, saturated in beer spills and tall tales. In 1974, one of the Boot Hill's tables hosted Bob Latford, Phil Holmer, and Joe Whitlock—all associated with NASCAR in one way or another—for a long session of drinking and calculating. By night's end, they had devised the point system that NASCAR would adopt for its Cup Series in 1975 and would use into the next century. Latford, a numbers wizard and a trusted NASCAR historian, built the core of the system, and his pals helped refine it using a stack of cocktail napkins.

The radical new system survived until 2004 despite its shortcomings, which emphasized solid consistency over winning. A victory earned a driver 175 points. Each driver who led a lap got five bonus points, and the driver who led the most laps received an additional five. Thus, the race winner earned at least 180 points. By leading the most laps, the second-place finisher could also pick up 180 points, making the race win worth no more than second place, at least in terms of the season-long run for the championship. That part of the system was often criticized, but the plan held firm for almost thirty years. Drivers, even those at out-of-the-way short tracks who dreamed of racing in the big time, came to know the concept as "point racing." In the long run, finishing third or fourth every week at your local track would beat scoring an occasional win.

And the Boot Hill, which later earned fame as a biker bar, gained its place in stock car racing lore.

Of equal status in the Daytona barroom category for the racing community was the Boar's Head Lounge, located in what once was the Howard Johnson's motel near Daytona International Speedway, several miles (11 km) from the ocean. The Boar's Head was a convenient after-work gathering spot for various individuals from the speedway garage area, including drivers, team owners, crew members, NASCAR officials, journalists, and assorted hangers-on. Friendly barkeepers and cheap beer attracted a long list of race-week regulars. It became a place where crew guys stayed too long, drank too much, and—sometimes after midnight—talked too much.

In the harsh sunlight of the next morning, with loud engines firing up in the Daytona garages and the race only hours away, a few secrets might have lost their value, having bounced from table to table at the Boar's Head. And to be sure, there were hangovers and headaches.

Before television networks began dictating race start times and innovative lighting systems opened the gates for night racing at big tracks, Daytona International Speedway's annual summer race was scheduled for morning starts (either 10 a.m. or 11 a.m.) on July 4. It was intended to be part of the nation's celebration of independence. The Firecracker 400—100 miles (161 km) less than its sister race, the Daytona 500, in February—typically was over quickly, giving fans (and some teams who lingered after the race in the oceanside resort) the afternoon to wander the beach and the boardwalk. Popular Daytona restaurants got an extra night of dining room overflow.

The schedule made sense and seemingly was a perfect fit for everyone, that is, except television executives who lusted for bigger ratings from night events. Lost in this rush to racing in the dark was the fact that afternoon thunderstorms are almost daily occurrences in the summer in Daytona Beach, soaking the track and delaying racing.

The concept of lighting a superspeedway for night racing was not even a thought in the summer of 1974, however, and so it was that teams arrived at the track at dawn on race morning July 4. Halfway through the season, it had been a Richard Petty–David Pearson kind of year. Petty won the Daytona 500 in February and followed up with victories at Rockingham, North Wilkesboro, Nashville, and Michigan, the final race before teams rolled into Daytona Beach for the Firecracker. Pearson had won at Darlington, Talladega, and Charlotte, giving the Petty-Pearson combination eight wins in the year's first fifteen races.

They were giants of the sport, and they were at their peak powers.

There was no reason to expect that anyone other than Petty or Pearson would win at Daytona, a track both drivers had mastered. In the previous year's Firecracker race, the story was about Pearson and Petty and no one else. They were the only drivers on the lead lap at the finish, Pearson taking the checkered flag six car lengths in front of Petty. They swapped the lead several times over the final fifty-six laps, but Pearson, whose Mercury was particularly strong that day, led the final twenty.

"I don't mind getting outrun, but I hate like hell to get played with," Petty said after the race. "Pearson played with me until the final twenty laps, then he just took off."

As on so many other race days, the final laps of the 1974 Firecracker 400 found the No. 43 and No. 21 wrestling for the win. They were one-two, Pearson in front, racing into the last of 160 laps.

Pearson had spent several of the final laps trying to entice Petty to pass him and move into first place. The 1970s at Daytona were all about the so-called slingshot, a maneuver in which the trailing car used the slipstream created by the lead car to make one final pass on the last lap. More than a few Daytona races were won using this "whip-around" method. Petty, of course, understood that second place typically was the position of choice entering the last lap at Daytona, and he was content to sail along in Pearson's wake and wait for the right moment to unleash the slingshot.

He never got the chance. Before the day was done, Pearson's nickname of the Silver Fox would be underlined.

Rolling toward Turn 1 after taking the white flag, Pearson suddenly slowed and dropped low on the track. Petty, assuming, in the heat of the moment, that Pearson's car had developed engine trouble or that the No. 21 had run out of fuel, zipped around on the outside and took the lead. He had little choice.

Mechanic Mike Hill, watching from Cecil Gordon's pit, saw the drama unfold. "They came around, and David was leading to take the white flag," he said. "Then he hit the cutoff switch. All the Pettys started jumping up and down like they've won the race. Then coming off Turn 4 David's under Richard and he's won the race. They were madder than hell. The Silver Fox had done it again. I remember hearing the car in the tri-oval. I thought it blew up, too."

After essentially forcing Petty to pass him at the beginning of the last lap, Pearson put his foot on the floorboard again and used momentum to zip around Petty into first place. A few seconds later, he ran under the checkered flag first, beating Petty by a half-car-length.

It quickly became clear that Pearson had executed one of the slickest moves in the history of NASCAR superspeedway racing, and Petty, his ultimate rival, was the victim. The grandstand crowd could barely be contained.

While Pearson rolled around the track on the cooldown lap, tempers boiled inside Petty's car and in the No. 43 pit. Although many celebrated Pearson's strategy, the Pettys took a critical view. Petty called Pearson's move dangerous, and there were a few comments that the engine that allowed Pearson to make up so much ground on the final lap might have had some "extra" firepower.

It was one of the few times in Petty and Pearson's long rivalry that real animosity emerged. Petty made the unusual move of visiting the press box after the race to tell his side of the story, and he and Pearson, who was doing the winner's interview, had some uncomfortable verbal exchanges. Petty repeated his charge that Pearson's move had been dangerous, and Pearson eventually suggested that Petty build a faster car so he could compete.

"Oh boy, that's probably the only time Richard was mad at him that I know of," Dale Inman said. "I think what upset Richard the most was that he almost hit him [Pearson]. It was that close. I thought he had run out of gas or had something go wrong. Richard said he could have taken both of them out."

Pearson took the view that he had done everything he could to win the race.

"That was the only way I could beat him," he said. "I had done everything in the world. I knew I couldn't pass him. I had to do something. The way it was then, you had to slingshot to win. The best thing I knew to do was make like mine quit with the engine or like I was out of gas. I threw up my hand [to let Petty know he was slowing down] and went to the inside. When I saw him go by me, I mashed the gas back down. I caught him coming off four. He was mad, but he got over it. He said it was dangerous what I did, but it wasn't. I got out of his way."

In an interview years later, Petty said Pearson's move temporarily damaged his confidence level in his top rival, but the situation didn't fester.

"We had raced together more than anybody," he said. "As far as racing each other, if he went down in the first turn and turned right, I would have followed him. That's how much confidence I had in him. I thought something had really happened to his car that day. If you look at the film, when he came off the second corner, he was two football fields behind me. He was fast enough to be able to catch me and pass me. The way he figured, he was going to run second, so I'll try this. If I still run second, at least I tried.

"It hurt the confidence I had in him. But that was just one incident. I got the confidence back."

Kyle Petty said his father moved on quickly after such incidents. "Dad always gets over stuff, and I think Pearson did, too," he said. "They didn't look at stuff like that. I think their relationship probably took a hit from a confidence standpoint. I think he always had confidence David would race a certain way, and David had confidence he would race a certain way."

The Pearsons, the Wood team members, and the Pettys were close off the track. After long practice and qualifying days, Dale Inman frequently visited area movie theaters, and Eddie and Len Wood often tagged along. Members of both teams once attended an NFL game together and made trips to Atlantic City, New Jersey, while racing nearby. Kyle Petty grew up at racetracks with Larry and Ricky, Pearson's oldest sons. "Larry and Ricky were dragged to the racetrack with their dad, and I came with mine," Kyle said. "Ricky and Larry taught me to swim in Daytona Beach at the Sea Dip motel. We were always together, stayed at the same hotels. That one we called the Flea Dip. But it was a great place."

Across his long career, Pearson rarely was involved in controversy, but he stood his ground. Among his admirers was longtime crew chief Tim Brewer, who matched wits with Pearson and the Woods.

"There was nobody smarter, nobody tougher," Brewer said. "He would race for 100 miles [161 km], ride for 300 miles [483 km], then in the last 100 miles [161 km] he was going to kick your ass. He would let somebody else lead until it was time to get paid."

Among those Pearson raced late in his career was Tim Richmond, who detoured to NASCAR from a promising run in IndyCar racing and quickly became a star. Brewer was Richmond's crew chief during a race at Daytona and remembered the two drivers having an off-track encounter after Richmond had given Pearson a one-finger salute while they were racing.

"Richmond called me on the radio and said, 'What kind of trouble am I going to be in? I stuck my finger at Pearson,'" Brewer said. "I said, 'You don't stick your finger at David Pearson. He'll whip your ass.' After the race, I see Pearson on pit road. He said, 'Brewer, you ought to do something about that son of a bitch Richmond. He stuck his finger at me. He's over there in front of the truck. I slapped him.' I walked over there, and Richmond is sitting there. He had a handprint across his face. 'What did he do?' I asked him. He looked up and said, 'He hit me.'"

Early in his career, Pearson had a mini-feud with future Hall of Fame driver Ned Jarrett, one that accelerated to the point that Pearson yanked the steering wheel from his car after a crash at Tar Heel Speedway in North Carolina and threw it at Jarrett on the next lap.

PEARSON KNEW VIRTUALLY EVERY BUMP ON THE DAYTONA TRACK AND RAN IN THE OFTEN-DANGEROUS DRAFT AS IF HE WAS ROLLING ALONG A COUNTRY ROAD.

Pearson's move to beat Petty in the 1974 race is considered by many longtime NASCAR travelers as one of the coolest in the sport's history. The race often is ranked as one of the top twenty across NASCAR's seventy-five years.

Pearson knew virtually every bump and other trouble spot on the Daytona track and ran in the often-dangerous draft as if he was rolling along a country road. Darrell Waltrip finally won the Daytona 500 on his 17th try and later talked about discussing the draft with Pearson. "I'd ask him questions about the car, about the track, what might happen during the race, and he'd always tell me exactly what was going to happen," Waltrip said. "I appreciated that about him a lot."

Petty totaled ten wins for the 1974 season and won the championship. Cale Yarborough was second. Pearson finished third in points despite running only nineteen races while Petty and Yarborough logged thirty each. Pearson won seven times.

"Pearson was the craftiest of all the drivers," Buddy Baker said. "He was kind of like, if you hear a noise and you go, 'Where's the ghost at?' and all of a sudden, there it is. About 25 miles [40 km] from the end of any major race, if he wasn't in the mirror, you started asking, 'Where's he at?' One time at Charlotte I was leading the race, and I looked in the mirror and I didn't see him. I looked in the mirror again, and I said, 'Where's Pearson?' He was underneath the back of my car almost, and when I looked back, I was looking through his car."

At the highest point of his career, Pearson was described by an *Atlanta Journal* sports writer as typifying "that era in racing when they measured a race driver by how much of a man he was. By how much he could guzzle down, by how many garter belts hung around his rearview mirror, by how unruffled he could appear at the sight of blood on the backstretch and by how close he could come to that fourth turn wall."

A *Sports Illustrated* writer, reporting from Daytona that July, offered the idea that Pearson might fall asleep and still win.

There was another angle to Pearson's 1974 win at Daytona. He had won the Firecracker race the previous two seasons, beating Petty to the stripe each time. Word spread around the garage before the 1974 race that Petty was determined not to lose to Pearson again. "Maurice Petty's wife had told Daddy before the race that Richard said you're not going to beat him today," Ricky Pearson said. "Daddy said toward the end of the race that came to his mind and that he had to do something. He did what he had to do."

It was a race finish the gang at the Boar's Head would rehash for years to come.

Despite the occasional failure, Petty kept rolling. He won thirteen times and notched another championship in 1975. "It was one of those years where we really weren't doing anything that much different," Petty said. "Everything just came together. Without a bunch of circumstances falling your way, it doesn't make any difference how good you run.

You just parlay other people's mistakes or other people's misfortune onto your side of the ledger, and if it happens to be your day, then you get more than they do. Really, that's just the way the game is played. Nobody can control that kind of stuff."

The statistics from that 1975 dash through the schedule speak loudly for Petty. From May 25 to September 21, he ran eleven races, winning six times and finishing second in the other five. The streak began in the World 600 at Charlotte with Petty scoring his first win in NASCAR's longest race. "I remember things were going so well that I kept thinking about the Charlotte jinx that had haunted me since the first race back in 1960," Petty said. "I kept wondering what was going to happen this time."

"YOU JUST PARLAY OTHER PEOPLE'S MISTAKES OR OTHER PEOPLE'S MISFORTUNE ONTO YOUR SIDE OF THE LEDGER, AND IF IT HAPPENS TO BE YOUR DAY, THEN YOU GET MORE THAN THEY DO."

Petty ran all but one lap of the possible 3,188 laps during the string. That stretch stirred memories of his ten-race winning streak in 1967.

"Of a possible 4,700 miles [7,564 km] of racing, I ran all but 0.596 of a mile [0.959 km]," Petty said. "I reckon that's a real tribute to the crew. I know they're good, but a record of keeping the car running that strong for that long shows how good they really are." At the end of the year, the Petty crew members were presented with a watch engraved with the crewman's name and "1975—The Big Season."

Despite the successes of the 1975 year, it is a year that left a stain on the team and the Petty family. During the May race at Talladega, Petty pitted for service. Crew member Randy Owens, twenty-year-old brother of Lynda, Richard's wife, raced to help put out a small fire around one of the car's wheels. He was killed when a pressurized water tank exploded. Kyle Petty was also working on the crew that day. "It was a horrible thing to witness," Petty wrote in his autobiography. "I was standing right there. I was in shock. It happened so quickly there was nothing I or anyone could do to stop it. It was over before we even realized it had begun." The team pulled out of the track that evening carrying a heavy burden home to North Carolina. Kyle described it as the longest ride of his life. Owens was buried the following Tuesday.

The Pettys raced on.

The Petty family moved into a new 10,000-square foot (929-sq m) home near the team shop that year. The house, still home to Petty, has five bedrooms and a big basement where the Petty children and their friends used to roller-skate.

In September 1975, *The Charlotte Observer* reported in a banner-headline story that Petty and Pearson were expected to retire at the end of the year. The story said Buddy Baker would replace Petty in the No. 43 and Cale Yarborough would be the new driver for the Wood Brothers. The story was quickly denied by all concerned.

Pearson and Petty weren't even close to the end of the road. It was long and winding, with miles—and wins—to go.

ABC's Bill Flemming and Jackie Stewart are high above Daytona International Speedway describing the final laps of the 1976 Daytona 500. It is tense theater as Richard Petty and David Pearson move through the turns and lapped traffic at 200 miles per hour (322 km per hour), as yet another NASCAR race apparently will be decided by the drivers of the No. 43 and No. 21 cars.

ABC had joined the race with about an hour to go, standard practice in the years before the networks, NASCAR, and tracks worked out deals to broadcast events from start to finish. The abbreviated race coverage was part of ABC's popular *Wide World of Sports* program, and it was sharing Sunday afternoon time with the network's featured coverage of the Winter Olympics in Innsbruck, Austria.

As Petty and Pearson plotted strategy over the closing laps, so did ABC. The plan was to switch from Daytona Beach to Innsbruck as soon as the race ended. The timing of the switch was a matter of discussion between Dennis Lewin, a coordinating producer in New York City, and Roone Arledge, a producer at ABC's Olympic headquarters location in Innsbruck. "He asked me if we were going to run over into the Olympics' time," Lewin said. "I told him, no, that everything was fine. Everything was going along as expected."

In the den in the Pearson house on Hawthorne Road in Spartanburg, the tension was too much for Helen Pearson. She and her 11-year-old son, Eddie, were watching the race as her husband chased Petty. "When they threw the white flag, she got up and ran outside," Eddie remembered. "She said, 'I can't watch it.'"

Things were about to change—and in a big way—for the Pearson family, for NASCAR, and for the skiers and skaters a world away in Austria. ABC was minutes away from showing the checkered flag flying at Daytona and pushing buttons to take viewers to the Olympics.

"Then—wham!—so much for that," Lewin said. "We stayed with the race and ran over several minutes into the Olympics' time."

David Pearson and Richard Petty had moved the world—and Helen Pearson.

Entering the final lap, Pearson closed the gap between his car and Petty, the leader. Approaching the third turn for the final time, Pearson slipped to Petty's inside and took the lead. Petty responded as Pearson's car pushed to the high side of the track between the turns, moving alongside Pearson. They ran into the bumpy fourth turn side by side, the checkered flag and $50,000 first-place money beckoning.

Then they hit.

Forty-eight years later, Petty, sitting behind the sunglasses seemingly permanently affixed to his head, is watching video of the finish in an office at Petty Enterprises.

"Back it up, back it up further," Petty said. "Can you stop it there? See, he still had about 3 foot [0.9 m] to the wall. I knew I didn't crowd him to the wall. But it doesn't make any difference. Anyhow, we touched. With the draft and all that, the cars were so light all you had to do was just blow on it. I don't even think it left a mark on the car. That's how easy we hit. I thought I had cleared Pearson. I really did."

But he didn't. The contact, however light and brief, sent both cars sailing into the outside wall. Petty's car twirled along the frontstretch, and, for a moment, it appeared that he would cross the finish line backward in a blur of Petty blue and red, scoring a quite unlikely victory. But the car moved down the banking and stalled on the grassy area separating the track from pit road. Pearson's car also looped onto the grass, but it didn't stall. During the spinning, Pearson had depressed the car's clutch, thus keeping the engine fired and his victory hopes alive.

In the Wood Brothers pit, Eddie Wood was taking the wild ride along with Pearson. Wood, trying to keep his cool, was on the two-way radio with Pearson as he drafted behind Petty with one to go.

"I asked David if he could get him," Wood said. "Then they go off into Turn 1 and come off of 2 and head down the backstretch. We couldn't see, of course. There were no TV monitors in the pits then. About midway down the backstretch, the crowd started reacting. David passed Richard on the inside off Turn 3. They went up the track. David said, 'I got him.' The crowd was going nuts. We were going nuts. Then they came off four, and he said, 'He hit me.'"

Actually, Pearson said, "The bitch hit me." Wood edited his version of the conversation until years later, when Pearson, not necessarily always shy, confirmed its true nature.

Pearson had been eerily calm during the frantic seconds that elapsed between the Turn 4 crash and the finish of the race. "When David was spinning backward, he keyed his mic and said, 'Where's Richard?'" Wood said. "He was just as calm as if he was on the phone. He stopped, and then he said, 'I'm coming.'"

This sequence of events was complicated. In order to communicate with Wood while wrecking and trying to win a race at the same time, Pearson had to push the radio button on the shoulder harness near his chest while trying to regain control of his car with his other hand. There was no panic in his voice. "He was the coolest guy ever on the radio," Wood said.

Pearson, his battered car rolling along, crossed the finish line at about 30 miles per hour (48 km per hour), winning the biggest stock car race in the world for the first time at the slowest speed any winner had ever recorded.

Members of Petty's crew ran to his car and pushed it across the line, a rules violation that cost Petty a lap in the final race rundown.

Eddie Pearson ran outside his house to report to his mother. "It was crazy," he said. "I didn't think either one of them would make it to the line. I went outside and told Mom he had won. She came back in, was all excited, got to see all the replays. We were both shaking our heads. Couldn't believe it."

In the ABC booth, Flemming and Stewart were talking over each other trying to keep up with the history happening before them. For a few minutes, the Olympics weren't the biggest thing in the sporting world.

Ken Squier had the radio call on the Motor Racing Network. "They're going to be side by side as they exit the banking and head for the start-finish line," he said. "They both spin. They're in the wall. Petty is sliding, slamming into the wall. He's coming down toward the finish line. Will he make it? The car's stopped three-four-hundred feet [300 to 400 m] shy of the finish line. Pearson is still running. Here's Petty trying to fire to come across the line. David Pearson, moving down through.

As they come to the stripe, the winner is car No. 21. It's going to be, I believe, Pearson's victory. We'll just have to wait and see. An amazing finish. Richard Petty's car demolished in the front end as well as car No. 21. An unbelievable finish. A terrible crash. Both cars in the wall. Both drivers kept on going.

"It has been some kind of a day. It looks like a half-mile [0.8-km] night at Nashville, Tennessee."

There would be much analysis of the greatest finish in the history of NASCAR, but the key factor in the closing moments of the 500 was Pearson's spontaneous reaction and his decision to depress the clutch and keep his engine alive. Why was Pearson so quick to kick the car out of gear? Eddie Wood believes events from the previous year's 500 guided Pearson's alert response. "The year before he was about to win the race with three laps to go," Wood said. "Cale Yarborough was coming off the second turn running on seven cylinders. David was lapping him. I think Cale was trying to get back to him as quick as he could, but he spun him down onto the grass. The car wouldn't crank."

"THEY BOTH SPIN. THEY'RE IN THE WALL. PETTY IS SLIDING, SLAMMING INTO THE WALL. HE'S COMING DOWN TOWARD THE FINISH LINE. WILL HE MAKE IT?"

Benny Parsons inherited the lead after Pearson's misfortune and won the race, the biggest victory of his career.

Pearson would not forget. The loss of that 500 led to winning the next one.

Although Pearson's Mercury had sustained considerable front-end damage in the crash, he drove it around the track on the cool-down lap and then moved along pit road toward victory lane. Maurice Petty ran alongside Pearson's car, apparently thinking Pearson had wrecked his brother intentionally. "Maurice and Dale [Inman] came out and about threatened to whip us like we had something to do with it," team owner Glen Wood said. "I think somebody finally told Maurice it wasn't David's fault. Richard admitted later on that he just wasn't clear. He thought David would back out, and David didn't."

As might be expected, emotions were high in both the No. 43 and No. 21 camps. Kyle Petty, then fifteen years old, was among the Petty crew members who ran to the King's car as it sat lifeless. "Oh yeah, I was out there," Kyle said. "Me, Barry Dodson, Wayne Dalton, other crew guys. We're pushing the car. We're all around. We're getting ready to go to victory lane and kick some ass. We're pissed. I was fifteen years old, but, yeah, I'm going to go fight. Daddy doesn't scream, but he said, 'Stop, take this car, and put it on the trailer, go back to Level Cross and we'll go to Rockingham next week.' We all did exactly what he said. In that moment, it was over."

Broadcaster Chris Economaki had been roaming NASCAR pit roads for years and would for years to come. "I was the first guy to get to Petty's car," he said. "I ran up and asked him what triggered the whole thing. He was rather aggravated. I was standing in front of pit wall when it happened. I was surprised to some extent. I guess each one was figuring the other guy was going to back down."

Larry McReynolds, then an Alabama high school kid and later a Cup Series crew chief and motorsports broadcaster, was sitting in the front-stretch grandstand. "A buddy of mine and I decided to pack up and go to Daytona for Saturday and Sunday," McReynolds said. "We didn't have tickets. Back then, at 7 in the morning, they put some tickets on sale. We slept in lawn chairs in line to be able to get tickets. We weren't sitting near the finish line, but, as the race progressed, we moved down the grandstands. By the time the race ended, we were kind of amongst them. It was crazy. That's going to be a tough Daytona 500 to ever duplicate. It was pretty classic. The third-place car [Benny Parsons] was far enough behind first and second that the top two could wreck and still beat him. You won't ever see that again."

Pearson and Petty were a lap in front of Parsons, giving them time to smash their cars and still battle for the win while Parsons was late to the finish.

Although there would be various interpretations of the finish in the few hours after the race and the years to come, Pearson was matter-of-fact about the whole thing, as he was on so many race days. "We didn't touch until we came off four," he said. "He hit me there in the left front fender with his back end, and I hit him after I came off the wall. Soon as I hit the wall, I pushed the clutch in and held my car wide open so it wouldn't choke down. When I stopped in the infield, I put it in low and took off. I didn't have time to be angry. If he had beat me to the finish line I might be telling a different tale. I'm sure he didn't do it for meanness."

Petty said he overcorrected after his car hit the wall. "The car looked like it was straight, but the front wheels weren't responding correctly and I didn't know it," he said. "I had one ulcer before the race. Now I have two."

The photo of Pearson's Mercury limping to the win with Petty's damaged Dodge in the background has been reprinted hundreds of times. "I sign that picture all the time," Petty said. "There's not a day goes by that somebody doesn't send it in. It was just one of those moments."

The team that would win the 1976 Daytona 500 woke up that morning in a yellow cinder-block house on Taylor Road outside Daytona Beach, several miles (11 km) from the speedway. It was economically efficient lodging for one of motorsports' leading operations.

Team owner Glen Wood loved it. His sons, Eddie (23) and Len (19) Not so much.

"Dad thought it was the greatest thing in the world, to have a place to stay in Daytona Beach," Eddie Wood said. "A man owned the house, and the interstate [I-95] was about to come through, so he had to sell it. Dad bought the house for about a thousand dollars. It cost $10,000 to move it about a mile [1.6 km] away. We had been staying in a single-wide trailer."

All of the Wood Brothers Racing team members stayed in the house, with the exception of Delano Wood, Glen's brother and the team's jackman. "Delano said he had allergies and couldn't stay there," Eddie Wood said. "I didn't think of that."

The least memorable thing about the place was the shower. "The water was sulphur," Wood said. "Taking a shower in that stuff. It was awful. We came out of there smelling like sulphur."

By sunset, they would be smelling like roses.

Two months before the Daytona 500, Eddie and Len had driven to Banjo Matthews' shop near Asheville, North Carolina, to pick up the new Mercury that Pearson would drive in the race. Eddie remembers the day more for the stock market than the stock car. "Len and I had just gotten into buying stocks," he said. "On the way over, we heard a stock market report, and stock we had bought in a natural gas company on somebody's recommendation had dropped to five dollars from ten dollars, this the day after we bought it."

A few minutes later, they would pick up gold from Matthews' shop, where many NASCAR Cup cars began their lives in those days.

"I have pictures of that car going together," Eddie said. "It was the first time we painted the roll cage and the interior red. It was a special car to begin with, and we didn't get new cars very often."

PEARSON CLAIMED HE NEVER DROVE A RACE CAR CARRYING NITROUS OXIDE. "BUT I KNOW THERE HAVE BEEN A LOT OF THEM. G. C. SPENCER HAD A BOTTLE, AND IT WENT OFF SITTING THERE IN LINE. 'THERE WENT 50 HORSEPOWER,' HE SAID."

Although Pearson and Petty would be the focus of that year's 500, they were not in the middle of news coverage a week earlier when qualifying was held for the race. Fast laps by A.J. Foyt, in Hoss Ellington's car, and Darrell Waltrip, in an entry from DiGard Racing, put them in the front row for the race. Temporarily, that is. NASCAR inspectors found nitrous oxide bottles, used to provide a short but powerful boost to speeds, hidden in both cars, and their speeds were disallowed, lifting

United States Auto Club (USAC) driver Ramo Stott into the pole position, a rare spot for him. Foyt, irascible by nature, was incensed. The next week, at the Rockingham race, he said he probably would never race at Daytona again and criticized "substandard" driver facilities at the track. He was back in the lineup in the July race at the track, however, and finished fourth.

The nitrous oxide story dominated the rest of the February race week until race day, when the green flag found Petty starting sixth and Pearson seventh.

Pearson claimed he never drove a race car carrying nitrous oxide. "But I know there have been a lot of them," he said. "People put them anywhere—in the frame of the car, anywhere. I remember one year at Talladega we had the cars sitting in line to qualify. G.C. Spencer had a bottle, and it went off sitting there in line. It smoked everywhere. 'There went 50 horsepower,' he said."

The controversy over the qualifying violations was soon forgotten as Pearson and Petty entertained more than 100,000 in the grandstands and big numbers on television. The truncated race coverage attracted 18 million viewers. The 1979 Daytona 500, featuring a last-lap crash involving Cale Yarborough and Donnie Allison, Richard Petty's upset win, and the off-track fight between Yarborough and brothers Bobby and Donnie Allison, generated more publicity than the Petty-Pearson finish three years earlier but couldn't match the television audience. Fifteen million watched the 1979 race.

Among those watching the 1976 Daytona 500 on television was Robin Pemberton, a New York kid who would land in stock car racing as a crew chief and later a NASCAR executive. "It's etched in my mind," he said. "Every time you turn around and they're showing some of the greatest highlights in the history it shows up. They were two crafty guys, and they understood what it took to get by each other. You saw a lot of racing in 5 miles [8 km], that's for sure. Two of the greatest."

Dale Jarrett, a Cup champion who would win the Daytona 500 three times, called the Pearson-Petty finish "just incredible. It was just a great racing moment to me. That's what the Daytona 500 is about—doing everything that you can to win and having it come down to literally the last 300 yards [274 m] of the race."

Despite the disappointment of the day, Petty said the finish fueled the sport for months to come. "It was good for racing because everybody wanted to see it again," he said. "Everybody wanted to know about it. Everybody wanted to know what happened, so it wasn't a deal where on Monday it said Pearson wins and Petty runs second. It kept it in the paper for a lot of different times, and we've been hashing it around for all these years."

Darrell Waltrip, then blazing a path to the top level of Cup racing, said Pearson "played it right to the last lap or two. I don't think he expected Richard to come back on him like he did. I think it probably surprised David more than anybody. I think it was just a racing incident—two guys going for the win. Things like that happen. I wouldn't want to blame Richard or blame David."

Waltrip said Pearson was not as enamored of Daytona Beach and its various entertainment venues as other drivers. He was there to race. "I was staying on the beach, and I asked him where he was staying," Waltrip said. "He said he was at a Holiday Inn near the track. I said, 'Why aren't you on the beach where you can hear the ocean?' He said, 'If I want to hear the water, I'll turn the shower on.'"

Although damaged heavily, Pearson's winning Mercury and Petty's second-place Dodge would live to race again.

Pearson crashed the Mercury again at Talladega Superspeedway that year. Neil Bonnett would drive the refurbished car later, and the Wood team eventually loaned it to the R.J. Reynolds Tobacco Company as a show car painted in the red and white colors of Winston cigarettes. It was returned to the Woods' shop, where it sat for years before being sold for $200 to a driver who planned to turn it into a dirt-racing car.

"We didn't see the car for years after that," Eddie Wood said. "Then I got a call from a guy in Fort Lauderdale, Florida who restores old cars. He said he thought he had found the car in a junkyard. I didn't think so, but he sent me a couple of Polaroids of it. I recognized a bracket on the car's radiator because I had made the bracket. It was the car."

The Mercury was restored in Florida and eventually bought by the Museum of American Speed in Lincoln, Nebraska, where it is on display, along with a video and information about the 1976 race. "We got the car around 1996, and it's been here ever since," said Bob Mays, the museum's historian. "It's a beautiful car. We didn't have to do anything to it. It was in great shape when it arrived. Somebody fired it up and drove it into the museum, and I think that's the only time it's run since then. The car always draws a crowd. It's big and mean-looking."

Petty drove the Daytona Dodge again in the next week's race at North Carolina Speedway in Rockingham, winning by two laps over Darrell Waltrip. "We had to get home to get the car ready for Rockingham," Petty said. "We were in the shop Monday morning working on it."

Crew chief Dale Inman said the damage was limited to sheet metal. "When the wreck happened, it just drained me," Inman said. "Took away all the adrenaline I had. I was stunned. After the race, Richard said it was our best car, so we had to run it at Rockingham."

As the team reworked the car for Rockingham, crew members tossed some of the damaged sheet metal in a pile behind the shop. The left front fender, rescued from oblivion, now is owned by Mike Dozier, a former Petty crew member and a racing memorabilia collector. He said he paid $3,700 for the piece.

> "I came across it on eBay," Dozier said. "A guy was advertising it as a fender from Richard's 1976 Daytona car. I have at least 10,000 photos of Richard and different cars, and I have a lot from that race. They put the contingency decals in different places on the car every race, and I was able to verify it from those. I'm always skeptical. That's why I put so much time looking into all the photographs. In a book there's an actual closeup after the crash, and I could see a ripple in the front part of the fender. I saw that exact ripple in the fender. After I got it, I took it up to Dale Inman's house. He looked at it and said, 'That's it.' Most of the damage was on the right front fender. The left side just had a bow in it."

In a 1977 article provocatively titled, "Hot Blood Down In Dixie," *Sports Illustrated* magazine explored the dynamics of the racing talents and styles of Petty and Pearson. "I think David Pearson is a better pure driver than I am, probably the best ever, but I'm as good a racer because I work better within a team and put the combination of driver and car and crew together," Petty told the magazine. "That's what produces the results. . . . When he's [Pearson] in a position to win, he's the toughest driver I've ever had to beat. He doesn't always drive hard, but he drives smart. . . . He can handle a car so smooth it's a pleasure to see."

Maurice Petty told author Peter Golenbock that Pearson was "our real nemesis. . . . Either Richard won or he did. We went 'round and 'round on that, too. David was just smooth, a hard driver but smooth. If Richard and him were running, you could depend that if one was on the inside, they weren't going to take each other out. They were there to race each other, and whoever came out on top came out on top. Not like some of the other drivers, who would try to run into you, try to drive you out. If you're going to race side by side with somebody, you want to race someone like David."

Pearson would go on to win ten times in twenty-two races in 1976. By early August, when the tour stopped at Talladega Superspeedway, he had won seven times. In the garage area on that race weekend, three reporters were walking along the line of Cup Series team trucks. Pearson, sitting in the back of the Wood Brothers truck, yelled, "Hey, are you guys tired of writing about me?" "No," one reporter said, "Give us another reason." Pearson laughed.

There would be other reasons.

Although Cale Yarborough won the Cup championship, Pearson was named American Driver of the Year for the second time. That year he won the NASCAR Triple Crown, defined then as the Daytona 500, World 600, and Southern 500. He became the first driver to win forty superspeedway races and forty superspeedway poles (superspeedway was defined as any track at least 1 mile [1.6 km] in length) in a career and the first driver to sweep all three California races (two at Riverside and one at Ontario) in a season. Another highlight of the season occurred in the 24 Hours of Daytona endurance race in February.

Pearson teamed with his son, Larry, and Gary and Jim Bowsher, sons of car owner Jack Bowsher, to win the Grand International class. They finished 16th overall.

On December 11, Pearson flew to New York City to pick up the Driver of the Year award and, not incidentally, the accompanying $10,000 check. The winner of the award was chosen by a 10-member panel of auto racing journalists. Appropriately, the luncheon celebrating Pearson was held at the 21 Club (named for its location on 21st Street). Looking uncomfortable in coat and tie, Pearson leaned against a doorway waiting on the festivities to begin. "Always fun to be in New York, but just for a little while," he said. "It's better when you're here to pick up some cash. And to be around people I respect and care about."

FOR DECADES, THE COLOR GREEN WAS CONSIDERED BAD LUCK BY DRIVERS. DARRELL WALTRIP PICKED UP A LUCRATIVE SPONSORSHIP FROM GATORADE EARLY IN HIS CUP CAREER. HE SAID PEARSON CHALLENGED HIM FOR SHOWING UP AT A TRACK "WITH GREEN ON YOUR CAR."

Pearson and about fifty guests, including team owner Glen Wood and NASCAR president Bill France Jr., dined on Manhattan chowder, escallopine of veal chareroi, and French peas etuvees. Pearson perhaps would have been happier with a steak and mashed potatoes. As for the check, he passed it along to Glen Wood as payment on a new Lincoln Mark V from the Woods' car dealership in Virginia.

Money was practically the only green thing Pearson allowed around him at racetracks. For decades, the color green and peanuts were considered bad luck by drivers. Pearson claimed he wasn't superstitious, "but why take a chance?" He would drive out of his way to avoid crossing a street after a black cat. Darrell Waltrip picked up a lucrative sponsorship from Gatorade early in his Cup career, and Waltrip's cars glowed with Gatorade green. He said Pearson challenged him for showing up at a track "with green on your car."

Pearson's 1976 season was also saluted by the City of Hope charities as part of a Las Vegas program that also honored other top athletes from that year. Ricky, Pearson's middle son, was along for the ride. "I met Kenny Stabler, Jerry Pate, even shook Joe Louis' hand," Ricky said. "That was a big deal to me. Daddy took it in stride, like it was nothing."

As Pearson raced deep into his second decade at the top level of NASCAR, he remained in excellent physical condition, in large part because he concentrated on strength and endurance exercises. When he was home, he visited the Spartanburg YMCA almost every morning, mixing a workout with a cup of coffee with friends. He also frequented the steam room. "I'd sit in there for hours at a time getting used to the heat," he said. "Then it didn't bother me in the race car. It wasn't bad to sweat."

By 1977, Petty, with fifteen more years to race, already had been the subject of two biographies. It was that season that saw the last of sixty-three one-two finishes by Petty and Pearson. Petty won the World 600 May 29, beating Pearson to the checkered flag by 30.8 seconds. The race was not a classic. Petty led 311 of the 400 laps. Pearson, who won the pole, led sixty-four.

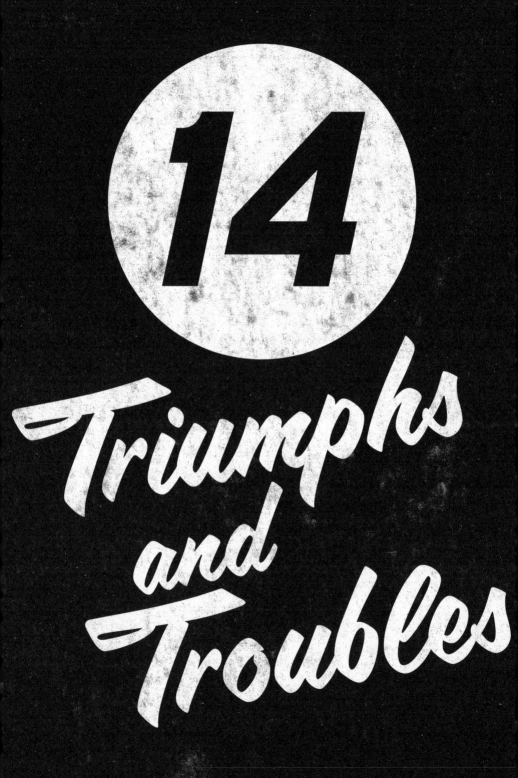

Kyle Petty was nineteen years old when he followed his grandfather and father into the Cup Series, making his first start in the Talladega 500 on August 5, 1979, at Talladega Superspeedway. It was a typically hot and humid race day in Alabama. Even the trees were sweating. Although he was seven laps behind winner Darrell Waltrip, Kyle scored a respectable ninth-place run, a finish boosted by the fact that twenty-one drivers—more than half the starting field—failed to complete the race because of crashes or mechanical issues.

Petty wasn't concentrating on that after the race. He was thinking about survival. About his next breath.

"My ass was kicked," he said, as he found a place to collapse on a concrete wall. Petty team members poured water on his face to offer some relief from the heat. David Pearson casually walked by, drinking a beer. He nudged the younger Petty in the ribs. "You're going to have to get a lot tougher to run with us," Pearson said. He walked on.

"Boy, those guys were so tough between the ears," Kyle said.

Pearson had finished second to Waltrip that day. Richard Petty was fourth, five laps in front of his son but two behind Waltrip.

The 1979 season, Kyle's first in the Cup Series, would be one of the most eventful in NASCAR history. Richard Petty won the Daytona 500 for the sixth time in wild circumstances that would propel NASCAR into a brighter spot on the national sports stage. Petty also won his seventh—and last—championship. On a day of high drama at Darlington Raceway, the stunningly successful partnership between Pearson and the Wood Brothers would end in an embarrassing failure that shook the auto racing world. And a rough, raw-boned kid named Dale Earnhardt, like Pearson a product of a Carolinas mill town, would emerge as the sport's next superstar.

But first, there was 1978 to plow through.

TRIUMPHS AND TROUBLES | **165**

The phone rang in the sports department of the Spartanburg, South Carolina Herald-Journal on a June afternoon in 1978, a Cup mechanic was on the line. "There's something you need to know," he said, "and you won't believe it. It's big."

It was big—headline news. Only a handful of people knew that Richard Petty, a Chrysler devotee, was a few days away from making a dramatic mid-season switch to Chevrolets. The Petty team had bought a Chevrolet from team owner and driver Cecil Gordon to replace its Dodge Magnum, a car so bulky and blocky it had been described as a cereal box on wheels. In the Petty pit, there were worse names for it. The car might have been great for hauling groceries, but for racing it was a stinker. The team had struggled with the Magnum from the start of the season, making futile efforts to turn a flying rectangle into a real race car. There were no wins through nineteen races, and Petty, stuck in a thirty-one-race winless streak that began in the 1977 season, ultimately made the drastic move to try a Chevrolet, as readers of *The Herald Journal* would discover in a shocking headline the next day. The word quickly spread through the rest of the racing community. Gordon said Maurice Petty had called him inquiring about purchasing a car. "It was such a shock I couldn't give him an answer right then," Gordon said. "But I called back later, and we worked it out. Richard came over with the truck and they got the car." Gordon, who raced from 1968 to 1985, scoring twenty-nine top-five finishes but no wins, was respected in NASCAR circles as a driver who fielded reliable cars. And the Chevrolet Petty bought was brand new.

The Magnum, Petty said, could not be salvaged. "It was about as tough a decision as any of us in the Petty crew have ever had to make in racing," he wrote in a column for *Stock Car Racing* magazine. "On top of it all, I wasn't feeling all that great about that time, and I had some lingering doubts deep down inside of me whether it wasn't Richard Petty that was at fault instead of the Magnum. . . . The Magnum is a big, bulky car that is so much wider, taller, broader, and thicker than anything we ran against that its very shape was a big strike against it."

"There was no way the Magnum was going to be competitive the way the rules were set up," Petty said after the switch. "I'm sure a lot of people are disappointed because we're leaving Chrysler, but I think if they're going to go to a race to see me, they'd rather see me win in a Chevrolet than lose in a Dodge. I still don't want racing to become an all-General Motors show, but I'm going to have to make it one way or another. I have to run by what the rules dictate."

Although there was a certain amount of relief in ditching the Dodge, Petty's troubles continued. He finished 1978 without a victory, marking the first season since 1959 he went winless. It was a decidedly un-Petty year.

The team's fortunes changed almost immediately in 1979 and in a bizarre way that would impact NASCAR forever.

Richard Petty wasn't supposed to win the Daytona 500 that year. He shouldn't even have been in the race. He was still in recovery mode from off-season stomach surgery and raced at Daytona against the advice of doctors. Petty had had marvelous success at one of NASCAR's marquee tracks, but, for this 500, he wouldn't be listed among the favorites. The race should have been decided between Cale Yarborough and Donnie Allison, who were wrestling for first place in the third turn on the last lap. Famously, they crashed, and their cars dropped off the banking, stock car racing's biggest prize lost. Wait a second . . . who's third? It's Richard Petty! He ran past the crash scene and took the checkered flag in front of Darrell Waltrip, scoring one of the oddest wins of his long career.

While Petty and his legion of fans were celebrating, Yarborough and Allison, and Donnie's brother, Bobby, who had stopped at the wreck scene, were engaging in fisticuffs, all for the enjoyment of a national television audience. It was "water cooler" stuff of the highest order, and NASCAR moved up a rung in the national consciousness. Contributing to the response to the crazy and complicated finish was a weather system that had dumped snow across much of the country, putting vast numbers of potential television viewers on their couches for the afternoon. CBS was the beneficiary; the network having agreed to make that year's 500 the first major NASCAR event televised flag-to-flag. The storm left Delaware covered with 26 inches (66 cm) of snow, and major cities in the Northeast and Midwest also were hammered. More than a foot (30.5 cm) of snow fell in parts of North Carolina. Meteorologists called it the worst storm to hit the Mid-Atlantic states in sixty years.

Watching television was a pleasant diversion, and people who had little knowledge of or interest in the sport suddenly became aware of this thing called stock car racing.

As the race rolled to a conclusion, Petty had been mostly forgotten. He led only twelve laps and was about a mile (1.6 km) behind the two leaders entering the final lap. Of the last 129 laps, he led only one—the last. When Allison and Yarborough crashed, Petty's crew chief Dale Inman yelled into the team radio, "Go for it. The leaders just wrecked."

CBS cameras followed both the race for the win and the brouhaha brewing on the track apron at the site of the Allison-Yarborough crash. "There were a lot of heated words," said track safety worker David Reep, one of the first to arrive at the wreck scene. "Next thing you know, it's a full-blown fight. It started with Cale and Donnie but got out of control when Bobby came up. You could tell that Cale was upset with Bobby. They had some heated words and then started fighting. The first part was Cale swinging his helmet around. Bobby was the first to get involved with the actual fisticuffs. Donnie was in it a little, but the main deal was Bobby and Cale."

After the race (and the fight), Yarborough called the accident "the worst thing I've ever seen in my life in racing. I started around Donnie and Donnie pulled out and carried me down into the grass. My car started spinning, and then we both started spinning. I had the race won. There are no ifs, ands, or buts about it. And he knew it, too." Allison said it was a case of the immovable object meeting the irresistible force. "I made up my mind to go low in the third turn," he said. "He was going low regardless. He wasn't going to give, and I wasn't going to give. As God is my witness—and on my mother, who was a very good lady—I never intended to block Cale. He had all the room he wanted on the outside. If he'd gone out there, I wouldn't have gone up there to block. But he hit me in the back bumper before he hit me in the side. He put himself on the apron, not me. I was determined that he wasn't going to get under me going down that backstretch. I had that position, so he was going to have to go around me. I wasn't getting into Turn 3 with him inside me. But I didn't put him on the apron, and I didn't block him."

For decades after, Allison and Yarborough, who mended fences and became close friends, would disagree on their confrontation in the third turn, each blaming the other. It was Allison's last, best chance to win a Daytona 500. Yarborough won four.

CBS Sports president Neal Pilson was overjoyed. The network's gamble to buy rights to the race and broadcast the entire 500 miles (805 km) had paid huge dividends. "It was a perfect storm, a watershed moment, one of the events you'll always remember," he said. "The way it turned out was one of the most incredible days of my life."

Petty appeared in the speedway press box for the winner's interview, his smile a mile wide. His first comment: "Where's the fight?" He had approached the race's closing laps with no designs on winning. He was protecting third place from the charging Waltrip. "I had to worry about Darrell," he said. "It was me and him. A.J. Foyt was a little behind us. All of us were running for third place. We were just in the right place at the right time. I wasn't thinking as much about winning the race as I was about beating Darrell."

PETTY APPEARED IN THE SPEEDWAY PRESS BOX FOR THE WINNER'S INTERVIEW, HIS SMILE A MILE WIDE. HIS FIRST COMMENT: "WHERE'S THE FIGHT?"

Waltrip said he wasn't sure where Yarborough and Allison were entering the last lap. "Then the caution lights came on when we were in one and two," he said. "I remember all three of us [Waltrip, Foyt, and Petty] let up for a second, then we took off again. We go on around, and I see two cars down there in the mud. Holy crap! I've got a chance to win this thing. I made a little dive at Richard at start-finish. I was elated how we ran. I couldn't believe the car ran like it did all day long. I think everybody was in the same boat—shocked. I couldn't believe those two knuckleheads wrecked each other coming to get the checkered. They were down there in the mud wrestling around, fighting. It didn't take long to figure out what happened. They were all wallowing around.

More power to them. We didn't care because we finished second."

Where was David Pearson during all this fun and frolic? Maybe on the way home to Spartanburg. He crashed out of the race on lap fifty-three, finishing 37th. He would not win another Daytona 500 after the spectacular finish with Petty in 1976.

Considering the background of Petty's sad 1978 season, the 500 victory meant more than most. Kyle Petty compared the scenario with 1961, when Lee and Richard Petty both crashed in Daytona 500 qualifying races and the team rolled home to North Carolina with no race cars and little cash. "We came off a bad year in 1978," Kyle Petty said. "We had fewer people working. We had cut the budget. Steve Hmiel and Richie Barsz put the body on that car. I helped put it together. That race in a lot of ways epitomized what Petty Enterprises was. We never gave up, never stopped pushing. That win meant a lot to our business."

The Petty victory also meant a lot to North Carolinian Dan Breuer, who won a little cash because he had made a bet with his father that Petty would win. With one lap to go and Petty nowhere near the lead, Breuer was a doubter, however. He handed a dollar to his father to pay off the bet. Then Petty won. "Son, the first thing you better learn is that it's never over," his father said. "Why did you give up on the white-flag lap? Why did you quit? Mr. Petty didn't quit." That story was repeated forty-five years later when Breuer received an award from the Mooresville-South Iredell (North Carolina) Chamber of Commerce. Petty was also honored at the chamber's annual meeting, and Breuer used the occasion to split his winnings with the King. Breuer's dad had told him if he ever met Petty that he should share the prize.

The sudden 500 win ended a spectacular week for the Pettys. Kyle, eighteen years old, made his racing debut the previous weekend, winning an Automobile Racing Club of America event at Daytona. He had a better car than practically everybody in the field—it was prepared at Petty Enterprises, after all, but the win was still a major moment for the Petty family. A victory in the boy's first time out? Impressive.

Watching anxiously for the one hour and thirty minutes of the race to reach an end were mom Lynda and Pattie, Kyle's wife of one week. And there was another anxious person—Dad. Richard Petty watched the race from atop the Petty team truck, sharing the space with fellow drivers Cale Yarborough and Donnie Allison, buddies for the moment but bitter rivals a week later. "It was very emotional, and I think everybody got caught up in it," Richard said. "I was probably more enthused about him winning than me. It was special to win races, but when you have a son coming along and he wins races, it's a special deal."

Petty said his son's win surprised him. "I told him when the race started to kind of get out of everybody's way, let eight or ten of them go and see what they do," Petty said. "They came by on the first lap and he was in front. He had never been in any kind of race car. He didn't have a clue."

Kyle Petty got a check for $4,150, a total he would remember for decades. And he got a "Hey, that's great, you did good," from his father. This was high praise from a Petty.

Richard and Kyle had left Level Cross earlier that month to test the car at Daytona, and they had not followed Mom's instructions. "I told you when you left here not to let him off the apron of the track," Lynda said.

It was around that same time that Richard Petty became the figure that thousands of race fans would come to recognize as the King. Kyle Petty had opened several shoe stores under the Kyle Petty's Boot Barn name, and a man hoping to sell cowboy hats in the stores delivered one for Kyle's inspection. It was a Charlie 1 Horse hat, enhanced with feathers and a fancy hatband. "That's where the hat started," Richard said. It would be the first of hundreds of Charlie 1 Horse models Petty would wear down through the years, and the image of the King with the cowboy hat and wrap-around sunglasses became his signature. "I usually have twelve to fifteen hats around," he said. "I'll wear one a while and then autograph it and give it away to a charity."

A cowboy hat on David Pearson's head? A rare sight, indeed.

After the February zaniness in Daytona provided enough drama to cover a season, there was much more two months later. The April 1979 race at Darlington Raceway would be a landmark event for both Pearson and Petty—and not for positive reasons.

With sixty-six laps remaining in the grueling 500 miles (805 km) on NASCAR's toughest track, Pearson, in contention for the win, pitted for fuel and tires. In a rare mistake, there was miscommunication between driver and team. Pearson thought the crew was changing two tires. The

Woods planned a four-tire change. Trying to beat leader Darrell Waltrip out of the pits and onto the track, Pearson bolted from the pit without lug nuts being tightened on his left-side wheels. The No. 21 crashed on pit road after the wheels fell off, a moment of major embarrassment for one of racing's slickest teams, one that had practically invented the modern pit stop.

Pearson's collapse left the race to Petty and Waltrip, and they engaged in one of the sport's great late-race chases. Petty led at the white flag. Waltrip drove underneath him in Turn 1, and Petty retaliated down the backstretch, taking first into Turn 3. Petty's momentum carried him high between the turns, and Waltrip ran to his inside, retaking the lead and winning by several car lengths.

The Darlington pit road incident wrote finish to one of racing's greatest partnerships. During the next week, team owner Glen Wood called Pearson and told him a parting of the ways would be best.

"It was a bad situation," rival crew chief Tim Brewer said. "Pearson told me later that he should have said he just made a mistake and that he'd have been in that car the rest of the way."

The Pearson-Woods split rocked the NASCAR world. They seemingly had the super team, and suddenly it was history. "I don't know what to say," Petty said. "They have had some tough luck, but you can't blame David or them. The only other story that would be as big would be me quitting Petty Enterprises." (A few years later, that statement would be draped in irony, as Petty indeed would leave home.)

At Charlotte Motor Speedway that week, a florist delivered a package from a group of Pearson fans. It contained twenty-one carnations—all painted black.

Although the trouble on pit road at Darlington was the flashpoint, it was not the only problem between Pearson and the team. After Darlington, both Pearson and team members talked about other issues that had popped up over the preceding months. The Darlington wreck was sort of the last act. Years later, Glen Wood admitted that "there had been a little friction where maybe that shouldn't have been. There shouldn't have been, but there was. Then they had a little problem and left the wheels loose, and he left the pits before they got them tight, and I guess all of that put together was why. But it was a bad decision to split then. We shouldn't have ever done that, but that's hindsight."

Helen Pearson, David's wife, told writer Bob Myers that the split disturbed her husband, who normally was calm and took virtually everything in stride. "You know, David never shows any emotion," she said. "But this hurt."

Forty-five years after the Darlington incident, Len Wood confirmed that other issues played into the sudden change. "Younger fellows were coming into the sport, guys like Darrell Waltrip and Dale Earnhardt," he said. "They were running hard from the start. Pearson's laid-back style had worked for years, but it was starting to not work as well. I think that was part of it. You're used to winning ten races a year; now you're winning three. I think times were changing. Winning fixes

"PEARSON'S LAID-BACK STYLE HAD WORKED FOR YEARS, BUT IT WAS STARTING TO NOT WORK AS WELL. YOU'RE USED TO WINNING TEN RACES A YEAR; NOW YOU'RE WINNING THREE."

things. If you're not winning . . ."

After Pearson's spectacular 1976 season (ten wins and the American Driver of the Year award), he dropped to two wins in 1977 and four in 1978. The highlight of his 1978 season was a win in the summer race at Daytona, his 48th superspeedway victory. It came at the expense of series point leader (and eventual champion) Cale Yarborough, then riding high with Junior Johnson's team. Pearson masterfully used the slower car of Baxter Price as a pick on the last lap to prevent Yarborough from making what probably would have been the winning pass. "I had him set up just like I wanted to, and he moved over on a slow car going down the backstretch and I didn't see it," Yarborough said. "I'm not mad about it because that's racing. Pearson used Price intentionally. But that's the Silver Fox. That's racing." Pearson said he planned his move laps ahead. "I had looked at the situation for two or three laps," he said. "I knew where Price was running. I knew I had to do something to get Cale off my back. What I did just happened to work to perfection."

Earlier that year, Pearson had recorded his landmark 100th Cup win, dominating the March race at Rockingham. Pearson led 219 of the 492 laps, including the final thirty-five, and outran Bobby Allison to the finish by 1.3 seconds. Richard Petty was fourth, two laps down. The win was one of the toughest of Pearson's 100, largely because of a late-race encounter with Benny Parsons. With about forty laps to go, Pearson had the lead in front of Parsons and Donnie Allison. Parsons drove low on the front straight to challenge for the lead, and he and Pearson collided in the first turn. Pearson's tires smoked as he spun out, while Parsons and Allison drove on. The caution flag flew, and Pearson, whose car wasn't damaged in the spin, pitted for fresh tires along with Parsons and Allison. Irritated by the contact, Pearson charged to the front and led the final thirty-five laps. "I was hot, as hot as I've ever been in racing," Pearson said. "He [Parsons] knocked the you-know-what out of me. But I had to realize before I tried to pass him that it was stupid to go and do something crazy. I wasn't going to knock him out, but I was determined to pass him." Pearson was stoic about reaching the century mark in wins, simply saying he would get started on the next hundred.

The start of the 1979 season didn't hold promise for Pearson. After finishing second at Riverside, California, in the opener, there were trials. Pearson crashed in the Daytona 500 and failed to finish at Rockingham and Atlanta because of engine failures. Darlington was next.

Glen Wood "felt I wasn't pushing the car at Darlington, that I wasn't as interested as I used to be," Pearson told reporters the week after the pit road crash. "That flew all over me. I told him to put somebody else in it and let them do the best they can." Alabama driver Neil Bonnett replaced Pearson in the No. 21 and eventually won nine races with the team.

Years later in an interview with NASCAR Images, Pearson provided some detail about the Darlington incident. "They did not tell me that they were going to change four tires, just a two-tire change," he said. "So, when I came in and made the pit stop, I did not see the guy squat down and take the left front wheel off because Glen was there leaning over the car cleaning the windshield. Darrell Waltrip was leading the race and come in right in front of me. So, they told me that I had to beat Darrell out. . . . The left side was loose and I didn't know that, so when they dropped it [the jack], I took off and made it down to the end of the pit road.

"That's not the reason we broke up. It was coming. I had been there long enough. We had already got to where we would argue about little things. . . . But we're the best friends of all right now. I guarantee, I think the world of them, all of them. . . . After I left them, I knew I could still drive."

There was a lot of back and forth during the week after Darlington, but the Woods and Pearson cleared the air quickly, and both parties soon realized the split was the biggest of their errors. "All of that just kind of happened," Eddie Wood said. "That probably wasn't the biggest mistake that's ever happened in our team's history. It's probably the first and second biggest mistake. I can't really explain how it happened. There was not a lot of conversation going on before that."

At that point, Pearson had 103 Cup victories. Forty-two of his forty-nine superspeedway victories had been scored with the Woods.

By the summer, Pearson was busy running Late Model Sportsman races at short tracks scattered across the country, picking up stacks of appearance money and thoroughly enjoying himself. He called it his second childhood. Pearson was the nationally known superstar riding into town to challenge the track regulars. He won some; he lost some. He always left with a pocket jammed with cash. And it was always that—cash. No checks accepted.

In August of that year, Pearson lost his best friend in racing, 1970 Cup champion Bobby Isaac. From similar backgrounds and with similar demeanors around garage areas, Isaac and Pearson became fast friends. Isaac died of a heart attack a day after pitting during a Late Model Sportsman race at Hickory Speedway (North Carolina) and collapsing after climbing out of the car. He was 45. "David talked to me about Bobby after that," Dale Inman said. "He said me and him were Bobby's best friends in the garage. I could tell it hit him hard."

If Pearson, who seemed very satisfied running short-track races for appearance money, needed redemption on the Cup circuit, it soon arrived, thanks to the misfortune of a young, bold driver on the rise—Dale Earnhardt.

Earnhardt, a rough-and-ready, square-shouldered throwback to the gritty days of intense short-track racing, had clawed his way up the ladder on Carolinas backwoods tracks to get a shot at Cup racing in 1975. Almost desperate to get his feet on the pedals of a Cup car, Earnhardt, at twenty-four years old, made the unfortunate move of choosing the exhausting, never-ending World 600 at Charlotte Motor Speedway for his first race. Driving a tired No. 8 Dodge owned by veteran driver Norman Negre and serviced by a ragtag crew, Earnhardt had jumped into the deep end of the pool without learning to swim. He started 33rd and banged around in the middle of the pack throughout the long and hot afternoon, finishing 22nd, forty-five laps behind the leaders. His distress during the race reached the point that he made

FOR ANYONE WHO THOUGHT PEARSON MIGHT HAVE LOST THE MAGIC, HE AGAIN PROVED HIS WORTH AT ONE OF RACING'S TOUGHEST TRACKS AND IN ONE OF ITS CLASSIC RACES.

one pit stop simply to get a drink of water.

Four years later, after a total of only nine Cup starts, Earnhardt got the chance to show his skills as he picked up a ride in potent cars owned by California businessman Rod Osterlund. He wasted little time cashing in, winning in his seventh race with the team April 1, 1979, at Bristol Motor Speedway. Long-time crew chief Jake Elder, the heart of the team, told Earnhardt to stick with him "and we'll have diamonds bigger than horse turds."

The season derailed four months later, however, when Earnhardt was hurt badly in a crash at Pocono Raceway, breaking both collarbones and sustaining other injuries. Although drivers often raced despite injuries, it was clear Earnhardt, racing through his rookie season and gaining fans weekly with an aggressive racing style, would be sidelined for at least a few weeks. Osterlund called Pearson, who agreed to fill Earnhardt's seat.

In Pearson's first race in the No. 2 car, he finished second at Talladega Superspeedway. Next was a fourth at Michigan International Speedway and then a seventh at Bristol. Next on the schedule was Darlington, a track Pearson owned in all respects except the deed. It was there, of course, where Pearson had wrecked on pit road in April. Could he gain redemption at the same track where he had driven off a figurative cliff? Literally, he could.

For anyone who thought Pearson might have lost the magic, he again proved his worth at one of racing's toughest tracks and in one of its classic races, the Southern 500. He carried Earnhardt's No. 2 car to a two-lap victory over Bill Elliott and then handed the reins back to Earnhardt for the next race. "It's always nice to come back and win at the same track where the Woods and I had actually split," Pearson said. "Yeah, it was a thrill. It was a disappointment in April 1979 but a thing of beauty in September 1979."

Doug Richert, who was crew chief for the No. 2 car, said Pearson meshed well with the Rod Osterlund–owned team. "He was a very laid-back guy," Richert said. "It was one of those deals where he had the talent. He had done it so many times that he knew exactly what he wanted. Some drivers know what they need to feel in the car to be successful. He was one of them.

"I was a young kid in a big arena when I started racing around all those guys. I was just amazed to be hanging around guys like Pearson and Petty. They were just like everyday guys because you were all in the garage area together. Richard Petty would come by and say, 'Can I help you?' I was welding. Growing up around them made them like family."

The day was another one of superlatives for Pearson at one of his top tracks.

"I must have been asked a million times why I have been so successful at Darlington," Pearson said. "It's hard to explain. I don't even know if I can explain it. I just like to race at Darlington, and I just have found a way to stay out of trouble there. You just have to be very smooth and not take any chances. If you do, the odds are something is going to happen. That place has just too many ways to beat you."

One member of the Petty family has no love for Darlington. "They should flood the place and turn it into a bass pond," said Kyle Petty, who raced fifty-one times at the track with no wins and no top-five runs. Like Kyle, many drivers never figured out the solution at Darlington.

Pearson had yet another big trophy for his collection. In the middle of the 1978 season, the Pearson family had moved from its home near downtown Spartanburg to a bigger house in Boiling Springs, north of Spartanburg. The ranch-style house had more room but more importantly came with a lot of surrounding property. Pearson's purchase included an old building that had housed a country store and enough land to build a race shop and a landing strip for his airplane.

"We all pitched in and moved stuff from the other house," said Eddie Pearson, David's youngest son, then in high school. "Before that, we had trophies scattered everywhere. We moved a lot of them into the old store building. It became sort of a trophy room and game room." Eddie and his high school pals played ping pong and pool surrounded by Pearson's race hardware.

Petty drove on to the championship in 1979, winning a fierce fight with Waltrip, the series' brash newcomer, in the final week. It was a season of joy for the 42-year-old Petty, who had been considered past his prime by many in the sport. He drove with a particular kind of aggression across much of that season, showing late-race strength at tracks where he might have faltered in previous runs. Waltrip scored more race wins (seven to Petty's five), but Petty had eighteen other finishes in the top five to Waltrip's twelve, and the NASCAR point system used that season loved that consistency. "We didn't win as many races as we did in some years, but we were as consistent as we've ever been," Petty said. "The only engine failure we had was in the opening race at Riverside, and the only other ones we didn't finish was when the car wrecked at Rockingham and Dover. So, we were running at the finish in twenty-eight of the thirty-one races and ended up in the top five twenty-three times, which says a lot for the team." He overcame a 229-point deficit in the final eleven races. "That was one of the greatest feats that our crowd has ever accomplished," Petty said.

Waltrip stormed into the series in 1972 and became a transformative figure. In a sport in which new drivers were expected to show a certain amount of deference to veterans, Waltrip took a different route, telling his story to anyone who would listen, stepping on toes as he climbed the ladder, and firing race-team members he considered below the performance level he expected. He was a man in a hurry. By the 1979 season, he had won fifteen times and seemed ready to win his first championship. As the season raced to a close, the title would be decided between Waltrip and Petty, the pretender against the King.

Waltrip, as he would admit years later, was still a work in progress that season. "I learned so much about myself that year—not so much about racing but about myself," he said. "I had become kind of arrogant, and I was determined to beat Richard, the King. I'll never forget Darlington when I beat Richard on the last lap, making a slingshot move out of Turn 4. I was determined to dethrone the King. He was all I ever heard about. It was a great opportunity to show my talent versus his talent. We traded the lead in the last ten laps. I ended up winning the race, passing him on the last lap. I probably would have been better off if I hadn't won that race. It just made me that much more obnoxious. I thought, 'I'm going to knock him off. He can't be the King forever.' He is, but I didn't know that at the time. I thought I had an advantage—him being older, me being younger, him on the back side of his career, me on the front side of mine. I found out he still had a lot of fight.

"Then I got a huge point lead, but I kept worrying about Richard and where he was and what he was doing. The first thing you know, we're in a battle."

The last race of the season was held at Ontario Motor Speedway in California. When the green flag flew, Waltrip, driving for up-and-coming DiGard Racing, had a two-point lead over Petty. On the 38th lap, John Rezek spun in the second turn, and Waltrip looped his car to avoid a crash. He lost a lap. "All I had to do was finish ahead of Richard," Waltrip said. "I got a lap down, couldn't get it back, and Richard won the championship. I'm the prime example of 'Don't beat yourself.' I blew that championship. It was mine to lose, and I lost it. That was a real wake-up call."

Petty finished fifth in the race, and Waltrip was eighth. Petty won his seventh championship by eleven points over Waltrip. No one was close to the top two.

"I learned to be on guard all the time," Waltrip said. "I learned that the hard way. It cost me the championship. I applied that knowledge. I had on my dash for a long time a note to not beat yourself. I beat myself in 1979, and I was determined I wasn't going to do that any more. I learned so much about myself that year. I thought Bobby Allison was my friend. He kind of was and he kind of wasn't. Bobby was one of those guys who was your buddy as long as you couldn't beat him, but if you ever got to where you could race with him or beat him, not so much. Bobby and I became not enemies, but 'frenemies.'"

Petty celebrated what became his final championship. "Darrell was his own worst enemy," Petty said. "He'd shoot that crap off, and nobody paid any attention. He tried to use that psychological stuff on us. Hey, man, we've been racing thirty years, so that didn't bother us."

In the aftermath of the loss of the championship, DiGard fired crew chief Buddy Parrott. Two months later, he was rehired. It was good to have his job back, Parrott said, but it was tough to miss the Christmas bonus check. "But Darrell came to my rescue," Parrott said. "He came by my house and wrote me a check for Christmas." A few years later, Parrott would be turning wrenches for Petty on some very successful Sundays.

Robin Pemberton was a rookie crew member on the No. 43 team in 1979. "Back then I don't know if we had twenty-five people on the team," he said. "That included everybody. Everybody multi-tasked. It was crazy. And we drove everywhere—no planes. I worked five years in the sport before I ever flew to California. We had a truck and Comfort Coach vans. One group would leave on Wednesday or Thursday and the rest later. Some would show up the night before the race."

Pemberton worked with Richie Barsz, the team's lead fabricator. "Richie had no 'governor,'" Pemberton said. "He let you have it. I learned a lot from him, but, boy, he was critical of everything. He put you in your place quite a bit. But he was a real smart guy. Could do anything, and he'd get some stuff done."

Barsz didn't waste a lot of time, and he knew the expectations. "When I worked with Petty, it wasn't whether you were going to win, it was how much you were going to win by," Barsz said. "And you were pissed when you didn't win by that much. I never had a bad day work-

EVEN THOUGH LEE PETTY EVENTUALLY GAVE UP HIS ROLE AS TEAM LEADER TO SONS RICHARD AND MAURICE, HE CONTINUED TO SHOW UP AT RACETRACKS, WHERE HE OCCASIONALLY SERVED IN A SORT OF SPY ROLE FOR THE TEAM, OTHER DRIVERS SAID.

ing there. Everybody was great to work with. And Lee Petty—he was a borderline genius."

Even though Lee Petty, who drove for the last time in 1964, eventually gave up his role as team leader to sons Richard and Maurice, he continued to show up at racetracks, where he occasionally served in a sort of spy role for the team, other drivers said. Darrell Waltrip said Lee would casually stroll through the garage, smoking a pipe and now and then taking a sneak peek under and around cars of other teams. Team owner Bud Moore said Lee was following his own advice. "Lee Petty told me years and years ago, back about 1950," Moore said. "He told me to just look and see what you can see. He'd come up and look at my car and look around and all this kind of stuff. What he was doing is being observant and seeing what he could see. He would come up and I would have the hood up and we would start going through inspection. He would walk up and start talking and joking and all this stuff. All he was doing was looking to see what kind of springs, what kind of sway bar and what else we were doing underneath the hood of that car."

Lee also kept up on shop goings-on, Richard said. "Daddy's just got to know everything that's going on," he said. "If I'm talking to someone in the office, and he doesn't know exactly who it is or what the matter is, he'll open the door and flip the ashes off his cigar, just to find out."

Pemberton said team members spent virtually all their time on the road together, sharing meals and down time. He saw the Richard Petty phenomenon up close and personal. "In respect to his fans, Richard behaved in a gentlemanly manner," he said. "He'd never have a glass of wine or a beer at dinner. He was clean-cut in nature. He respected his fans."

Waltrip, who lost that championship battle to Petty before scoring three titles in the 1980s, also had his share of on-track tussles with Pearson. In August 1978, they were in a tight race for the win at Michigan International Speedway. Waltrip had the lead taking the white flag, but Pearson outran him on the last lap for the victory. "I had been within a few car lengths of lapping him when the caution came out," Waltrip said. "He comes around and gets caught up, and I look in the mirror and he's back there smoking a cigarette. I'm thinking, 'This is not a good sign.' He got by me and won the race.

"I think racers must have a really small brain because from one race to the next you forget about what happened before. David loved to do that. That was his trademark move. You didn't get him excited."

In 1981, NASCAR made a dramatic shift in rules for the Cup Series. In response to the general public's attraction to smaller passenger cars, NASCAR shortened the wheelbase of its Cup cars, changing many of the dynamics of race preparation for teams.

Drivers and crews arrived in Daytona Beach that February with many questions about how the new, smaller cars would perform in the draft. Bobby Allison surprised the rest of the garage area by showing up with a Pontiac LeMans, and his car was the class of the field in practice and qualifying. No one was close. Allison dominated the race, leading 117 laps, but circumstances would open the door for Petty to win his seventh and last 500.

The lead group made final pit stops with about twenty-seven laps to go. Allison and the other leaders pitted for fuel and tires. Dale Inman, realizing Petty's only chance at victory was a different strategy, called in Petty for fuel only. The short pit stop put Petty in front for the final twenty-seven laps—the only laps he led all day. Inman's confidence that Petty's tires would hold up to the checkered flag led to the victory.

Petty said Allison had the fastest car. "Under normal circumstances, he would have won easy," Petty said. "Then I came in but took on only enough fuel to go the distance and picked up maybe twelve to thirteen seconds on the others. The quick stop did two things. First, it put me in the lead, and second, it gave my car a chance to run better. It seemed as if the car handled easier and didn't jump around as much when it was running by itself. When we were in a crowd, like just before the pit stops, it wasn't handling all that good. Bobby made a heck of a run, knocking off almost a second a lap but couldn't catch me."

Petty won by three seconds, and he drove his car into a victory lane fired with emotion. Inman, the point man in the win, was in tears, and it wasn't because of the unexpected victory. A Petty team member since Richard's early days in racing, Inman had agreed to move to Rod Osterlund's team to become vice president and work with Dale Earnhardt. In 1983, Inman left there to join the Billy Hagan team, where he won the Cup championship with driver Terry Labonte in 1984. Inman returned to Petty Enterprises in 1986. In 2012, he became the first crew chief inducted into the NASCAR Hall of Fame.

*I*t was a homecoming of epic proportions, a moment burnished with nostalgia. David Pearson sat in the driver's seat of the Wood Brothers No. 21 Ford September 26, 1989, at Charlotte Motor Speedway. The whole scene looked natural, Pearson tightening his belt harness while members of the team put final touches on the race car.

David Pearson racing for the Wood Brothers again, a decade after their dramatic split following a pit-road mistake at Darlington Raceway? Indeed, that was the goal. Neil Bonnett, the Woods' driver, was injured, and Pearson had been invited to run the October 8 Charlotte 500-miler (805 km) in his place. It would be a reunion draped in sentiment and fun. But first Pearson, who hadn't run a long-distance race in three years, had to prove—mainly to himself—that he could do it.

The test runs proved positive, and Pearson left CMS that day planning to make his return to Cup racing with the team that had ridden with him to great heights in the 1970s. The next morning, those hopes were dashed. Pearson woke up with major back and neck pain. His back had been an issue for decades. "He had gone to several doctors over the years about his back," his son Ricky Pearson said. "I've seen him have to get down on the floor because of it. It would take him fifteen minutes to get up to where he could sit down. When it hit him, it hit him hard."

*P*earson was openly disappointed about missing the chance to race again with the Woods.

"I wanted to run one more time with them just as bad as they wanted me to run," Pearson said. "I felt like I could have done good there. The car ran really good, and I didn't try to run as fast as I could. But the next morning my back was hurting really bad. I knew then that I wouldn't be able to make 500 miles [805 km]. I could have started the race, but that wouldn't have been fair to them or the fans. I just said I wouldn't do it."

Ricky Pearson said his father "loved the Wood boys. It would have been a good deal if he could have driven that car that one last time."

Pearson finally had to bring the "R" word into the conversation. Although he was convinced he could drive a race car as well as anyone for some number of laps, he was also certain that his nagging back issues wouldn't allow him to compete through an hours-long race. Although he would run in mostly local short-track races now and then, Pearson's big-time racing career was over. He was retired. "I don't want to say it now," he said. "It's hard for me to say it, but, heck, I might as well go ahead. If I can't run at Charlotte, I can't run anywhere else. All this is making tears come to my eyes. I just don't know how to say it." For a man who rarely showed emotion, it was a dramatic public moment.

Pearson raced for the last time in the Cup Series on August 17, 1986, at Michigan International Speedway. Driving a Chevrolet from his Spartanburg shop, he finished 10th, a lap down. There was no prerace announcement that the race would be Pearson's finale, and thus there was no "farewell" observance, no public goodbye, no parting gifts, no farewell tour—no acknowledgement of a great career reaching an end.

Although he was fifty-one years old, Pearson wanted to keep the door ajar ever so slightly for the possibility of more racing, and he simply refused to admit—or even believe—that he was fifty-one.

When Pearson finally retired, there were those who suggested he still had the first dollar he had ever won. Pearson had a reputation as a man tight with money, a charge he often denied. "Members of the racing gang think I am a Scrooge," he said. "I'm really not. Truthfully, I enjoy spending money. I usually buy within reason what I want, and I don't hold back when it comes to doing what I want to do. I just don't throw money away, especially money I don't have." It was true that he wasn't wasteful with money, but if he wanted something he usually got it. When his friends talked about how fast their boats ran on a lake near Spartanburg, Pearson bought a faster boat. He owned a pontoon boat and a Jet Ski. When friends in his motorcycle group boasted about their rides, Pearson got a faster one. And, for no apparent reason, he bought a helicopter.

Already a pilot and owner of a small plane, Pearson became interested in helicopters. He traveled to Piney Flats, Tennessee, to meet Bob McNab, owner of a helicopter sales operation. Soon, he owned one, a Bell 206 with a price tag of $175,000. McNab introduced Pearson to John

Berry, a local instructor. "They took off and came back about an hour and 15 minutes later," McNab said. "I'm standing on the ramp at the heliport. John got out of the helicopter, and David took off in it. I said, 'John, what are you doing turning him loose already?' He said, 'I've never seen anything like it. The guy is so good. His hand-to-eye coordination is the best I've ever seen. We could have come back earlier, but I thought I'd give him at least an hour.' I never knew of anybody who had done what he did in less than eight or 10 [instructional] hours."

Years after he drove the last lap, Pearson said he didn't miss the racing. "It's the people you miss," he said. "Every once in a while, I'll watch on TV and wonder why in the world this driver doesn't do this or that. I'll see somebody trying to make a pass, and I'll say, 'Do this or that.' I see a lot of mistakes on TV that I think I could do different. Of course, it's altogether different when you're sitting in that car."

Richard Petty is many things—racer, businessman, philanthropist, product pitchman, father, grandfather, and great-grandfather. And he's a staunch Republican.

Petty has supported conservative Republicans and also has been involved directly in politics. He served sixteen years as a Randolph County commissioner. In 1996, North Carolina Republicans put him on the ballot for Secretary of State, a move widely seen as a prelude to a possible run for governor. But Petty's popularity as a race car driver wasn't enough. He lost by 200,000 votes to Democrat Elaine Marshall.

Petty politics include the 1980 presidential campaign and his endorsement of the candidacy of former Texas governor John Connally. More famous for having been wounded during the assassination of President John F. Kennedy than for any of his achievements as governor, Connally was a decided underdog in the race for the Republican presidential nomination, and the help of a beloved athlete like Petty was very welcome at his campaign headquarters.

Petty agreed to do a promotional spot for Connally's campaign, and it was shot in the media center at Daytona International Speedway during race week. The Soviet invasion of Afghanistan was a major issue during the campaign, and the script called for Petty to point out that Connally would be the best candidate to handle that issue, among others.

The spot took several takes to complete, largely because Petty's North Carolina drawl and the pronunciation of "Afghanistan" didn't mesh well. After a couple of misfires, Petty, a bit frustrated, looked at the group around him and said, "Heck, why does anybody want that place anyway?"

Connally's campaign fizzled quickly (through no apparent fault of Petty). Ironically, the man who beat Connally (and ultimately won the presidency), California governor Ronald Reagan, would share one of the major moments of Petty's long career only four years later.

It came on a hot summer day in 1984 in Daytona Beach. Reagan, recognizing a solid voter base when he saw one, planned a long day at Daytona International Speedway to meet drivers and fans and see the racing up close in the Firecracker 400. How close it would become, he had no idea. Neither did anyone else.

Reagan wasn't at the track for the start of the race, but he was part of the opening show, anyway. He gave the command to start engines from Air Force One as he flew to the speedway, landing at the airport adjacent to the track. Alert photographers got iconic shots of the giant white and blue airplane dropping onto the runway as Petty's No. 43 ran down the parallel backstretch. The president and the King in their favorite machines.

Cale Yarborough and Petty were the stars of the day. Petty led fifty-three laps, Yarborough seventy-nine. No one else led more than eleven. Over the final seventy-two laps, either Petty or Yarborough was in front. They wrestled into the final miles, with the grandstand crowd, a national television audience, and a president anticipating a dash to the checkered. That idea was modified with two laps to go when a crash in the first turn brought out the caution flag. Under rules in effect that season, drivers raced back to the caution flag. The field wasn't "frozen" as in current rules. The race to the start-finish line under the caution flag would determine the winner. Petty had the lead, but Yarborough passed him in Turn 3. Petty dropped to the inside, and they raced side by side, bumping slightly, as they raced to the finish line. Petty won by a few feet (1 m). Reagan watched the finish from a suite high above the track, later sharing his astonishment at competition that close at 200 miles per hour (322 km per hour).

Yarborough should have finished second, but in the excitement of the moment, he became the trigger to one of NASCAR's all-time great trivia questions. Who finished second in the 1984 Firecracker 400? It wasn't Yarborough. He rolled around the track and headed for pit road, assuming the race was over. There was another lap to complete, however, and before Yarborough realized his error and returned to speed, Harry Gant had taken second place and became the trivia answer.

"I THINK FOR THE LAST TEN OR TWELVE LAPS HE HAD FIGURED OUT WHAT HE WAS GOING TO DO, AND I WAS TRYING TO FIGURE OUT WHAT HE WAS GOING TO DO, TOO. HE DID EXACTLY WHAT I THOUGHT HE WOULD DO. HE JUST HAD TO DO IT QUICKER."

"It came down to Cale and myself," Petty said years later. "When we came across the start-finish line, someone was wrecking down in the first corner, and we knew it was the last lap. I think for the last ten or twelve laps he had figured out what he was going to do, and I was trying to figure out what he was going to do, too. He did exactly what I thought he would do. He just had to do it quicker. I think all of our strategy went out the window. We just pushed it to the floor, and I happened to get back first."

The win was Petty's landmark 200th—and his last. He joined Reagan in a speedway suite to celebrate the occasion, and Reagan later visited the garage area, where he dined on fried chicken with many of the drivers. It was a big day for NASCAR, and the race is remembered as one of the greatest races in the sport's history.

"I never doubted we could get the 200th win," Petty said years later. "After the 199th, we were fairly competitive in every race we ran. All we needed was the right circumstances. I don't remember that much about the race. I don't remember where Cale was. I don't even remember how we got together at the end. Cale had a really good car, and we did. The end of the race is what I really remember. Winning on the last speed lap, side by side, smoke flying on July 4 in front of the president. One thing it did that NASCAR hadn't had before—Reagan put us on the front page and we put him on the sports page."

Petty's 200th had been anticipated since he won No. 199 at Dover, Delaware, on May 20 of that year. In fact, some important people a figurative world away in Washington, D.C., had been looking toward No. 200 much earlier. Officials at the Smithsonian Institution had been made aware of Petty's march toward 200, and there was contact between Smithsonian representatives and members of Petty's team as early as 1983 about the possibility of the 200th win–car being obtained by the Smithsonian, the country's repository for historic items. Phone calls and letters bounced back and forth between museum officials, Petty team members, and car owner Mike Curb, leading to the car arriving at the Smithsonian. Petty and family members attended a ceremony at the Smithsonian in 1985 and later were guests of Reagan in the White House.

The car has been displayed in the National Museum of American History, one of several Smithsonian units on the National Mall in Washington. Most recently, it has been part of a National Air and Space Museum exhibit called "Nation of Speed." The exhibit also includes an IndyCar driven by Mario Andretti and a motorcycle from daredevil showman Evel Knievel's collection.

Petty said the Smithsonian wanted his car after the 200th win, but he said the team needed it to run at Talladega because it was the only superspeedway car in the stable. "I ran Talladega, and we didn't tear it up," he said. "We cleaned it up, put it on a flatbed trailer, and hauled it up to Washington. When we got there, we wiped it all down. In the museum, they had to use special lights and had to watch humidity levels with it. I said, 'Man, it ain't nothing but a race car.' But it's something special. Millions of people would like to give stuff to the Smithsonian that they don't even take. That they asked for it made it very, very special."

Petty came close to victory No. 201 on April 12, 1987, at Bristol Motor Speedway. He shadowed eventual winner Dale Earnhardt over the closing laps. "Near the end of the race, I was catching him a little," Petty said. "I talked to him when it was over. I told him I had already picked out a place on his left rear quarter-panel where I was going to pass him, but I never got close enough." Petty lost to the man who had replaced him at the top of the sport by 0.78 of a second. Earnhardt led the final 115 laps.

The Intimidator was steadily taking over from the King.

The seasons before Petty's 200th win were a tangle of emotions for both Petty and Pearson. There were fewer wins and more issues for both drivers as they rolled into their final on-track years. Both rejected repeated suggestions that they retire, Petty continuing to run full schedules and Pearson dropping in for sporadic starts.

After winning the 1979 Southern 500 while substituting for the injured Dale Earnhardt, Pearson ran nine races for longtime team owner Hoss Ellington in 1980. "People are saying a lot of things about Hoss and myself, but I can still win races," Pearson said. "I don't have to prove anything. We will be competitive and with a little bit of luck we will win a race." He did just that, finishing first in the spring Rebel 400 at Darlington, an appropriate location for the 105th and final checkered flag of his career. "The perfect time for him to quit would have been when he won that race," Ricky Pearson said. "I think he kept doing what he was doing because of us [the Pearson sons], to keep us in racing. He didn't have to do that."

In 1981, Pearson saw what appeared to be a great opportunity disappear in tragedy. New York real estate developer and speedboat racer Joel Halpern started a NASCAR team in 1980 and signed Pearson as driver for a limited schedule for the 1981 season. Pearson had run only three races when Halpern was killed March 28 in a collision between two racing boats being prepared for competition on Lake Ponchartrain in New Orleans. "What in the world can I say?" Pearson said after hearing about the accident. "I don't even know what to think about it. He was doing what he wanted to do just like I'm doing what I want to do."

Pearson ran a final race with the team, finishing eighth at Darlington April 12, before the operation closed. "Dad said the Halpern deal was one of the best he ever had," Ricky Pearson said.

From 1982 to 1984, Pearson ran twenty-eight races with team owner Bobby Hawkins of Travelers Rest, South Carolina. Pearson didn't win any races in the Hawkins cars, but he was up to his old tricks prior to the 1982 World 600 at Charlotte Motor Speedway, scoring a major upset by winning the pole—and its $16,200 prize—for the race. It was Pearson's first race for the team. "That wasn't bad for a car right out of the box with a has-been driver and a never-was crew chief," said team crew chief David Ifft, a longtime traveler of NASCAR pit roads.

Pearson raced eight times with Ellington's team in 1985 and then fielded his own cars from his Spartanburg shop for four races. He ran two races in 1986 in Pearson Racing cars. With sponsorship from Chattanooga Chew tobacco, Pearson jumped into the ownership game in 1985, dipping into the Cup Series for a few races but devoting full-time to the second-tier Busch Series, fielding cars for his oldest son, Larry. That family endeavor bore fruit, as Larry won Busch championships in 1986 and 1987 with brothers Ricky (crew chief) and Eddie (tire changer) assisting. Although David owned the team, Eddie was listed as the owner for NASCAR's purposes, meaning the owner's championship trophies for those years carry Eddie's name. They rest in his home, special products of pride from the Pearson racing years.

Larry Pearson sat in one of the toughest positions in sports—the son of a Hall-of-Fame athlete. His results always would be compared with his father's. It was a hard road to drive.

"But I didn't feel any pressure about it," Larry told *The Scene Vault*. "I always wanted to be like him or even outdo him. Of course, there was no way to do that, but I tried. Nothing wrong with being compared to David Pearson. My goal was to try to win as much as him, as many championships. It just wasn't meant to be, but I'm very satisfied with what I did in racing."

David served as Larry's spotter, a pairing that wasn't always ideal. "He offered help when I asked, but the biggest mistake we made was letting him be my spotter," Larry said. "It got so bad that we started giving Dad a radio that was half-charged . . . just so I wouldn't have to listen to, 'I'm going to tell you one more time, boy, how to get in that corner.' We were at Charlotte, and he came on the radio and said, 'Look here, getting into the first turn you have to get higher.' I said, 'I'm as high as I can go.' He said, 'No, you're not.' The caution came out. He said, 'All right, get up close to the wall.' I was up close. He said, 'Closer.' I scraped the wall. I said, 'I hit the wall.' He said, 'Why did you do that?' I said, 'You told me to keep getting closer.'

"I would get aggravated sometimes with him spotting for me, but I enjoyed everything he taught me. It was great to have him around."

Larry scored his first Busch Series win on October 13, 1984, at Hickory Motor Speedway in North Carolina in the Bobby Isaac Memorial. "That win was so special to me because Bobby and Daddy were such great friends," Larry said. "It was a close finish with Jack Ingram. He was right on my butt for the last 20 laps, bumped me a couple of times but didn't hit me hard enough to turn me." David said Larry's win was "no fluke. He beat Jack Ingram, Dale Jarrett, Tommy Houston, and Sam Ard in that order, and that's a strong lineup. He's coming on strong."

LARRY PEARSON SAT IN ONE OF THE TOUGHEST POSITIONS IN SPORTS—THE SON OF A HALL-OF-FAME ATHLETE. HIS RESULTS ALWAYS WOULD BE COMPARED WITH HIS FATHER'S.

Eleven years later, on March 25, 1995, Larry won a Busch race at Darlington Raceway, conquering the mean old track his father had mastered. "My first win was the most valuable to me, but Darlington was definitely second," he said. "I was a happy boy. Everybody was happy. It was a good deal to win there."

All three Pearson sons drove race cars of one kind or another. Ricky spent much of his career as a crew chief, and Eddie worked for several teams as a tire changer and mechanic.

Larry McReynolds worked with Pearson Racing as a mechanic in 1983 and 1984. He reported to the Pearson shop in August 1983. "I was maybe a little intimidated," McReynolds said. "David Pearson is one of the guys I'd go to Talladega to watch as a young fan. This was the Silver Fox, second winningest Cup driver to ever come along. I was probably more starstruck than anything."

McReynolds said Pearson generally took a hands-off approach to the building of the team's cars. "But he was there every day," McReynolds said. "He was so structured. At noon, it didn't matter if you were in the middle of putting an engine in, he'd cut the lights off and say, 'Let's go to lunch.' It was like clockwork." Lunch generally was at Jimmy's Restaurant near downtown Spartanburg. "David was a gambler," McReynolds said. "He would bet on which leaf was going to fall off a tree first. We'd match for lunch. He even did that with Jimmy [Boukedes], who owned the restaurant. There were a lot of Fridays that he'd shut the lights off and say, 'We're going golfing.' He wouldn't let you say no."

McReynolds worked on the car Pearson drove in the 1984 Daytona 500. "David had never run a qualifying lap at 200 miles per hour [322 km per hour] at Daytona his whole career," McReynolds said. "In January testing we were pretty quick. He had run 45.20 [seconds per lap], and 45 even was 200 miles per hour [322 km per hour]. We had 20 degrees of rear spoiler on the car. We knew we'd have more engine when we got back to Daytona for qualifying. I built a spoiler with 10 degrees. We unloaded with 20 degrees of spoiler and ran 45.15 in the first practice. Ricky [Pearson] and I made the decision to go with the 10-degree spoiler, which should make the car faster. I went to the truck and got the spoiler. David was standing there leaning against the garage. He said, 'What is that?' I said, 'It's a 10-degree spoiler.' He said, 'You might as well put that bitch back on the trailer. I'm not running with that.'" Pearson's qualifying lap was 45.03.

Johnny Davis, later a team owner in NASCAR's No. 2 series, worked on Larry Pearson's Busch Series crew in 1987. "David and I butted heads a lot," said Davis, smiling at the memory. "We were a lot alike.

That made it interesting. It was a good time. He was at the shop every day, and he kept saying we weren't working hard enough, that we couldn't have made it in his era. But he was one of the guys. He respected us and treated us like he did everybody else.

"I remember working in the shop getting ready to go to Daytona, and it started snowing. David came in and said, 'Did you bring any clothes to work?' I said, 'No, sir, I don't bring clothes to work.' He said, 'Well, you're not going home tonight. It's snowing, but we're going to work on these damn race cars. I don't want you saying you can't get to work because it's snowing. You'll just have to wear the same clothes tomorrow.' He wouldn't let me go home. Made me stay over in his house in the spare bedroom."

Davis said Pearson had a "fatherly pride" about his sons' success, "but he was not someone who blew his own horn. He was proud, but he didn't brag about it. No emotion. He was the same David morning and night."

The Pearson operation shut down in 1990, but Pearson had plenty to do. Among other things, he continued to own and manage numerous commercial rental properties in and around Spartanburg.

The 1983 season saw one of the Petty team's great failures, one that scarred the King's reputation and led to a circumstance few would have imagined—Richard leaving Petty Enterprises.

With a late-race charge, Petty won the October 9 Miller High Life 500 at Charlotte Motor Speedway. Along pit road, there was surprise at the increased speed Petty's car showed after the final round of pit stops. The reason quickly became evident. During the last pit stop, Petty's crew had switched tires, placing tires made for the right side on the left and tires made for the left side on the right, significantly improving the car's grip factor. This move was illegal. Compounding the problem was the size of the engine in Petty's Pontiac. It was much bigger than allowed, measuring at 381 cubic inches (6.2 L) instead of the NASCAR maximum size of 358 (5.9 L). Following long-standing practice, NASCAR allowed Petty to keep the win, lining up with NASCAR founder Bill France Sr.'s belief that fans who saw the finish at the track should leave the race knowing they witnessed the actual result. Petty was fined $35,000, then the largest fine in NASCAR history. He was also docked 104 points.

The drama began in victory lane, even as Petty started the celebration of his 198th career win. Whispers began that there was a major problem with the car. After victory lane photos were completed, Petty was escorted to the press box above the frontstretch for the winner's formal interview. While he was answering questions, a NASCAR official called from the inspection area, telling Petty team representative Steve Tucker that Petty should meet immediately with NASCAR president Bill France Jr. in a suite near the press box. There, France, accompanied by NASCAR executive Jim Foster, listed the issues. The win would not be vacated, France said, but there would be big penalties.

CHEATING WAS NOTHING NEW IN NASCAR, BUT FOR ONE OF THE SPORT'S BEDROCK TEAMS TO BE CAUGHT WITH MAJOR VIOLATIONS—A VERY FAT ENGINE?—WAS QUITE UNUSUAL.

"I came back to the press box and made the announcement that included that Richard had accepted NASCAR's penalty," Tucker said. Neither Petty nor Tucker took questions from media members. "I called my boss Ralph Salvino [of Petty team sponsor STP] and said, 'Hey, I've got some news for you. Richard won the race. But we have a little issue,'" Tucker said.

Not surprisingly, the Petty violations were big news across the world of motorsports. Fans of the No. 43 were staggered by the goings-on, and media members pressed team principals for weeks for definitive answers about what happened and why. Cheating was nothing new in NASCAR, but for one of the sport's bedrock teams to be caught with major violations—a very fat engine?—was quite unusual.

The day became known as Black Sunday. Petty left the track with the glare of television lights in his face and his right arm draped around the shoulders of his wife Lynda.

"When I got home from work Monday at my little apartment in Greensboro, there was somebody from *The Charlotte Observer* waiting on my doorstep wanting to talk about it," team co-crew chief Robin Pemberton said. "I didn't know about it. Obviously, there were people in the organization who knew. But I wasn't privy to that information."

Engine builder Maurice Petty took the blame for at least part of the problem. "I did it," he told media members a few days later. "And I'm not so sure I wouldn't do it again under similar circumstances. What I don't like is people calling my brother Richard the cheater. I'm the one who cheated. Not him." Maurice had responded to what he considered cheating by other teams, figuring if his competitors had oversized engines, he should have one, too. "We kept getting outrun," he said. "They kept hollering for more horsepower. It's kind of like that deal—when in Rome, do as the Romans."

Richard later said the Charlotte fiasco "may well have been the worst moment of my career. That was a black time at Petty Enterprises. It was tough on all of us." Petty said he had no knowledge of the big engine or the tire swap.

Bill France Jr. later underlined the blatant nature of the violations. "It was like a bank robber walking down the sidewalk waving a shotgun," he said.

Modern NASCAR inspections are much more detailed than those of the 1980s. "Now they've got what they call the room of doom that cars have to go through for inspection," longtime Petty crew chief Dale Inman said. "Back in the day, that thing probably would have burned down."

The Charlotte fiasco exacerbated some in-house issues that had been bubbling at Petty Enterprises. Petty started looking for other driving opportunities and wound up in discussions with car dealership owner Rick Hendrick, who was starting a team for the 1984 season, the beginning of what would become a multi-car championship juggernaut. "It was almost common knowledge in our compound that he was going to Hendrick," Pemberton said. "He actually drove a car around that had a Hendrick plate on it for a while." That deal fell through, however, and Petty eventually signed with Californian Mike Curb. In April 1984, the Petty shop closed, although the shutdown would be temporary. Maurice Petty opened Maurice Petty and Associates, a consulting firm, but he and Richard would reunite under the Petty team umbrella in 1986.

On July 18, 1991, Helen Pearson, David's wife, died at the age of 58 after a long battle with cancer. When the disease was diagnosed, Pearson became Helen's main caretaker, staying near her bedside and helping her through the darkest days. "Helen's ordeal is the hardest thing I've ever gone through," he said. "I cared for her for 13 months, doing things I never thought I'd be able to do, and I feel better about it because I did. When she died, she seemed to have a smile on her face. I'll never forget that. When you're married to someone 'all your life' it takes time to get over it."

Helen Pearson had surgery for a brain tumor, but doctors told the family she probably wouldn't live much more than a year. "That was hard on my daddy," Ricky Pearson said. "He did all he could do for her. She was in bed at home for months. He stayed with her."

NASCAR was changing dramatically as the 1990s opened. Most tracks boasted sellout crowds, and many added new grandstands. Bristol Motor Speedway, one of the tour's most popular stops, had 150,000 seats and still had a long waiting list for tickets. New tracks opened in Fort Worth, Texas; Fontana, California; Loudon, New Hampshire; and Las Vegas, Nevada. *Sports Illustrated* magazine, in a laudatory cover story, called NASCAR "America's Hottest Sport" and proclaimed it "an unspoiled bastion of Americana." New fans, far from the NASCAR stereotype, were drawn to the sport, making a wild and not always comfortable (but profitable) mix of the old and the new. Total attendance at Cup races in 1995 was reported to be about five million, more than doubling figures from the mid-1980s. *Sports Illustrated* noted that NASCAR merchandise sales totaled $400 million in 1994, a dramatic increase from $60 million only four years earlier. NASCAR also found more ways to get fans closer to their heroes, expanding spectator access to garage areas and pit roads, and speedways built "fan zones" to offer extra amenities. In many cases, driver autographs were easy to grab, and fans didn't have to pay for them like they did with those super-rich football and basketball players.

This period also saw a new emphasis on driver fitness. Much younger drivers were streaming into the sport, and most of them were on strict diets and tough exercise programs. For much of the sport's history, many drivers weren't exactly models of fitness. Some raced with big bellies pressing against the steering wheel. Stronger bodies, experts figured, were better for long-distance racing and endurance. Although such concepts became widely accepted in the NASCAR garage area, there were those who scoffed. Dick Trickle, winner of hundreds of short-track races, offered the opinion that the best way to get in shape to drive a race car is to drive a race car. Then he lit another Marlboro.

NASCAR's memorable past and its promising future met in one race as the 1990s surge gained momentum. Richard Petty's last race, the Hooters 500 on November 15, 1992, at Atlanta Motor Speedway, was the first Cup event for heralded newcomer Jeff Gordon, one of the newbies. It was an ideal coincidence, a sort of changing of the guard.

Petty, who had pondered retirement for years but resisted it with every fiber of his being, finally announced October 2, 1991, that the 1992 season would be his last as a driver. Dozens of media members and assorted hangers-on gathered at his Level Cross shop to hear the details. Questioned for years about retirement, Petty always responded that he would "gather a crowd, all of y'all," when it came time to make that announcement. He was true to his word.

Why retire? "Age has something to do with it," Petty, then 54, said. "Not winning races [he hadn't won since 1984] has something to do with it. . . . Maybe the burning desire isn't there that was there ten years ago. I still really, really enjoy driving the race car. That's going to be a tough, tough situation.

"The racing deal is what keeps me going. I get up every morning and I've got to come do this, got to go do that, got to go over yonder and do that. I don't know if it keeps me any younger, but it keeps me going."

Some drivers race for money, others for the thrill of close competition, and others for the ego boost. For Petty, money certainly was a key factor, but driving a race car was mostly about pure joy. It was an act that, despite the crashes and the injuries, and the near-misses at the finish line, made him happy. It was that he would be giving up.

But, as Petty said, it wouldn't be a farewell tour "because I'm not going anywhere." His final season would carry the label of the Fan Appreciation Tour, and when it ended, he would slide into his new role as strictly a team owner. Petty had decided to dedicate his last driving season to the fans, and various events were scheduled during and around race weekends to place him even closer to the disciples who had followed him for so long. And, not incidentally, Petty's last year would bring with it a mass of new Petty merchandise, including a die-cast model car made specifically for each race and scheduled to be sold only at that event. They moved across sales counters like ice cream on a hot day. The Fan Appreciation Tour would make Petty a much richer man, and there were few who would argue that he didn't deserve the bonus dollars. "He is NASCAR racing, as far as most of the fans are concerned," said Tom Chambers, president of Goody's Headache Powders, a long-time Petty sponsor.

NASCAR's popularity drew the attention of President George H. W. Bush, who visited Daytona International Speedway for the running of the Pepsi 400 on July 4, 1992. The race was Petty's last at Daytona. "Keep up the great work for American sports, American values," Bush said during the prerace drivers meeting. "We're very, very proud of you. And as for Richard Petty Day . . . they're saluting him all the way around the track here—I'm proud to be at his side on this very special day, too."

During his final season as a driver, Petty joined the list of garage-area regulars buying motorhomes for trips to most of the tour's tracks. The motorhomes typically were parked in speedway infields with easy access to garage areas. They became a major convenience for drivers, both as a place to escape from crowded garage areas and a place to share meals and evenings with family members. The motorhome was particularly important that year, Petty said, because his schedule was packed with appearances and fan events and the home away from home gave him a place to get away from it all.

Petty had opened that final season with a touch of realism. "If we win some races or a race, it'll be great," he said. "It would be a great way to end my career, but if I don't then I still think it's a pretty good career and we'll go out happy with what we've got in the last thirty-five years.

I've been fortunate to have had a lot of good times. Of course, there have been a lot of bad times, too. But it sort of equaled itself out."

Petty's last season ended with a best finish of 15th, scored twice at Talladega Superspeedway and once at Michigan International Speedway.

On the final weekend of his final season, Petty was swamped with well-wishers, trailed by media members and their cameras, and saluted by fellow drivers and officials. Cup Series director Dick Beaty, who was also retiring, commented on Petty's final run during the prerace drivers meeting, one of the most emotional of those gatherings in years. Petty presented a sterling silver money clip with a Petty blue center to every other driver in the starting lineup. The clips were engraved with this message: Thanks for all the memories, Richard Petty. "I really appreciate what y'all have done for us over the years," Petty told the other drivers. "Try not to hit me today, and I'll try not to hit you."

"I REALLY APPRECIATE WHAT Y'ALL HAVE DONE FOR US OVER THE YEARS. TRY NOT TO HIT ME TODAY, AND I'LL TRY NOT TO HIT YOU."

Receiving one of the clips was the kid starting his first race in the 21st position—Jeff Gordon. "Going into the race, we were focused on our own thing," Gordon said. "I was very nervous and anxious for the weekend because Rick Hendrick [team owner] took a risk on me. But when I got to the track, I thought, 'Hold on.' I watched Richard walk around the garage area being mobbed by fans, photographers, and media. It hit me as soon as I got to the track. It was fun to be a part of, very memorable."

For years, Gordon kept the money clip in a dresser drawer near his bed. "Then I realized I need to protect this a little more," he said. Now it's in a safe. "I can tell you right where it is," he said.

There was a 30-minute ceremony honoring Petty before the race. Then, he led the first pace lap as four Apache helicopters flew along as an escort. Lynda Petty, standing in the Petty pit, broke into tears in the seconds before the green flag flew.

Petty hoped for a strong finish for his last ride, but he crashed on the 95th lap as part of a multi-car accident. His car slid off the track, and fire erupted from underneath the car. The fire was quickly extinguished, and Petty was not hurt. His crew worked to repair the damage so that Petty could be on the track for his final checkered flag.

"It was probably one of the saddest days of my life," Dale Inman, then the team's spotter, said. "I think the girls and Lynda had told him just to survive it. We got in a wreck. I was spotting for him, and there was nothing he could do to miss it. We wanted him to finish the race, so the car was made ready."

Petty finished 35th in his 1,184th race, ending thirty-five years of driving. He failed to win over the final eight seasons. "He, A.J. Foyt, and Darrell Waltrip did run too long," NASCAR historian Buz McKim said. "But they were racers by nature. It's tough for guys to walk away. They just really enjoyed driving race cars."

After the race, Petty was swarmed by media members. He eventually made his way to the team hauler, where he was met by Lynda, his three daughters, and son Kyle. "We were all crying," said Rebecca Petty Moffitt, Richard's youngest. "I'm going to cry now just telling you about it. We told him we were proud of him. It was crazy, very emotional. It's still sad. But we were happy it was over."

Petty had to change his approach to life almost immediately, Kyle said. "As soon as he wasn't able to get back in a car, he changed," Kyle said. "Part of who Richard Petty was was put in a box and put on a shelf. That part of what he was is in a museum. When you're a kid and you lay down at night and dream, you dream of one thing—driving a race car and winning. You don't dream of doing commercials, doing interviews, getting a shoe deal or a big house. You dream about driving a race car. That's all he ever wanted to do, but that's the one piece he couldn't do any more. So, he is different. He had to take that dream and put it in a box."

At the beginning of the 1993 season, Petty, now strictly a team owner, faced a new landscape. "I would like to have a little more control of my life, but as far as it slowing down, I don't want that," he said. "I probably make the commitments I do to keep my life moving. I've been going at this pace so long that anything slower would be 'stop.' I've adapted to everything else for fifty-five years, so I don't see why I can't adapt to this."

Without Petty behind the wheel, the sport moved on. In 1994, NASCAR made a historic breakthrough, racing for the first time at Indianapolis Motor Speedway, a world-famous track previously reserved for Indianapolis-type open-wheel cars. More than 300,000 fans were in attendance, and drivers raced for a $5.4 million purse, NASCAR's richest ever. Jeff Gordon was a popular winner of the Indy inaugural.

The 1990s produced another big moment in February 1998. Dale Earnhardt, who had won virtually everything his sport had to offer other than the Daytona 500, finally made it to that victory lane, ending a twenty-year struggle. Petty won seven 500s. "The next race at Rockingham," Dale Inman remembered, "Earnhardt came by and grabbed me by the cheek. He said, 'I can whip you now. I've won the 500.' I said, 'And you're six behind.'"

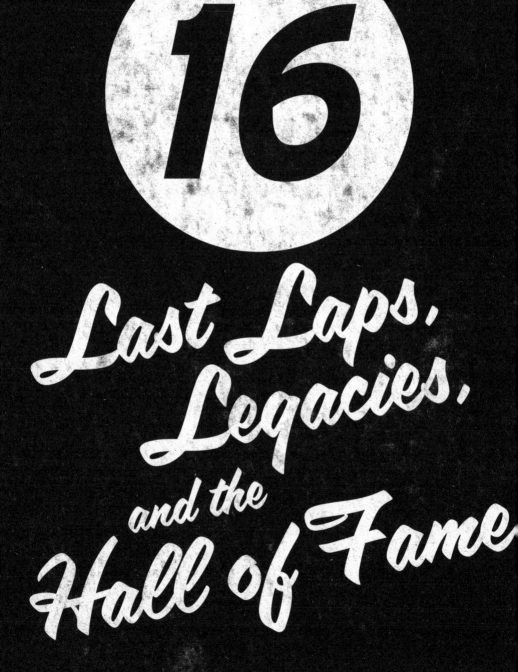

*T*he sudden roar of a Boss 429 NASCAR race engine came to life from over the hill and down the road. David Pearson, sitting near the driveway of his Boiling Springs, South Carolina, home, heard the noise. "What's that?" he asked no one in particular.

A few seconds later, the car rolled into sight. It was the No. 21 Wood Brothers Mercury Pearson had driven to the top of Cup racing so many years before. It's September 21, 2015, and Leonard Wood, Pearson's longtime crew chief, is at the wheel. "It's my Mercury," Pearson said, leaning to the side for a better view.

The car rumbled to a stop in the Pearson driveway, and Pearson, his three sons, and several members of the Wood Brothers team, including Eddie, Len, and Leonard Wood, and William Fulp, gathered around it, the memories bubbling of the time when this car and this driver and this outfit ruled NASCAR's fast lanes. There were a few tears.

Pearson had been in declining health for about a year, generally confined to his house. Eddie and Len Wood suggested they haul the Mercury to Pearson's house to relive a bit of the good times. "He thought it was a fake car to begin with, then he saw Leonard," Eddie Pearson said. "You couldn't believe the big smile on his face. They talked about everything. He could remember more about the past than what he had for breakfast."

"Leonard said, 'Hey, I brought my favorite car,'" Ricky said. "They shook hands and hugged. They really did right by my dad."

Pearson put his signature on the car, and the Woods and Pearsons sat down to reminisce about the good ol' days.

"You can't put into words what that was like," Eddie Wood said. "It was a very emotional day for everybody. We got him to sign the car, and he was the first. Since then, Cale Yarborough, Donnie Allison, A.J. Foyt, Dave Marcis, and all the Wood brothers have signed it."

Eight months later, the doorbell rang at the Pearson home and in stepped Richard Petty and Dale Inman, Pearson's old on-track antagonists and longtime friends. Pearson saw Petty enter from his bedroom on the other side of the house. "Richard Petty!" he yelled. "He loved seeing them," Ricky Pearson said. "He was talkative. He had had a stroke, but it never really affected him in that way. That visit was big. They talked about old times. Dale asked him if he was any good on dirt. Dad said, 'The best.' Richard said, 'That's the David I remember.' There's no doubt he had a special relationship with Richard."

Petty said seeing Pearson "felt good. A lot of years we were side by side whether we wanted to be or not. He lit up when he saw us come in. We probably stayed an hour and had a good talk. The big deal is that he recognized us. He looked good."

While Pearson was confined to his house, visitors came and went, but family members limited the number because he was sometimes weak and susceptible to infection. "Even then, he didn't talk a lot about what he'd done," Ricky said. "If somebody asked him, he'd answer. He just wanted to pass whoever was in front of him, that's all. Once he quit, he didn't talk about it much. He never outgrew the Whitney mill. He was a regular person."

There were no serious concerns about Pearson's health until October 2014. He, Ricky, and Ann, Ricky's wife, were visiting a restaurant in Boiling Springs near the family home when Pearson said he was feeling very hot. "He grabbed his stomach and then started passing out," Ricky said. "Ann reached and grabbed him. He had had an aneurysm. We got to the hospital, and the doctors came out looking very serious and said they would do what they could. They worked until after midnight to save him. He had congestive heart failure, and his heart was working only at 35 percent. That saved him. If his heart had been working 100 percent, he would have bled out."

Pearson later had a stroke and needed care around the clock. "We dropped what we were doing and worked in shifts and were with him 24-7," Ricky said. "We did all we could for him. It was hard to see him go from what he once was to that. He never was paralyzed, and he knew everybody who came in, but he kind of got worse over the years."

Pearson died November 12, 2018, at the age of 83. A private funeral was held a few days later in Spartanburg's Greenlawn Memorial Gardens. About fifty people, including family members, four members of the Wood Brothers team, and a few friends attended. Pearson was laid to rest in a crypt with a short but profound marker: Simply The Best.

"He didn't want a lot of attention," Ricky said. "He didn't want to put a lot of stuff on his marker. I figured that would be enough."

Pearson's three sons, Larry, Ricky, and Eddie, each own one of their father's three Cup championship rings.

Pearson's black Chevrolet pickup truck, a custom "Silver Fox edition" with fox emblems embroidered into the seats, remains in Pearson's shop, covered with a tarp.

In 1992, after several years of go-kart racing, 12-year-old Adam Petty, son of Kyle and grandson of Richard, sat on the back of a motorhome in the Daytona International Speedway infield and talked racing, his mother Pattie sitting nearby. "My dad never comes and watches me because he's too scared," Adam said. "He came and watched one night and told me some pointers. I want to do better. I've won some heat races, but those don't count."

Pattie said she and Kyle tried to blend Adam's enthusiasm for racing with their desire for him to have a "normal" kid's life. "We live at the beach in the summer, and that's just our time and my time to be Mommy with the kids and for him to be twelve years old and playing on the beach," she said. "We don't necessarily advocate spending every weekend at a go-kart track. He's twelve years old. There are other things."

By this time, Adam, who is listening, is restless. "It's my interview, Mom," he said.

Adam revealed that he handled most of his sponsor negotiations himself and that he had saved money to buy another racing kart but saw it disappear when he broke a house window hitting a tennis ball and had to pay to replace it. Among his money-raising enterprises, Adam said, was selling Grandfather Richard's autograph for $5.

It soon became evident that Adam had full possession of the racing gene that had carried his great-grandfather, grandfather, and father to victory lane. He progressed through short-track stock car series and into the second-level NASCAR Busch Series. On September 30, 1998, he won an Automobile Racing Club of America stock car race at Charlotte Motor Speedway. In 1999, he scored three top-five finishes in twenty-nine Busch Series races, and the Petty team planned a full season of Busch racing in 2000, along with Adam's debut in the Cup Series. He ran in the Cup race at Texas Motor Speedway on April 2, 2000, finishing 40th after blowing an engine. It would be his only Cup race.

Adam had the bright smile of his grandfather and the outgoing personality of his father and seemed destined for big things. After a series of down years at Petty Enterprises, Adam was seen as the rising star who would right the ship. "He has a lot of untapped potential," Kyle Petty said of his teenage son. "You can't teach racing. You can teach somebody the fundamentals of how to get through a corner and what it's like, but you don't teach racing. There are certain people who have a natural ability to race. How he refines that ability will depend on how his mindset works."

At eighteen years old, Adam said he tried to race outside the pressure of being a Petty. "There's so much to live up to in my family that I kind of decided at a young age that I'm not going to try to live up to it," he said. "I'm just going to try to do the best I can. Every time I buckle up, I try to do that."

Then came May 12, 2000, at New Hampshire Motor Speedway. Adam was practicing in his Busch Series car on the one-mile (1.6-km) oval when the throttle apparently hung, sending the car full-force into the outside wall. Only nineteen years old, Adam did not survive the crash.

The NASCAR family, competitive but also compassionate in moments of tragedy, gathered around the Pettys in their days of grief. Beyond the loss of Adam and the dark days for the Petty family, his death changed the future for the family racing team. "The basic deal was that Kyle and I were putting everything in Adam's hands," Richard Petty told *Autoweek* in a 2016 interview. "He was going to be the one who rejuvenated Petty Enterprises. He had the personality and the ability and the smarts to be very competitive. It just didn't work out. It was a way bigger personal loss for the family than it was a professional loss for racing."

Family members dealt with the loss in different ways. Kyle decided to drive his son's Busch cars for the rest of that season as he and Pattie struggled to move forward. Richard Petty, always very much a public figure, escaped into a silent world.

"When Adam got killed," Richard said, "it was probably the lowest point of my life. I didn't leave the house for five or six days. I'd get up in the morning and just sit there. My world quit. A lady wrote to me and told me not to put a question mark where God has put a period. I came back to the real world. Before that I was blaming myself because if I hadn't been in racing Adam wouldn't have. I was blaming myself for his accident. She lifted a burden off me."

"WHEN ADAM GOT KILLED, IT WAS PROBABLY THE LOWEST POINT IN MY LIFE. I'D GET UP IN THE MORNING AND JUST SIT THERE. MY WORLD QUIT."

Adam had visited a Florida camp for children with chronic illnesses and developed the idea of building a similar camp in North Carolina. Kyle and Pattie supported the concept, and months after Adam's death, the Petty family jumped full force into planning what became the Victory Junction Gang Camp in memory of Adam. Richard and Lynda Petty donated seventy-two acres (29 hectares) near their home for the camp, and construction took more than two years. The camp opened in 2004. NASCAR drivers, team owners, sponsors, and sanctioning body officials donated to the cause, and fans from around the world sent in money, many matching Adam's car number of 45 with $45 donations. Bob Bahre, owner of the New Hampshire track where Adam was killed, became the first million-dollar donor to the camp. The camp's centerpiece is Adam's Race Shop, a building designed to look like his race car. The camp provides a free summer camp experience for thousands of children.

"The camp has come out of it, so Adam's life was worth something," Richard said. "I'm a big believer in fate. The good Lord put us here. He knows where we're going and what we're doing."

"You don't realize how big your community is until you have something like Adam's accident happen," Kyle Petty said. "That community reached out and gave something back, gave the kids something. When Adam's accident happened, it came back to us 10-million-fold and continues to this day."

A year after Adam's death, Kyle Petty said the pain of his son's loss did not diminish with time. "Some days you do have bad days, and there's nothing you can do about it," he said. "You don't know what triggers it. I don't think anybody knows. It's just a memory or a look or you hear somebody's voice or you hear somebody talk about something. It's not that we never talk about Adam because we talk about him all the time. We encourage other people to talk about him. It's not a taboo subject. We don't want you to think it's off limits because he was part of our life. At the same time, those are the easy parts to talk about. The hard part is when you're by yourself."

David Pearson and Richard Petty were locks for early selection when NASCAR announced it would open a Hall of Fame, and there was considerable grumbling in certain circles when Petty was chosen for the first class in 2010 and Pearson was not. Petty and Pearson had been inducted into numerous halls of fame over the years, but the NASCAR hall became the prominent one for stock car racing almost as soon as it was announced. Joining Petty in the first class were seven-time champion Dale Earnhardt, owner-driver Junior Johnson, NASCAR founder Bill France Sr., and NASCAR president Bill France Jr. Many, especially Pearson's devoted fans, were of the strong opinion Petty and Pearson should have gone in together and were disappointed that Pearson had to wait until the second class a year later. Like Jeff Gordon, Jimmie Johnson, Cale Yarborough, and Bobby Allison, Petty and Pearson forever will remain in the conversation concerning the best driver in NASCAR history.

Pearson was invited to the public announcement of the first class and was left in an awkward position when he wasn't chosen and was surrounded by numerous new media representatives seeking his reaction. He hid his disappointment well, but Pearson family members and friends confirmed that he was hurt by the results of the voting. "He said you always want to be first," said longtime Pearson friend Willis Smith. "It hurt him. I never heard him fuss about it, but it hurt him." Petty, asked about Pearson's response to not making the first class, said, "It bothered him a little bit. But he's a big-enough man to suck it up and move on down the road. You have to look at it like you would a race. He didn't win this one. He'll win that one."

The panel choosing members of the hall changes virtually every year, but generally it is made up of speedway owners, NASCAR officials, drivers, crew chiefs, and journalists.

As the sport's all-time winner, a seven-time champion and the face of NASCAR for decades, Petty was a no-brainer for the first class. In talking to hall officials and others before the first voting day, Petty sort of campaigned against himself, however. He and Pearson agreed on the process. Both expressed the opinion that some of the pioneers of the sport—for example, team owner Raymond Parks, a key figure in NASCAR's first years, and successful drivers from the 1950s—should be chosen in the first class. Pearson offered the idea that the two Frances, both instrumental in the growth of stock car racing, should be named the first two members of the hall without a vote because of their stature and impact. There was no doubt that Petty and Earnhardt, both immensely popular during their careers, would be two of the five members of the first class.

Inexplicably, NASCAR and hall officials said the vote totals from the first hall class balloting are not available despite the historic nature of the process. There is a widespread assumption, however, that Pearson missed being elected by a narrow margin.

Pearson easily strolled into the hall at the top of the second class, receiving 94 percent of the vote, and gave a gracious speech at the induction banquet, thanking, among others, Richard Petty. Among the items in Pearson's spotlighted display area in the hall was the Pure Oil shirt he wore while driving to his first Cup win at Charlotte Motor Speedway in 1961. Also included in the display was a bronzed shoe Pearson wore while racing from 1972 to 1977. Pearson's wife Helen had the shoe bronzed as a gift to Pearson. Petty's Hall display as part of the first class included trophies, championship rings, helmets, and the Presidential Medal of Freedom, presented to Petty in 1992 by President George H.W. Bush.

A year after his induction into the hall, Richard Petty participated in the induction of his father Lee to the second class. "Get to talking about the things that Lee Petty was—he was tough, OK?," Petty said during the ceremony. "He was pretty good with the grandsons and stuff like that, but pretty hard on me, but real hard on the outside world. He lived in his world, and he didn't want anybody to tell him how to live in his world. His big deal was to take care of his own. If you got in the way, didn't make a whole lot of difference to him, he got you out of the way."

Pearson went into the hall in the same group with Lee Petty. Leonard Wood introduced him. "The next inductee is all you ever want in a race car driver," Wood said. "He had so much talent, takes the perfect line, knows when to back off, knows when to get on the accelerator to bring him off the corner with the most speed and carry him down the straightaway. . . . If the car wasn't running, you better work on it because it sure wasn't the driver." In bringing Pearson on stage, [Leonard] Wood said, "Now it is my great pleasure to introduce to you the greatest driver in the history of NASCAR, Mr. David Pearson."

IN BRINGING PEARSON ON STAGE, [LEONARD] WOOD SAID, "NOW IT IS MY GREAT PLEASURE TO INTRODUCE TO YOU THE GREATEST DRIVER IN THE HISTORY OF NASCAR, MR. DAVID PEARSON."

One of Pearson's grandest honors had arrived late in 1999 when *Sports Illustrated* magazine named him NASCAR's Driver of the Century. A voting panel that included drivers, crew chiefs, team owners, and journalists chose Pearson over Dale Earnhardt in a close vote. Pearson edged Earnhardt by two points. Richard Petty was third. The magazine called Pearson's talent "incalculably uncommon."

"I didn't have any idea I would win," said Pearson, who was on the voting panel. "I figured somebody like A. J. Foyt would win it. I voted for him because he has run all kinds of races and won in all kinds of cars. It meant a lot to me. It made me feel good that the people who voted thought enough of me to vote for me."

In 2011, the year Pearson was inducted into the hall, NASCAR asked him to travel to Daytona Beach to attend Daytona 500 activities and to do interviews about the hall. He traveled to Florida with friend Willis Smith. "We always stayed at an old motel down there," Smith said. "It was clean, but you wouldn't think he'd want to stay there. They called and told him they had him a room at the Hilton. 'I'm not staying at the Hilton,' he said. 'Send me the money and I'll get my own room.'"

Pearson could be quirky. Eddie Wood of the Wood Brothers team called him a "professional aggravator. You're not going to get the best of him. You think you've got him, and you don't. I've been down that road."

Few in the racing community knew about a side of Pearson that came late in his life. Smith bought a vacation place in a campground in Myrtle Beach, South Carolina, and Pearson, after traveling there with Smith, also bought a small house there. "There was a preacher who lived in the community near us who did mission work in St. Thomas, Virgin Islands," Smith said. "We got to talking to him and became friends. He invited us to go down there, and David went several times, laying block for a church they were building. He started going to Whitney Baptist Church and later bought pews for the church and a van. One day the pastor, who knew about the St. Thomas trips, asked if anyone wanted to stand up in church and talk about them. I said to myself, that ain't never going to happen with Pearson. But he did. He got up and talked and cried like a baby. He told them what it meant to him to be over there to do that, what it meant to his life. I would never have believed that he would have spoken in that church."

The Pearson family's resilience was tested in March 2010 when Larry Pearson, then 56, was seriously injured in a race crash at Bristol Motor Speedway. He was driving in a "legends" race whose field included numerous retired drivers, among them his father. Harry Gant, Cale Yarborough, Jack Ingram, and Dave Marcis also participated. Larry's car blew a tire and hit the wall, and former Cup driver Charlie Glotzbach slammed into the driver's side of the car at full speed as it dropped down the track banking. Larry suffered a broken leg, ribs, hand, and wrist. He underwent six surgeries in twelve days, was hospitalized for weeks, and worked through months of rehabilitation.

"That was a scary day," said Ricky Pearson, who was at the track. "It was absolutely one of the worst days I've had, not knowing what to expect when I got to the car."

David was sitting in his race car in the first turn while medical workers attended to Larry and Glotzbach at the Turn 2 crash site. "I didn't know how bad it was," David said later. "Eddie [his youngest son] came over to my car and told me Larry had broken his leg and that I needed to come on and go with them to the hospital. I saw him blow the tire, and I went around him on the outside, so I didn't see what happened. I talked to Charlie that night at the hospital for a long time. He said he didn't have time to back off at all, that he hit him full blast."

Russell Branham, who worked in public relations with Pearson Racing and became a close friend of the family, was also at the race. "David was visibly shaken," Branham said. "And well he should have been. That was his son. I think Larry's wreck drew all of them closer than they ever had been. It was a time of need and hurt and question marks, and David sort of took the reins and kept them all together. David spent a lot of time at Larry's house during the recuperation process. He needed help. He was struggling."

In hindsight, scheduling a race for retired drivers at a fast track like Bristol wasn't an especially wise move. Speeds on the high-banked half-mile (0.8 km) leave little time for reaction when there are incidents. Larry Pearson, however, has no regrets about competing in the race. Indeed, he's ready to do it again. "Oh, God, yes," he said in a 2024 interview. "Absolutely, I'd do it again. I wish they'd do it every year. I loved it."

In many NASCAR infields and racetrack campgrounds, Confederate flags flew—sometimes above the American flag on some poles—with predictable regularity until NASCAR made some aggressive moves to expel the symbol. Still, the coarsest of the coarse found ways to express themselves. This was no more evident than at Talladega Superspeedway, Alabama's fast track and a gathering place for wild and beer-soaked legions since its opening in 1969. After the rise of Donald Trump and the subsequent election of Joe Biden in 2020, the race-day infield at Talladega boasted flags that were none too subtle: "Fuck Joe Biden and Fuck You If You Voted For Him."

At a track famous for close finishes, beer parties, and women baring their breasts in exchange for cheap bead necklaces, Talladega in 2020 became the flashpoint for NASCAR's long racial divide. In late June of that year, during the COVID pandemic, Cup teams gathered at Talladega for the Geico 500. On June 21, the day the race was scheduled (it was postponed to Monday because of weather), a pull-down rope fashioned into a noose was discovered in the garage stall of the Richard Petty Motorsports team and its driver Bubba Wallace, the Cup Series' only black driver.

The sport was already operating in a tension-filled environment. NASCAR had announced two weeks earlier its decision to ban the Confederate flag from its tracks, a move that had been pushed along by Wallace. "No one should feel uncomfortable when they come to a NASCAR race," Wallace told CNN. "So, it starts with Confederate flags. Get them out of here. They have no place for them."

On the scheduled race day, protesters who opposed the flag ban gathered outside the track, flying the Confederate flag and saying their NASCAR fandom had reached its end.

The Federal Bureau of Investigation (FBI) sent agents to Talladega to investigate the possibility of a hate crime. Meanwhile, Wallace's competitors rallied around him and in a nationally televised show of support unlike anything ever seen in the sport, walked behind Wallace's Chevrolet in a group as the car was pushed along pit road prior to the start of Monday's race. Defending series champion Kyle Busch was at the front of the group. Petty, who wasn't originally scheduled to attend the race because of the COVID pandemic, traveled to Alabama to support Wallace. Wallace climbed out of his car when it reached the end of pit road and rested his head on the roof of the car. Petty came over to console him.

"I didn't have to think about whether I'd go because at that time we were really involved team-wise," Petty said. "I said, 'Hey, there's trouble down there and I need to go see about it.' I thought it was really neat that all the racing people got behind him, saying this isn't right. Even though it turned out not to be a real problem, it showed that racing people back racing people whether they're red, white, or purple."

In his autobiography, Kyle Petty wrote, "I was proud to see my dad standing at Bubba's side, helping to lead the sport they both loved into the next chapter."

The FBI concluded that the noose had been in the garage stall since the track's previous race in October 2019, meaning that it could not have been directed at Wallace. According to NASCAR, FBI investigators visited every Cup track and examined every garage stall. They found eleven pull-down ropes with knotted ties but none similar to the one at Talladega. The FBI decided that there had been no hate crime. Before all of the evidence was in, NASCAR president Steve Phelps had called the placing of the noose a "heinous act."

NASCAR's racial history doesn't read well. Minority drivers often were refused entry to events in the early years, and Wendell Scott, the Cup Series' most persistent African-American driver, had a race victory taken away from him in 1963 at a short track in Florida. Officials originally awarded the win to Buck Baker, in part to prevent Scott from appearing in victory lane with a white race queen. The decision eventually was reversed and Scott was awarded the win. Although Scott had significant support in NASCAR garage areas over the years, his family faced discrimination on the road. Scott and his wife and children often ate picnics on the road because they weren't allowed to dine in segregated restaurants. In the 1950s, black fans attending some tracks were greeted with restroom signs reading Negroes Not Allowed. Some drivers refused to participate in races if black drivers were allowed.

NASCAR has attempted to put the Confederate flag, once a prominent symbol at many of its Southern tracks, out of sight and mind. Items such as trophies or souvenir program covers that include flag imagery are not included in public display areas at the NASCAR Hall of Fame. NASCAR includes videos of many of its past races on its website along with this disclaimer: "The races you are about to see appear as originally broadcast and may contain imagery that is offensive and doesn't align with NASCAR's values. NASCAR has since permanently banned the display of the Confederate flag at all events."

After he retired from driving, Richard Petty retained a crowded travel schedule, attending most races and making sponsor appearances. But he was also able to devote more time to family matters. In 1993, the Pettys bought a vacation house in Alpine, Wyoming, south of Yellowstone National Park. The extended family spent Christmases there, and Richard and his wife Lynda used the house, named Winner's Retreat, as a central location from which to tour popular vacation spots in the West. Alpine became a great escape for Petty, a place where he was a visitor in the wilderness, not a famous race car driver. "He enjoyed going out there with my mom because I think that's one of the only places he has ever gone where he was Richard and she was Lynda," Kyle Petty said. "Nobody made a big deal or stopped him for autographs."

One Petty trip to Wyoming underlined his love for racing—and almost no other pursuits. "My son-in-law and a couple of boys who work for me, they packed up a big trailer and truck with camping gear to go up into the woods behind the house to go hunting," Petty said. "I went with them. They got to where they wanted to go and put up the tent and everything. They said, 'What are you going to do?' I said, 'I'll see you in the morning. I'm going back to the house.' So, I rode my little horse back down to the house, went in, took a shower, ate supper, watched TV. I got up the next morning, got on the horse, and went back up there. It's snowing. I just like to wander around in the woods and see stuff. Didn't care about bringing home hunting trophies. That's the wrong kind of trophy."

The Alpine house became a refuge of sorts when Lynda was diagnosed with a debilitating illness.

"She'd have good days and bad days," Richard said. "We'd go to Wyoming and spend three or four days. When she was so sick, I forgot about the rest of the world and the rest of the family. It was about whatever she needed. I spent a lot of time taking her to Duke [University Medical Center], doing whatever. She got to be the center of my life instead of racing. I look back and think about what if I had taken her to different doctors. But you can't change that. It is what it is. We did everything that we thought was possible at that time.

"She was the love of my life. We lived three lives. She lived a life. I lived a life. And we lived a life together. When we lost her, I got back in one of Richard Petty's shells. I didn't go anywhere. Wasn't interested in anything. My daughters all came in one day and said, 'Daddy, you have to get your butt up and do something. You can't sit here for the rest of your life.'"

Petty had revealed Lynda's illness in an emotional press conference at Daytona International Speedway in February 2010. A media member asked Petty if there was anything those attending could do for him. "Pray for Lynda Gayle," he said.

Lynda Petty died in 2014. She was cremated, and her ashes were placed in five urns—one large and four small for each of the Petty children. When Richard Petty dies, the family plans to add his ashes to the urns.

"When I lost Lynda, I had to learn how to live a different life," Petty said. "She always took care of so many things." That included choosing Richard's shirt and jeans every day and placing them out for him.

The Wyoming house was a special project for Lynda. "Everything you see in here, she did or picked out," Petty said during a 2015 trip to Winner's Retreat. "The colors, the floor, the chairs, the paintings—everything."

Petty sold the Wyoming house in 2019 "because once we lost Lynda it just wasn't as interesting to be there," he said. But parts of that experience live on in the Petty home in Level Cross. One room has "Lynda's corner," a space that includes her favorite chair from the Wyoming house. "The house out there was very sentimental to Mom and Dad," Richard's daughter Rebecca said. "He moved as much as he could into the room and her corner—her knitting stuff, pictures of her."

For decades, the Pettys have been involved in a wide range of charitable work, from helping build athletic fields in their community to contributing to hospitals, veterans' organizations, and various scholarship funds. The Petty Family Foundation was created in the 1980s to oversee those efforts.

Petty continued a rigorous travel schedule well into his 80s, attending races and supporting sponsors with appearances and autograph signings. Jodi Meeks, his executive assistant, coordinates his travel. Petty's hearing is not good, so he doesn't have a cellphone. His schedule, which typically is completed months in advance, is recorded on index cards that he keeps in his wallet.

"Racing and being at a racetrack and being around race people is who Richard Petty is," Kyle Petty said. "If you take all of that away from him, there's no doubt he would have sat down in a chair and passed away. But he just had the driving part taken away. It took him a while to deal with that, but once he did, he's still Richard Petty. That's who he is and what he does. It was his single focus, all he's ever wanted to do. That was the case with all of the Pettys. It was all about racing. None of them had any hobbies. I'm the anomaly of the group. All I had was hobbies."

The 2020 COVID pandemic hit Petty hard. He went from traveling to a race site almost every week to sitting at home, wondering what was next. Petty estimated that he had either attended or driven in 2,300 of the Cup Series' first 2,500 races, including the very first one in 1949. "But it was a good thing in a way," Petty said. "I suddenly realized that I didn't have to be at a track for them to have a race. Everything went on anyway."

The Petty Enterprises team declined in Richard's final years as a driver and in the years that followed. There were sporadic moments of strength, including wins by drivers John Andretti and Bobby Hamilton, but the days of competing consistently were gone in the dust.

"We got behind because of money, technology, and key personnel," Kyle Petty told writer Bob Myers in a 2002 interview. "When we fell behind, we struggled. Through the struggle, we stayed constant. We never got ahead again. The sport began to grow and passed us by. We became just another team."

After Richard left the home team to drive for Mike Curb in 1984 and 1985, Kyle eventually joined the exodus, leaving to drive for the Wood Brothers in an ironic pairing of long-time rivals. He won races there in 1986 and 1987.

Over the years, the Petty team went through a series of iterations in attempts to funnel more money and improved operational strength into the organization. Various individuals and groups obtained portions of the team through a dizzying sequence of mergers and acquisitions, and the team shop moved from Level Cross to other locations in North Carolina. In 2008, Petty Enterprises, as it had been known for decades, closed its doors, a victim of the times. "I'm sad for the people," Dale

Inman said. "The people were Petty Enterprises. I just think it's the way progress goes and about the things that happened to us along the way." Andretti, who drove for the team for seven seasons, said his heart was broken. "It's amazing to think we'd ever be talking about this day," he said. "It's the end of a long era."

The final reorganization of the Petty team resulted in the Petty name being removed from the team and Petty's involvement being limited to a role as ambassador and advisor.

The history of the Petty family's racing is celebrated in the Petty Museum at the former Petty Enterprises location in Level Cross. Race cars, trophies, driver uniforms, photographs, and assorted memorabilia from four generations of racing Pettys fill several rooms. Items continue to come in.

"A guy recently brought in a spring that he had gotten from Daddy's wreck at Pocono when he broke his neck," Rebecca Moffitt said. "We get people in from all over. There was a woman touring the museum recently. I was showing someone else around. When she was leaving, she said to Sharon [Rebecca's sister, who works at the museum], 'I saw Richard Petty's daughter. I know that was her because she called him Daddy.' Sharon smiled and said, 'I call him that, too.'"

A back room in the museum includes storage shelves and a long table. The table is reserved for items for Petty to sign: hats, shirts, diecast cars, sports cards, and photographs. For many years, Petty has retreated to this room at least once a week to try to keep pace with the requests, which arrive in the mail daily from all corners of the world. He signs and signs and signs, repeating the famously flowing autograph that means a certain kind of magic to those receiving it. The autograph mail has not declined despite the fact that Petty hasn't raced in more than thirty years; in fact, Petty said the sport's increasing exposure has doubled the total over a few years ago.

"That he remains so popular speaks to how he is with people," Dale Inman said. "He is so recognized that it's unreal, even if he's wearing a baseball cap. And that's everywhere. We left London one time and went to Nova Scotia. They practically closed down one little town there and everybody gathered in the middle of the street to talk to him. He was recognized even there."

Years after he retired from Cup racing, David Pearson dabbled in short-track runs: sometimes for money, sometimes for entertainment. In October 2002, at the age of sixty-seven, he ran in an old-timer's race at the old Piedmont Interstate Fairgrounds track in Spartanburg. The cars for the charity race were provided by the race organizers, and Pearson didn't win. This didn't sit well. Before another race was held at the track, Pearson had rebuilt a 1937 Ford coupe. He won the next race—and thirteen more in the car.

Other than occasional on-track activity, Pearson spent much of his retirement time simply being David. "He was just an ordinary guy in a lot of ways," Len Wood said. "He let his on-track abilities speak for him rather than being the one seeking out commercials or trying to be a star. I don't think he intended to be a star, but he was good and he wanted everybody to know that. I don't think he needed the limelight. The last 10 laps of a race, that was his time."

At the Darlington spring race in 2023, the track celebrated its annual Throwback Weekend, in which teams are encouraged to enter race cars with popular or noteworthy paint designs from previous seasons. As part of prerace ceremonies, Ricky Pearson drove the No. 21 Wood Brothers car that his father had driven to victory at Darlington and many other tracks. The car had been restored to its original race form, including the seat that David Pearson sat in. "I cried like a baby," Ricky said. "It was all I could do to get through it. A very emotional thing for me."

The Petty story rolls on. His travel is somewhat limited, but he might show up at a track or a supermarket or an automotive parts show near you.

Pearson rides on in the rich history of the Wood Brothers. "We'd look forward every morning to him coming to the track just so we could talk to him," Len Wood said. "Whatever he said was gold. We believed it. He was our hero. Still is."

EPILOGUE

The Debate

If there's one thing sports fans value more than a high grandstand seat at the Daytona 500 or a 50-yard-line spot at the Super Bowl, it's the debate.

Who's better, David Pearson or Richard Petty? Best NBA team of all time—Celtics, Lakers, or Bulls? Tom Brady or Joe Montana? Babe Ruth or Mickey Mantle? Best dynasty—Yankees or Patriots?

The list goes on forever. As do the arguments. They have fueled long nights at neighborhood bars, ended long-standing friendships, fractured marriages, and—in the case of stock car racing—produced more than a few grandstand debates that ended with a Petty fan punching a Pearson fan in the nose. Sometimes, the fan fights were more entertaining than the on-track competition, especially at tracks with muddy infields.

Was Petty better than Pearson? Was Pearson better than Petty? And who's the best NASCAR driver of all time? Where do Petty and Pearson rank in that discussion?

These are questions that can't be answered by numbers alone, and in Petty's oft-spoken view, they can't be answered with any sort of certainty using any kind of measurement.

"You can't compare the eras," Petty said. "The cars were different, some of the tracks were different, the teams have changed, the way people raced was different. Trying to compare the guys from the 1950s to the 1980s just really can't be done."

Of course, that doesn't stop people from doing it. It's an entertaining game for the television couch or the corner bar.

Asked by *Autoweek* magazine which American racers would be on his Mount Rushmore of drivers (assuming he would fill one of the four spots), Petty listed A.J. Foyt, Mario Andretti, and David Pearson.

In an interview in 1979, Pearson said Petty "has to be at the top." Not necessarily first, but at the top.

"Fireball Roberts, Joe Weatherly and Junior Johnson were the top drivers when I started," Pearson said. "So was Lee Petty. Richard Petty, of course. And Bobby Allison. They have been around a long time. Then you have Cale Yarborough. There's Donnie Allison and Buddy Baker. I'm not ranking them. No one should think I've listed them in order. I'm not going to, but Richard has to be at the top. There have been some drivers who could be top drivers if they had the equipment of top drivers. You have to have a good car, good crew, good mechanics, and a little bit of luck."

Donnie Allison, a ten-time winner in Cup racing, described Pearson as "extremely intelligent but also very patient. He was as good a driver as we had. Bobby [Allison] and I were talking about the fact that Bobby and Richard [Petty] beat each other's fenders off, and David went on and won the race."

Junior Johnson said in a 1977 interview with journalist Benny Phillips that Curtis Turner, Bob Flock, Fonty Flock, Fireball Roberts, and Richard Petty were the best drivers he competed against on-track. What about the years since Johnson's 1966 retirement from driving? He listed Cale Yarborough, Bobby Allison, Darrell Waltrip, and Richard Petty.

"Petty and Bob Flock compare," Johnson said. "Both will beat you racing but had really rather beat you mentally first of all, if they can. They will wait and try to play with your mind and then make a run for it late in the race. Fonty Flock and Pearson compare. They keep it all mixed up. They may race hard at any time, or they may wait around to see what is going to happen."

No less an authority than Bill France Sr., the sport's founder, declared in the 1960s that Curtis Turner, the master of the dirt-track powerslide and a man who knew no limits (on track and off), was the best ever. Of course, many fine drivers appeared in the post-Turner years. In most current rankings of drivers by people closely involved with the sport, Turner rarely appears even in the top 10 all-time.

Pearson gets the vote of virtually everybody connected to Wood Brothers Racing, which fielded the No. 21 cars he drove to incredible successes in the 1970s.

Waddell Wilson, who built engines for Pearson during his Holman-Moody years, said Pearson "wanted to win as badly as any driver I was ever around. He would work us and work us in practice. He was sandbagging himself. He would make it look like we were behind everybody, then he'd out-qualify people by a half-second."

Wilson said Pearson's competitive side emerged even in rental cars. "We all had rental cars leaving the track in Michigan one day," he remembered. "We must have been running something like 120. Darel Dieringer was on my right, and Pearson was behind me. So, Pearson comes up and bumps me in the rear bumper and pushes me on past Dieringer. I think Pearson probably invented bump-drafting right there."

"[PEARSON] WOULD WORK US AND WORK US IN PRACTICE. HE WAS SANDBAGGING HIMSELF. HE WOULD MAKE IT LOOK LIKE WE WERE BEHIND EVERYBODY, THEN HE'D OUT-QUALIFY PEOPLE BY A HALF-SECOND."

Pearson and Petty put up the kind of numbers that should keep their names out front for decades to come, but not everyone knows the history. Kyle Petty remembered a garage-area incident that illustrated that fact. "Tony Glover [a long-time NASCAR mechanic and later a series official] and I were talking in the garage area," Petty said. "Pearson walked up, and we talked to him for twenty to thirty minutes. This guy came over and said, 'It was pretty nice of you guys to spend so much time talking to that old man.' Glover said, 'Give me your hard card [garage pass].' He made the kid give him his pass. Then he said, 'You go to the NASCAR truck and figure out who that is, and you'll get it back.'"

Drivers can also be fans. That was the case for longtime Cup competitor Dave Marcis, who traveled south from Wisconsin in 1968 to try his hand at Cup racing. He described Petty as "my hero. We're not that far apart in age. People laugh when I say that, but it's true. [Petty is four years older]. He was down here racing when I was up in Wisconsin shoveling snow, and I only wished I could be here. I loved blue race cars, I guess because Richard's car was always blue. All my early race cars—unless a sponsor wanted otherwise—were painted blue."

Where would Pearson rank himself? "No. 1," he said emphatically in a 2009 interview with *The Scene Vault*. "If you don't feel like you're the best out there, you're going to get beat. No doubt about it. Every time I got in a race car, even the [1961] World 600, I'm sitting there in Ray Fox's car getting ready to start the race. I'm thinking, this car, these people, don't know who's driving this car. I felt like if they can do it, I can do it. And I ended up winning the race.

"Rusty Wallace one time said Dale Earnhardt is the best guy out there. I said, 'Rusty, if you don't feel like you're the best one out there, he's going to beat you every time.' And Earnhardt like to have killed him three or four times."

Over the years, various news media outlets with an interest in stock car racing have attempted to decide the question of which driver is the greatest of all time by assembling expert panels to consider the candidates. These groups typically include drivers (active and retired), crew chiefs, NASCAR officials, team owners, and journalists.

In 2023, The Athletic website conducted one of the most comprehensive surveys of key racing personalities regarding the sport's greats. Richard Petty finished first, followed by Jimmie Johnson, David Pearson, Dale Earnhardt, and Jeff Gordon.

Sports Illustrated magazine ranked Pearson No. 1 in a December 1999 issue and went a step beyond to name the three-time Cup champion Driver of the Century. In that voting, Earnhardt was second, Petty third, Bobby Allison fourth, and Gordon fifth.

A year earlier, *Sports Illustrated,* apparently using a difficult calculation, had named Junior Johnson the best all-time, followed by Pearson, Petty, Allison, and Earnhardt.

Inside NASCAR, a magazine published by NASCAR, named Earnhardt the best ever in a June 1997 issue, with Petty second, Pearson third, Cale Yarborough fourth, and Allison fifth.

Using a 10-9-8-7-6-5-4-3-2-1 point system to combine the results of those four rankings, Petty and Pearson tie for first with 37, Earnhardt is third with 34, and Bobby Allison is fourth with 27.

Numbers alone clearly establish Petty in the No. 1 spot. He won 200 Cup races; no one else won more than 105. Petty also won seven championships, a mark reached by only two other drivers—Dale Earnhardt and Jimmie Johnson. This is more than enough evidence to consider Petty the greatest of all time, but those who favor other drivers often point out that Petty's superb equipment generally outclassed many fields, particularly in the 1960s when he stacked up dozens of victories on tiny tracks with limited competition. That line of thought leads some to this conclusion: Anybody could have won in Petty's cars. Still and all, he actually won all those races. Others just talk about them.

Pearson sometimes is criticized for winning "only" three Cup championships, although he ran what might be considered full seasons only four times. If Pearson had run as many races as Petty, Pearson disciples will point out, he probably would have won as many times—or more. But he didn't. A plus for Pearson is the fact that his winning percentage (18.3 percent) is third all-time, behind only 1950s era stars Herb Thomas (20.9) and Tim Flock (20.8). Petty's winning percentage was 16.8.

Veteran motorsports journalist Jonathan Ingram compared Pearson and Petty: "Like many journalists as well as fans, I admired Petty for his ability to sustain so much demand for his time and attention with humor, cheer, and grace. As a driver, he put his emphasis on smoothness, too, and was never so much a rabble-rouser as a driver who let the race come to him and his often outstanding equipment. But for me, Pearson was in a class of his own when it came to shepherding a field of cars around a high-banked superspeedway all afternoon as if they were sheep, before picking up the trophy."

Mechanic Richie Barsz won races and championships with Pearson at Holman-Moody and with Petty at Petty Enterprises. Which driver was better? "I think Petty was better because he had a better-handling car, and I don't think his heart beat twice in a minute and he just was laid back and still is, but I think Pearson had more natural ability," Barsz said.

Although Pearson wasn't Petty's match in the world of public relations, he was proud of fan approval. "I could win at Indianapolis or in Europe and make money if I ever got the right car," Pearson said. "But it wouldn't mean as much to me as any little old victory in NASCAR. These people are my fans. They know me."

Earnhardt's driving style and fierce ambition to lead every lap no matter what stood in his way earned him an intensely loyal fan base and kept him atop many fans' ratings of the all-time best. He was considered the toughest of the tough, a driver who would crash even one of his best friends (Terry Labonte, in a famous encounter at Bristol Motor Speedway, for example) to win a race.

Earnhardt won 76 times and was still in pursuit of a record eighth championship when he was killed on the last lap of the Daytona 500 in 2001. He ruled the sport for much of the 1980s and 1990s, his "Intimidator" image selling T-shirts practically as fast as they could be printed.

Earnhardt cultivated that tough-guy image to the extreme, rarely showing what some of his closest friends called a sensitive side. Near the peak of his career, he spoiled a major news media event at Daytona International Speedway, refusing to speak to a gathering of about 200 media members who had flown to Daytona Beach to cover NASCAR preseason testing. Charlotte Motor Speedway had organized the trip as part of its annual preseason media tour, and CMS public relations official Eddie Gossage argued with Earnhardt about his refusal to take some time from test runs to meet with the media. "He was just as mad as could be," said Gossage, who later became the first president of Texas Motor Speedway. "He was poking me in the chest. 'I'm not talking to you guys; you're interrupting my work,' he said. I got back in his face. They wound up separating us. My mom passed away that week, and I went home to Tennessee for the services. I was back in the office early the next Monday to catch up. The hallway was dark, but the light was on in the office. I rounded the corner, and Dale was sitting there. He said, 'I'm sorry about your mom. Tell me about her.' He got tears in his eyes. He started talking about his dad and started crying. We must have talked 45 minutes with tears running down our faces. He said, 'I'm sorry we had a fight. I brought you a peace offering.' And he gave me one of his helmets. He said, 'I've got to go.' He looked at me and said, 'Don't you ever tell anybody.'"

The Intimidator was intimidated.

Earnhardt, Petty, Pearson, Gordon, Allison, and Yarborough built huge fan bases over the years and generally for different reasons. Earnhardt, Allison, and Yarborough were respected for their toughness, Petty for his class and perpetual winning, and Pearson and Gordon for race smarts. Allegiance often leads fans to extremes. Many stand in blocks-long lines for hours to get an autograph, spend thousands of dollars on collectible items featuring their driver, and will argue relentlessly with anyone who doesn't think Driver A is the best. And tattoos? Yes, some strange ones are out there. More than a few fans have had their favorite driver sign his name on one of their arms and then have had a tattoo artist make the signature permanent.

And some fans make incredible journeys. In September 2017, Ted Lee drove 16 hours from his home in Norman, Oklahoma, to Pearson's home in Boiling Springs, South Carolina. A Pearson fan for decades, Lee hoped to visit Pearson, who by that time was generally confined to a bedroom in his home because of illness.

"I knew he was sick, and I was hoping I could see him," Lee said. "Nobody was giving out much information about him. I drove there and talked to Ricky [Pearson's son] out in the yard. I couldn't see David, and that was all right."

Lee said he had visited Pearson in Boiling Springs years earlier and that he got to know the driver and his family well.

"It was a burning desire to go see him," Lee said. "I always studied him, read the stories, read the books, watched from afar. It's great when you have a hero and you get to meet him and he's really what you wanted him to be all along."

Why Pearson? "Because of his persona, the way he carried himself," Lee said. "He was so smart. When he pulled that move to beat Petty at Daytona in the summer race in 1974, I had never seen anything like that. And then for him to win the 500 at Daytona in 1976 in the greatest finish ever.

"The Pearson-Petty rivalry was what made the sport, made it grow. Most of the time people had either a Pearson hat or a Petty hat. I wanted to beat Richard Petty so bad every time, and his fans thought the same. Their rivalry was clean and respectful, but on a track they each wanted to beat the other in the worst way."

Lee said he and his father, Joseph, were devoted to Fords as long as Pearson raced them. "When he and the Woods split up and David drove a Chevrolet for Hoss Ellington, I told Dad, 'We're going to have to drive a Chevrolet Monte Carlo now because that's what David is driving.' And he got one."

Chase Whitaker of Franklin, Tennessee, is on the other side of the Great Debate. His life is painted Petty blue.

"THE PEARSON-PETTY RIVALRY WAS WHAT MADE THE SPORT, MADE IT GROW... THEIR RIVALRY WAS CLEAN AND RESPECTFUL, BUT ON A TRACK THEY EACH WANTED TO BEAT THE OTHER IN THE WORST WAY."

"My uncle got me into racing, and that got me into Richard Petty," Whitaker said. "The winning didn't hurt. Every time you opened a newspaper, you'd see another headline he had won. The winning, that was it, and the way the car looked. I remember seeing the car glowing under the lights at Nashville Speedway in the 1970s. That memory is burned in my mind. I started reading all I could about Petty, and the more I read it cemented for me that this is a guy I want to be a fan of. I clipped every article I could find from *The* [Nashville] *Tennessean*. It was almost like having a King James Bible. Every time Richard or Kyle's name was mentioned, I'd underline it in red ink."

An accountant with a leaning toward research, Whitaker, 59, spins Petty tales via blogs and X (formerly Twitter) and has built an archive of Petty information that might be among the best in the country. In one form or another, he has written about all the wins scored by Richard and Lee and the other drivers who raced Petty Enterprises cars. "He knows more about my family than I do," said Rebecca Moffitt, Richard's daughter. Whitaker has articles, souvenir programs, newspapers, magazines, patches, decals, books, diecast cars—most Petty-oriented.

"I'm a committed fan," Whitaker said. "I've enjoyed it for what it is. I remember my heart coming out of my chest when I realized he was going to win the 1979 Daytona 500. Even now, I can't keep my eye off the [No.] 43. I have to know where it is. There have been some lean years to be a Petty fan, but a lot of people don't have any idea about the domination the team had."

David Blake's family vacationed every summer in Daytona Beach. When he was fifteen years old, in 1978, he was playing in the pool at the Treasure Island hotel on the beach when Richard Petty, who was also staying at the hotel for that week's race, walked out of his room and jumped in the pool. They talked for a while, Blake said, and Petty joined in a pool volleyball game. The next day, one day before the race, Petty spoke to Blake again. On the morning of the race, he invited Blake to accompany him to the track. After getting his mother's approval, Blake rode with Petty team members to the track and watched the race from the pits.

This goes a long way toward explaining why David Blake is the current president of the Richard Petty Fan Club, which continues to be a thing despite the fact Petty hasn't driven a race car since 1992.

"Since those days in Daytona, we've been friends," Blake said. "He has had a big impact on my life as far as how you should treat people and what to do when you meet people. To me he's a legend, an icon, a John Wayne, a Babe Ruth. He's one of those people who has transcended his sport. He's the same guy he was forty-five years ago. People like him come along once in a lifetime."

This reasoning also works for Bryan Ramey, but he lands on the Pearson side of the chasm. Ramey, an attorney in Upstate South Carolina, has sponsored races and race cars at area short tracks for years and has been a Pearson fan virtually since the first time he heard a loud race engine.

Ramey met Pearson in 1980 at Greenville-Pickens Speedway in Easley, South Carolina, when Pearson, Petty, Earnhardt, Jody Ridley, and Bobby Allison raced in a special event at the track. "I followed him around the pits, listened to him talk to people," Ramey said. "I heard him cuss out a woman for having peanuts near his race car [peanuts in the pits were a no-no for superstitious racers]."

In 2008, Ramey's law firm sponsored a race at Greenville-Pickens, and track operator Tom Blackwell, a long-time friend of Pearson's, helped Ramey secure Pearson's services as grand marshal for the race. "Tom said, 'If you give him a thousand dollars, he'll do it,'" Ramey said. "I came to the track that night with a thousand dollars in my pocket. Pearson came walking through the gate, and he and Tom commenced to cuss each other. I'm standing there with my mouth open. Pearson looked at me. I said, 'Nice to meet you, Mr. David. I couldn't be more excited if you were Elvis.' He said, 'You give me a thousand dollars, and I can sing.'"

"ALL THOSE YEARS OF SITTING ON THE PIT WALL AND SIGNING AUTOGRAPHS... YOU DIDN'T REALIZE WHAT YOU WERE DOING THEN WAS BASICALLY PLANTING A SEED. THEN IT GREW INTO A TREE, AND NOW IT'S GROWN INTO AN ORCHARD."

Pearson drove Ramey's Mercedes for some hot laps before the race. Ramey was on board. "He went into Turn 3 at 105 miles per hour [169 km per hour], driving with his left hand, his right hand on his thigh, talking a mile a minute," Ramey said. He asked Pearson to sign the car's sun visor. "When I traded the car, I kept the sun visor," he said.

Mike Hart was a member of Petty's weekend pit crew from 1978 to 1985 and, noting his prejudice, says Petty was the best driver "by far."

"It was like being the bat boy for the New York Yankees," Hart said. "I carried tires, changed tires, jacked for a pit stop at Nashville, gassed the car. When I was a kid, I had a toy racetrack. I'd listen to the races and move the cars around according to where they were running.

"To work with the team was something I couldn't have imagined. I was never anything but a Petty fan. Ever."

Russell Branham was never anything but a Pearson fan. He was three years old when he met Pearson, who had landed his small airplane at Branham's Airport, which was operated by Rudy Branham, Russell's uncle, in Darlington, South Carolina. Pearson took a few minutes to talk to Russell, and that was that. Pearson fan forever.

"I remember as a child being mesmerized by that white car and the gold foil number [21], going to races with my uncle and seeing that race car, and being able to see the man himself when he would fly his plane to my uncle's airport," Branham said. "That was all overwhelming for a child. We'd go to races, and if the 21 car had problems or fell out, I was ready to leave. The rest of it didn't matter to me."

Branham later lived a Pearson fan's dream. In 1988, after working as a sports writer in Florence, South Carolina, he was named public relations director for Pearson's racing team. Later, Branham worked in various executive positions for NASCAR and kept his connections with the Pearson family.

"He was a very simple, good man who just happened to be an extremely good race car driver," Branham said.

In the ultimate endorsement, Branham named his son, Pierson (with a different spelling), after his hero.

So, who's best?

"All those years of sitting on the pit wall and signing autographs, all those years of making appearances and doing things when NASCAR and the tracks asked—you didn't realize what you were doing then was basically planting a seed," Kyle Petty said of his father. "Then it grew into a tree, and now it's grown into an orchard. Fans saw him for the first time and became Petty fans. They knew people, and they became fans, and so did their sons and grandsons. When Adam died, the outpouring from people was as if somebody in their family had passed away. I think that's the way they feel about him and always have. He's just that guy from Level Cross who won a bunch of races. The winning is not how he kept his popularity. He kept it by being who he is."

Darrell Waltrip raced against both Petty and Pearson and appreciates the special nature of both sides of the Petty-Pearson divide.

"Because of who Richard Petty is and what he has done, he elevated the sport more than anybody else could have done," Darrell Waltrip said. "He was the right guy at the right time. There's nobody who's come along who did anything like Richard did. I know they'd go to Islip or some little track like that and nobody might have a car anywhere close to his and he'd win. But he won 200 races.

"In my opinion, David Pearson was the greatest driver ever to drive a stock car. I think he was just a little better than Richard, but Richard had 200 wins and David had 105. So, what do you do?"

SOURCES

Benyo, Richard, "Superspeedway: The Story of NASCAR Grand National Racing," 1977 (New York, NY: Mason/Charter)
Blake, Ben and Conway, Dick, "Richard Petty: Images of the King," 2005 (St. Paul, MN: Motorbooks International)
Bongard, Tim and Coulter, Bill, "Richard Petty: The Cars of the King," 1997 (Champaign, IL: Sports Publishing, Inc.)
Bourcier, Bones, "Foyt Andretti Petty–America's Racing Trinity," 2015 (Newburyport, MA: Coastal International Inc.)
Chapin, Kim, "Fast as White Lightning: The Story of Stock Car Racing," 1998 (New York, NY: Three Rivers Press)
Cotter, Tom and Pearce, Al, "Holman Moody: The Legendary Race Team," 2002 (St. Paul, MN: MBI Publishing Company)
Craft, John A., "Bud Moore: Man and Machine," 2009 (Holly Hill, FL: Carbon Press)
Cunningham, Scott, "The World of King Richard," 1987 (Atlanta, GA: Rand & Ezor Sports Enterprises)
Cutter, Robert and Fendell, Bob, "The Encyclopedia of Auto Racing Greats," 1973 (Englewood Cliffs, NJ: Prentice-Hall, Inc.)
Edelstein, Robert, "Full Throttle: The Life and Fast Times of NASCAR Legend Curtis Turner," 2005 (New York, NY: Overlook Press)
Edelstein, Robert, "NASCAR Generations: The Legacy of Family in NASCAR Racing," 2000 (New York, NY: HarperCollins Publishers LLC)
Edelstein, Robert, "NASCAR Legends: Memorable Men, Moments, and Machines in Racing History," 2011 (New York, NY: The Overlook Press)
Fielden, Greg, "Forty Years of Stock Car Racing (four volumes)," 1988 (Surfside Beach, SC: The Galfield Press)
Fielded, Greg (with Bryan Hallman), "NASCAR: The Complete History," 2009 (Lincolnwood, IL: Publications International, Ltd.)
Gabbard, Alex, "NASCAR's Wild Years: Stock-Car Technology in the 1960s," 2005 (North Branch, MN: CarTech, Inc.)
Golenbock, Peter, "The Last Lap," 1998 (New York, NY: Macmillan Publishing)
Golenbock, Peter, "NASCAR Confidential," 2004 (St. Paul, MN: Motorbooks International)

Hinton, Ed, "Daytona: From the Birth of Speed to the Death of the Man in Black," 2001 (New York, NY: Warner Books, Inc.)

Hunter, Don and Pearce, Al, "The Illustrated History of Stock Car Racing," 1998 (Osceola, WI: MBI Publishing Company)

Hunter, Jim (with Lyle Kenyon Engel), "Racing to Win Wood Brothers Style," 1974 (New York, NY: Arco Publishing Company)

Hunter, Jim (with David Pearson), "21 Forever: The Story of Stock Car Driver David Pearson," 1980 (Huntsville, AL: The Strode Publishers, Inc.)

Jensen, Tom, "Cheating: An Inside Look at the Bad Things Good NASCAR Winston Cup Racers Do in Pursuit of Speed," 2002 (Phoenix, AZ: David Bull Publishing)

Kelly, Godwin, "Ray Fox: Sly in the Stock Car Forest," 2006 (Daytona Beach, FL: Carbon Press)

Libby, Bill (with Richard Petty), "King Richard: The Richard Petty Story," 1977 (Garden City, NY: Doubleday & Company)

Langworth, Richard M. and Norbye, Jan P., "The Complete History of Chrysler Corporation 1924–1985," 1985 (Skokie, IL: Publications International)

McReynolds, Larry (with Bob Zeller), "Larry McReynolds: The Big Picture," 2002 (Phoenix, AZ: David Bull Publishing)

Menzer, Joe, "The Great American Gamble: How the 1979 Daytona 500 Gave Birth to a NASCAR Nation," 2009 (Hoboken, NJ: John Wiley & Sons, Inc.)

Neely, William, "Daytona U.S.A.," 1979 (Tucson, AZ: Aztex Corporation)

Petty, Kyle and Henican, Ellis, "Swerve or Die," 2022 (New York, NY: St. Martin's Press)

Pierce, Daniel S., "Real NASCAR: White Lightning, Red Clay, and Big Bill France," 2010 (Chapel Hill, NC: University of North Carolina Press)

Petty, Richard and Neely, Bill, "Grand National: The Autobiography of Richard Petty," 1971 (Chicago, IL: Henry Regnery Company)

Poole, David, "Race with Destiny: The Year That Changed NASCAR Forever," 2002 (Tampa, FL: Albion Press)

Riggs, L. Spencer, "Langhorne! No Man's Land," 2008 (Zionsville, IN: Pitstop Books)

Teter, Betsy Wakefield (editor), "Textile Town: Spartanburg County, South Carolina," 2002 (Spartanburg, SC: Hub City Writers Project)

Thompson, Neal, "Driving with the Devil: Southern Moonshine, Detroit Wheels, and the Birth of NASCAR," 2006 (New York, NY: Crown Publishers)

Vehorn, Frank, "A Farewell to the King," 1992 (Asheboro, NC: Down Home Press)

Waltrip, Darrell (with Jade Gurss), "DW: A Lifetime Going Around in Circles," 2004 (New York, NY: G.P. Putnam's Sons)

Yates, Brock, "NASCAR Off The Record," 2004 (St. Paul, MN: MBI Publishing Company)

Young, Anthony, "Hemi: History of the Chrysler Hemi V-8 Engine and Hemi-Powered Cars," 1991 (Osceola, WI: MBI Publishing Company)

Publications, websites, archives, and podcasts:
Autoweek
Inside NASCAR
NASCAR Illustrated (ceased publication 2016)
NASCAR Scene (ceased publication 2010)
www.racing-reference.info
The Scene Vault NASCAR podcast
Sports Illustrated
Stock Car Racing Collection, Appalachian State University

ACKNOWLEDGMENTS

Many thanks to three "editors-at-large" who read various versions of the manuscript and made it better: New York City man-about-town Rob Edelstein, who managed to simultaneously read a manuscript and welcome granddaughter Lottie into the world; Tom Layton, North Carolina man-of-the-mountains and a fellow traveler in the pages of another book; and Scott Derks, who survived university life with me in a roach-infested $90-a-month apartment and can sling adjectives with the best of them. All read with a practiced eye. Any mistakes in the book are theirs. Just kidding.

A salute to library and archives staffs everywhere and, in this particular case, thanks to Bill English and Kate Sayers at the NASCAR Archives and Research Center in Daytona Beach, Florida; Susan Wise at the Appalachian State University Stock Car Racing Collection in Boone, North Carolina; and Ken Martin, director of NASCAR Productions Historical Content.

I once worked alongside stock car racing journalist and historian Gene Granger, whose insight and research into David Pearson's career are important to anyone studying the driver's life and times.

Thanks to all who agreed to be interviewed for this book, especially Richard Petty, Kyle Petty, Rebecca Petty Moffitt, Larry Pearson, Ricky Pearson, Eddie Pearson, and Willis Smith. Dozens of conversations with David Pearson and Richard Petty over the years, from the dens of their homes to garage areas from coast to coast, filled the heart of this book.

Invaluable for baseline information about two of racing's all-time greats are books by Jim Hunter (*21 Forever: The Story of Stock Car Driver David Pearson*) and Bill Neely (*Grand National: The Autobiography of Richard Petty*). Also, a nod to the two best books ever written about NASCAR: *Fast as White Lightning: The Story of Stock Car Racing* by Kim Chapin, and *Daytona: From the Birth of Speed to the Death of the Man in Black* by Ed Hinton.

A long career chasing race cars has landed me in forty-eight states, four countries, and more than a handful of journalism outposts. I have shared press box and media center space with some of the best people I know, talented journalists who tell great stories under tough deadlines and write the hard stories with professionalism and dedication when tragedy clouds the track. They are far too many to list here, but the ride with them has been fun. In a time in which journalism has become a whipping boy, the people I know continue to make it a noble profession.

And a big thank you to Polly, the kids, and the grandkids, who gave me the space and time to travel on the long and winding road that is a book.

INDEX

A
Alabama International Motor Speedway (AL), 106–109
Allen, Johnny, 74
Allison, Bobby, 11, 18–19, 73, 90, 108, 119, 131, 138–139, 167–168, 182–183
Allison, David, 23
Allison, Donnie, 75, 119, 158, 167–168, 174, 224
Andretti, John, 219
Andretti, Mario, 95
Arledge, Roone, 151
Athletic website, 227
Atlanta Constitution, The, 61
Automobile Racing Club of America (ARCA), 87

B
Bahre, Bob, 209
Baker, Buck, 23, 27, 41–42, 44, 126
Baker, Buddy, 54, 137, 147
Barsz, Richie, 84–85, 101–102, 113–114, 116, 138, 180–181, 229
Batson, Gary, 111
Beaty, Dick, 201
Beauchamp, Johnny, 51, 56–57, 68
Benfield, Henry, 136–137
Bennett, Joe, 130–131
Berry, John, 187
best driver debate
   Donnie Allison's on Pearson, 223
   Athletic website survey and, 227
   Richie Barsz on, 229
   Earnhardt as contender, 229–230
   fan thoughts about, 229–232
   Bill France, Sr. on, 223
   Mike Hart on, 232
   Jonathan Ingram on, 228–229
   Inside NASCAR on, 228
   Junior Johnson on, 223
   knowledge of current fans and, 226–227
   Ted Lee on, 230–231
   number of wins and, 228
   other contenders, 229–230
   Pearson's best drivers, 223, 227
   Petty's best drivers, 222
   Bryan Ramey on, 233–234
   Sports Illustrated on, 227–228
   Darrell Waltrip on, 233
   Chase Whitaker on, 231–233
   Waddell Wilson on, 226
   win percentage and, 228
   Wood Brother's on, 223–224
   Leonard Wood on, 226
Blackwell, Pete, 38
Blackwell, Tom, 38, 233
Blake, Ben, 93
Blake, David, 230–231
Boar's Head Lounge (Daytona Beach), 141–142
Bodine, Brett, 117
Bonnett, Neil, 111, 133, 159, 185
Boot Hill Saloon (Dayton Beach), 141
Bowsher, Gary, 162
Bowsher, Jack, 162
Bowsher, Jim, 162
Branham, Russell, 214
Breuer, Dan, 170
Brewer, Tim, 85, 145–146, 172

Brickhouse, Richard, 108, 127
Brigance, Buck, 114
Bristol Motor Speedway, 21, 120, 176, 198
Busch, Kyle, 215
Bush, George H. W., 200, 211
Byron, Red, 23, 71

C

Canadian National Exposition (CNE) grounds, 47
Carter, Jimmy, 57
Chambers, Tom, 200
Charlotte Fairgrounds track, 41
Charlotte Motor Speedway, 23–24, 63, 72, 111, 134, 176, 185
Charlotte Observer, The, 63
Chevrolet, NASCAR and, 15
Chrysler, 14–15, 79–81, 97–98
    Plymouth Superbird, 127
City of Hope charities, 163
Clardy, Buck, 41
Clark, Jimmy, 133
Columbia (SC) Speedway, 28, 39, 47, 72, 99, 125
Confederate Motor Speedway, 34
Connally, John, 187–188
Cotter, Tom, 104
COVID pandemic, 215, 219
Cowley, John, 133
Curb, Mike, 198, 219

D

Darlington Raceway (SC), 51, 72, 90, 100, 103, 114–115, 129, 165, 171–172
Davis, Johnny, 194
Daytona 500 (1959), 51, 56–58
Daytona 500 (1961), 67
Daytona 500 (1964), 79–80
Daytona 500 (1965), 81
Daytona 500 (1968), 8
Daytona 500 (1970), 127
Daytona 500 (1974), 142
Daytona 500 (1976), 13–14, 151–156, 158–159, 231
Daytona 500 (1979), 158, 165, 167–169, 232
Daytona 500 (1984), 194
Daytona 500 (1988), 117
Daytona 500 (1998), 203
Daytona 500 (2001), 55
Daytona International Speedway (DIS), 44–45, 51–58, 67, 105, 111, 119
Depression, 26, 29
DeWitt, L.G., 87
DiGard Racing, 157, 180
Dixie Motor Speedway (AL), 43
Dodge
    Dodge Charger Daytona, 106
    Magnum, 166–167
Dover International Speedway (DE), 105
Dozier, Mike, 160
drag racing, 82–83
driver fitness, 199

E

Earnhardt, Dale, 11, 20, 55, 84, 111–113, 173, 176–177, 183, 191, 203, 210–212, 229–230
Earnhardt, Dale, Jr., 91
Earnhardt, Ralph, 39
Economaki, Chris, 63–64, 112, 117, 155
Elder, J. C. "Suitcase Jake," 101–102, 116, 176
Ellington, Hoss, 157, 191
Eubanks, Joe, 56

F

Federal Bureau of Investigation (FBI), 215–216
Firecracker 400 (1969), 105
Firecracker 400 (1974), 142–147, 231
Firecracker 400 (1984), 189–191
Firestone, 106–107
Flemming, Bill, 151, 153
Flock, Tim, 23, 25, 44, 89–90
Ford
  hemi and, 80
  Holman-Moody and, 104
  NASCAR and, 14–15, 21, 80–82, 95, 102
  Petty's switch to, 15, 97–99
  Wood Brothers and, 133
Fox, Ray, 64–66, 227
Foyt, A. J., 99, 129–130, 133, 157–158, 169, 202, 212
France, Bill, Jr., 128, 162, 196–197, 210–211
France, Bill, Sr., 23–24, 32, 52, 56–57, 66, 106–108, 123–124, 129, 195, 211, 224

G

Gazaway, Joe, 135
Geico 500 (2020), 215
General Motors, 14
Glotzbach, Charlie, 213–214
Golden Strip Speedway (Fountain Inn), 37
Goldsmith, Paul, 79, 81, 91, 95
Goodyear, 106–107
Gordon, Cecil, 166
Gordon, Jeff, 11, 20, 135, 199, 201, 203

Gossage, Eddie, 229–230
Granatelli, Andy, 125–126
Grand National Illustrated, 76
Gray, Charlie, 135
Greenville-Pickens Speedway (SC), 38, 125
Gurney, Dan, 133

H

Haight, Neil, 49
Halifax County 100 (1971), 87
Halpern, Joel, 191–192
Hamilton, Bobby, 219
Hamilton, Pete, 108, 115, 127
Hart, Mike, 232
Hawkins, Bobby, 192
head-and-neck restraints, 112–113
Heidelberg Raceway, 27
Helton, Mike, 10, 20
hemi engines, 78–80
Hendrick, Rick, 197
Hickory Motor Speedway (NC), 125, 193
Hill, Harley, 36
Hill, Mike, 36–37, 143
Holman, John, 104
Holman-Moody (H-M) team, 84–85, 94, 99–101, 103–104
Holmer, Phil, 141
Hooters 500 (1992), 199
Hopes, Olin, 66
"Hot Blood Down In Dixie," 161
Hunter, Jim, 35
Hunter, Lester, 55
Hutcherson, Dick, 90–91, 102
Hutchins, Sonny, 105–106
Hyde, Harry, 127
Hylton, James, 85

I

Ifft, David, 192
Indianapolis 500 (1964), 72
Ingram, Jack, 90, 193
Ingram, Jonathan, 228
Inman, Dale
  career after Petty Enterprises, 183
  childhood with Petty family and, 27
  Daytona 500 (1979) and, 168
  early years of racing, 42–43
  on Earnhardt, 203
  on Isaacs' death, 175
  on Maurice, 43–44
  as mechanic, 89, 93, 105
  move to Osterlund team, 183
  NASCAR Hall of Fame and, 183
  1981 rule changes and, 182–183
  1967 season and, 94
  on Pearson, 12, 44, 77, 131
  on Petty, 131, 220–221
  on Petty crashes, 111, 113–114, 116–117, 160
  on Petty and Jarrett, 78
  Richard Petty's first racing car and, 29
  visit to Pearson in 2016 and, 205–206
  Wood Brothers and, 145
Inside NASCAR, 228
International Race of Champions (IROC, 1978), 119
Irwin, Kenny, 111
Isaac, Bobby, 20, 39, 74, 81, 116, 130, 138, 175
  Bobby Isaac Memorial, 193

J

Jarrett, Dale, 133, 158
Jarrett, Ned, 78, 81, 113, 146
Johns, Bobby, 59
Johnson, Jimmie, 11
Johnson, Junior, 59–65, 67, 77, 123, 128, 136–137, 210, 224
Jones, Parnelli, 133

K

Kennedy, Joe, 134
Kennedy, Ross, 48
Kite, Harold, 72

L

Labonte, Terry, 8–9, 91
Lakewood Speedway (GA), 61
Langhorne Speedway (PA), 111
Langley, Elmo, 90
Latford, Bob, 141
Lee, Ted, 228–229
Letterman, David, 117–118
Lewin, Dennis, 151
Littlejohn, Joe, 31–32, 64
Lorenzen, Fred, 82, 91, 100

M

McDonald, Dave, 72
McKay, Jim, 113
McKim, Buz, 202
McNab, Bob, 186–187
McReynolds, Larry, 155, 194
Mann, Larry, 111
Marcis, Dave, 227
Marshall Tucker Band, 36
Martinsville Speedway (VA), 109
Maryville Speedway (TN), 125
Matthews, Banjo, 39, 157
Meeks, Jodi, 218

Memphis-Arkansas Speedway (AR), 119
Mercury, 130, 159–160, 205
Michigan International Speedway, 186, 201
Miller High Life 500 (1983), 195–197
Millikan, Joe, 116
Moffitt, Rebecca Petty, 115, 118, 202
Moody, Ralph, 104
Moore, Bud, 54, 56, 64, 73, 100, 123, 129, 135–137, 181
Moore, Paul "Little Bud," 39
Moose, John, 63
Museum of American Speed (NE), 160
Myers, Bob, 104
Myler, Red, 29

N

NASCAR
 car makers and, 13, 78, 80–82
 changes in racing, 41, 44
 checkered flag decals and, 38
 Confederate flag ban and, 214–216
 Convertible Division, 44, 47
 Daytona International Speedway (DIS), 55–57
 deaths in, 72, 111–112
 formation of, 32
 health protocols, 117
 hemi engines and, 78–81
 Late Model Sportsman races, 45
 1990s era and, 198
 noose at Geico 400 race and, 215–216
 point system, 141
 racial history and, 216
 R.J. Reynolds Tobacco Company (RJR) and, 123–125, 136
 safety efforts and, 72, 112–113, 116
 sponsorships and, 123–125, 128
 Strictly Stock Series, 24–27
 Sweepstakes events, 61
 See also best driver debate
NASCAR Cup Series
 beginning of, 31, 41
 Lakewood Speedway race (June 14, 1959), 61–62
 last dirt track and, 125
 Maurice Petty and, 43
 1949 championship, 71
 Petty's first start in, 47
 rule changes of 1981 and, 182
 schedule, 42
 season of 1965 and, 81
NASCAR News Bureau, 44
National 500 (1967), 94–95
National Museum of American History, 190
Negre, Norman, 176
Nemechek, John, 111
Nichels, Ray, 79, 129
nitrous oxide, 158
North Carolina Motor Speedway, 139
North Wilkesboro Speedway (NC), 139
Nowland, Mose, 133

O

Ontario Motor Speedway (CA), 179
Orr, Rodney, 111

Osterlund, Rod, 176–177
Owens, Cotton, 48, 64, 76, 82–84, 94, 99–100
Owens, Randy, 149
oxygen, 74–75

P

Panch, Marvin, 120
Pardue, Jimmy, 72
Parks, Raymond, 71, 211
Parrott, Buddy, 180
Parsons, Benny, 87, 154–155, 174
Paschal, Jim, 81
Passino, Jacque, 91
Pearce, Al, 62
Pearson, Ann, 206
David Pearson Appreciation Day, 130–131
Pearson, Bill, 34
David Pearson Boulevard, 33
Pearson, Danny, 138
Pearson, David
  American Driver of the Year Award, 131, 161–162
  autograph requests and, 33
  avoidance of accidents, 120
  background of, 12–13, 31, 34
  back troubles of, 185–186
  on best driver debate, 223–224
  Chattanooga Chew tobacco sponsorship, 192
  crashes, 120, 151–156, 152–153, 159, 174
  Darlington pit road incident, 172, 174–175
  death of Helen and, 198
  death of, 206–207
  drag racing and, 82–83
  first Cup Series win, 63–65
  flying and, 138, 178, 186–187
  Grand National racing and, 58–59
  Holman-Moody and, 98–100, 103–105
  Larry's 2010 crash and, 214
  Late Model Sportsman races, 175
  Little David the Giant Killer nickname, 38
  NASCAR Hall of Fame and, 19, 65, 210–213
  NASCAR rookie of the year, 13, 59
  NASCAR Triple Crown (1976), 161
  Pearson Racing and, 192–195
  personality of, 8–9, 16–17, 33, 84–85, 177
  on Petty's racing style, 19
  post-retirement life, 186–187, 192–195, 221
  pranks and, 137–138
  races in the 1960s and, 72, 72–74, 76–77, 81–84, 100, 102–103, 105–106
  races in the 1970s and, 129–130, 134, 142–147, 151–156, 165, 171–174, 177–178
  races in the 1980s and, 185–186, 191–192, 194
  racing for Osterlund and, 177–178
  racing style and, 18–19, 75–77, 146–147, 161
  record of, 10, 13, 17, 69, 72, 134, 161
  relationship with Petty, 10–11, 17, 20, 116, 145
  retirement and, 149, 186–187

Silver Fox nickname and, 132
Sports Illustrated Driver of the
 Century Award, 212
visit from Petty and Inman,
 205–206
Wood Brothers and, 8, 129–
 131, 134, 165, 172–175,
 185–186, 221
Pearson, Eddie, 153, 178, 192,
 194, 207
Pearson, Eura, 33
Pearson, Helen (Ray), 35–37,
 151–153, 173, 198
Pearson, Larry, 20, 36, 162,
 192–193, 207, 213–214
Pearson, Lennie, 33
Pearson Racing, 192–194
Pearson, Ricky, 147, 186, 191–
 194, 198, 205–207, 214, 221
Peckham, Peck, 49
Pemberton, Robin, 102, 158, 180,
 182
Pepsi 400 (1992), 200
Petty, Adam, 111, 207–210
Maurice Petty and Associates,
 198
Petty, Elizabeth, 75, 116
Petty Enterprises
 decline of, 219–220
 drag racing and, 82–83
 growth of, 67
 Lee's retirement and, 73,
  181–182
 mail to, 15
 Miller High Life 500 (1983),
  195–197
 1967 season and, 92, 94
 Petty blue and, 126
 Richard's departure from,
  195–198

season of 1965 and, 81
STP sponsorship, 125–127
Talledega 500 (1969), 108
Petty Family Foundation, 218
Richard Petty Fan Club, 232
Petty, Julian, 12
Petty, Kyle
 Barsz and, 138
 birth of, 63
 on current lack of knowledge of
  Pearson, 225–226
 on Darlington, 178
 Daytona 500 (1976) and, 155
 on Holman-Moody, 101
 on Lee Petty, 26
 memories of childhood at track
  and, 80
 on 1968 season, 170
 on Randy Owens' death, 149
 on Pearson, 16–17
 on Petty Enterprises, 219
 on Petty's fans, 233
 racing career of, 115, 165, 170
 on relationship with Pearson
  family, 145
 Richard's retirement and, 202,
  219
 on Richard's support of Bubba
  Wallace, 216
 on rivalry, 20, 145
 son Adam and, 207–210
 on switch to Ford, 98
 Wood Brothers and, 134, 219
Petty, Lee
 as businessman, 12, 61–62
 as competitor, 61
 crashes, 67–68, 119–120
 on Daytona International
  Speedway (DIS), 55
 golf and, 51

NASCAR Hall of Fame and, 62, 212
personality of, 74
racing career of, 12, 23–28, 42–45, 48–49, 51, 56–57, 59, 67–68
retirement of, 73, 181–182
as team manager, 45, 47, 181
Petty, Lynda (Owens), 44, 63, 115, 117, 170–171, 197, 201–202, 209, 217–218
Petty, Maurice, 12, 25
  Daytona 500 (1976) and, 154–155
  on fight with Jarrett, 78
  on hemi engines, 78–79
  on Lee's absence, 69
  Miller High Life 500 (1983), 197
  on 1967 season, 91–92
  on Pearson, 161
  Petty-Allison feud and, 139
  racing career and, 42–44
  Richard's 1970 crash and, 114
Petty Museum, 88, 220
Petty, Pattie, 170, 207–209
Petty, Richard
  on Adam, 208–209
  background of, 12, 15–16, 23–24, 27–29
  on best driver debate, 223
  Charlie 1 Horse hat and sun glasses and, 171
  crashes, 111, 113–119, 151–156, 159, 202
  death of Lynda and, 217–218
  drag racing and, 82–83
  Fan Appreciation Tour, 200
  fans and, 16, 73–74, 126, 233
  father's racing career and, 12, 23–28

first Cup Series win, 62–63
Geico 500 (2020) and, 215–216
Hall of Fame and, 210–211
handwriting and, 44, 126
health issues, 119
injuries and, 111, 113–116, 118
King Richard nickname, 88–89
Kyle's racing debut and, 170–171
marriage to Lynda and, 44
Miller High Life 500 (1983), 195–197
mind over matter attitude and, 118
NASCAR debut and, 28–29
NASCAR News Bureau file and, 44
NASCAR rookie of the year, 13, 59
1967 season and, 89–95
on Pearson's racing style, 19, 77
Petty-Allison rivalry and, 138–139
politics and, 187–189
post-retirement life and, 217–221
Professional Drivers Association (PDA) and, 106
races in the 1960s and, 72–73, 77–78, 81, 85, 102, 105–106, 115–116
races in the 1970s and, 87–88, 125–126, 142–148, 151–156, 165–170, 178–180
races in the 1980s and, 189–191, 195–197
racing style of, 75–77, 161
Rebel 400 crash, 111, 113–115

record of, 9, 13, 17, 69, 72, 88, 129
relationship with Pearson, 10–11, 17, 20, 145
retirement and, 117–118, 149, 199–202
return to Chrysler, 127
switch to Chevrolet, 166
switch to Ford and, 15, 97–99
as team owner, 202–203
visit to Pearson in 2016 and, 205–206
Winner's Retreat house and, 217–218
Phelps, Steve, 216
Phillippi, Howard, 49
Phillips, Russell, 111
Piedmont Interstate Fairgrounds (SC), 31–32
Pierce, Dan, 124
Pilson, Neal, 169
Plymouth, 15
Belvedere (1967), 88
Pocono Raceway, 116, 176–177
Pontiac LeMans, 182
Poor, Bill, 49
pranks, 137–138
Price, Baxter, 173–174
Professional Drivers Association (PDA), 106–108
Pruitt, Gerald, 35–36
Purcell, Pat, 57

R

Ramey, Bryan, 231–232
Randleman High School, 28
Reagan, Ronald, 188–190
Rebel 400 (1970), 111, 113
Rebel 400 (1980), 191
Reep, David, 168

Richert, Doug, 177
Richmond Raceway (VA), 76, 118
Richmond, Tim, 145–146
Riddle, Paul, 36
Riverside International Raceway (CA), 98–99
R.J. Reynolds Tobacco Company (RJR), 123–125, 136, 159
Roberts, Fireball, 54, 59, 65, 72
Robertson, Don, 125
Robinson, Bill, 88
Rogers, Edmund, 58–59
Roper, Tony, 111
Rutherford, Johnny, 119

S

Sachs, Eddie, 72
safety measures, 72, 112–113, 116
Salter, Nate, 49
Salvino, Ralph, 196
Sawyer, Ralph, 58–59
Scene Vault, The podcast, 20, 192, 227
Scott, Wendell, 130, 216
Simonsen, Troy, 79
Skeen, Buren, 72
Smith, Jack, 41–42, 45, 59
Smithsonian Institution, 190–191
Smith, Virginia, 38
Smith, Willis, 37–38, 210, 213
soft walls, 112–113
South Boston Speedway (VA), 87
Southern 500 (1967), 90
Southern 500 (1979), 177, 191
Spartanburg, SC, 31–32
Spencer, G. C., 158
sponsorships, 123–128
Sports Illustrated, 161, 198, 227–228

Squier, Ken, 154
Starr, Bart, 127
Stewart, Jackie, 151, 153
Stewart, Tony, 11
Stock Car Racing, 166
Stott, Ramo, 158
Strictly Stock Series, 24–27
superstition, 162–163

T
Talladega 500 (1969), 106–108
Talladega 500 (1979), 165
Talladega Superspeedway (AL), 106–109, 112, 116, 159, 177, 201
Taylor, Elizabeth, 137
Teague, Marshall, 54
Thomas, Herb, 23, 44
Thomas, Jabe, 125
Thomas, Larry, 77
Thornburg, Wade, 118
tires, 26–27, 106–108, 195–197
Tomlin, Bill, 35
Trickle, Dick, 199
Truelove, Russ, 52
Tucker, Steve, 74, 118, 196
Turner, Curtis, 23, 133, 223
24 Hours of Daytona (1976), 161–162
24 Hours of Daytona, 8–9, 161

U
Unser, Al, 119

V
Vallo, Chris, 129
Victory Junction Gang Camp, 209
Volunteer 500 (1969), 21

W
Wade, Billy, 72
Wallace, Bubba, 215–216
Waltrip, Darrell
  accidents and, 116, 179
  on best driver debate, 233
  on dangers of early racing, 112
  Gatorade car and, 163
  on Pearson, 19–20, 146–147
  on Petty, 20
  racing career and, 157–159, 165, 167, 169, 170, 178–180, 182
  racing style of, 173
  retirement and, 202
  rivalries and, 11
  on sponsorships, 128
Warren, T. Taylor, 56–57
Wasson, Roger, 136
Watkins Glen International racetrack, 21, 73
Weatherly, Joe, 56, 72, 91
Welborn, Bob, 29
West, John, 130
Wheeler, H. A. "Humpy," 134, 137
Whitaker, Chase, 229–230
White, Rex, 62–63
Whitlock, Joe, 58, 141
Wide World of Sports (ABC), 151
Williams, "Ozark Ike," 38
Wilson, Waddell, 226
window nets, 116
Winston All-Star Race, 124
Wood Brothers
  accusations of cheating, 133–134
  NASCAR and, 135–136
  Pearson and, 8, 129–132, 135–136, 172–175, 185–186, 221

    Kyle Petty and, 134, 219
    rivalry and, 10
    visit to Pearson house with the
        Mercury, 205
Wood, Delano, 156
Wood, Eddie, 152–154, 156–157,
    159–160, 175, 205, 213
Wood, Glen, 45, 129–130, 132–
    133, 162, 172–174
Wood, Len, 156–157, 173, 205,
    221
Wood, Leonard, 18, 130–136,
    138, 156, 205, 212, 224–225
World 600 (1961), 63, 74
World 600 (1975), 148, 176
World 600 (1977), 137, 163
World 600 (1978), 134
World 600 (1982), 192

Y
Yarborough, Cale
    Daytona 500 and, 51, 158,
        167–168
    on Daytona International
        Speedway, 54
    other styles of racing, 119
    as Petty driver, 73
    racing career of, 134–135, 147,
        154, 161, 173–174, 188–190
    racing style of, 19, 131
    Wood Brothers and, 133
Yarbrough, LeeRoy, 105–106,
    119, 135
Yates, Robert, 84
Young, Anthony, 79